Single Parents and Child Welfare in the New Russia

Single Parents and Child Welfare in the New Russia

Edited by

Jeni Klugman

and

Albert Motivans

United Nations Children's Fund
Innocenti Research Centre
Florence, Italy

First published 2001 by
PALGRAVE
Houndmills, Basingstoke, Hampshire RG21 6XS and
175 Fifth Avenue, New York, N.Y. 10010
Companies and representatives throughout the world

PALGRAVE is the new global academic imprint of
St. Martin's Press LLC Scholarly and Reference Division and
Palgrave Publishers Ltd (formerly Macmillan Press Ltd).

ISBN 0–333–77360–8

This book is printed on paper suitable for recycling and made from fully managed and sustained forest sources.

A catalogue record for this book is available from the British Library.

Library of Congress Cataloging-in-Publication Data
Single parents and child welfare in the new Russia / edited by Jeni Klugman and Albert Motivans.
        p. cm.
    Includes bibliographical references and index.
    ISBN 0–333–77360–8 (cloth)
        1. Single-parent families—Russia (Federation) 2. Child welfare—
    —Russia (Federation) 3. Russia (Federation)—Social conditions—
    —1991– 4. Family policy—Russia (Federation) I. Klugman, Jeni,
    1964– II. Motivans, Albert, 1960–

    HQ638.2 .S56 2001
    362.7'0947—dc21
                                                    00–054526

10   9   8   7   6   5   4   3   2   1
10 09 08 07 06 05 04 03 02 01

Printed in Great Britain by Antony Rowe Ltd, Chippenham, Wiltshire

Contents

Acknowledgements   vi

Contributors   vii

List of Tables   viii

List of Figures   x

1 Single Parents and Child Welfare in the New Russia
  Albert Motivans and Jeni Klugman   1

PART I: THE DEMOGRAPHIC CONTEXT   25
2. Family Formation, Stability and Structure in Russia
  Albert Motivans   27

3. The Living Arrangements of Russian Children
  *Michael Swafford, Elena Artamonova
  and Svetlana Gerassimova*   53

PART II: SOCIAL POLICY AND THE SINGLE PARENT   87
4. Single Parents, Poverty and Social Welfare Policies in the West
  Sheldon Danziger and Marcia Carlson   89

5. Social Policy for Single-Parent Families: Russia in Transition
  Jeni Klugman and Alastair McAuley   121

PART III: POVERTY, WELFARE AND SINGLE PARENTS
              IN THE TRANSITION   151
6. The Welfare Repercussions of Single-Parenthood in Russia
  in Transition
  Jeni Klugman and Alexandre Kolev   153

7. Family Structure and Child Welfare Outcomes
  Aline Coudouel and Mark Foley   191

Bibliography   225

Index   245

Acknowledgements

This volume would not have been possible without the support of a number of people. John Donohue, Director of the UNICEF CEE/CIS/Baltics Regional Office helped to provide funds to organize a workshop in Florence. The continuing encouragement and valuable insights provided by John Micklewright, Head of Research at the Innocenti Research Centre in Florence, were instrumental to the final product.

Special thanks go to our colleagues in Moscow who provided expertise and assistance on the single-parenthood issue, especially Ludmila Erosina, Elena Feoktistova, Elena Kuprianova, Marina Mozhina, Lydia Prokofieva, and Olga Remenets. The editors are also grateful to Leonid Sokolin and his colleagues at the State Statistical Committee of the Russian Federation for facilitating the access to micro-census data.

The volume also benefited from useful advice from Sheila Marnie, Bruce Bradbury, Jeanine Braithwaite and Pierella Paci. Finally, we are grateful to Eve Leckey who managed the editing and contacts with the publisher with grace, patience and her characteristic good humour.

Contributors

Elena Artamonova is a scientific Researcher at the Institute of Sociology, Russian Academy of Sciences, Moscow.

Marcia Carlson is a post-doctoral Research Fellow at the Center for Research on Child Well-Being at Princeton University.

Aline Coudouel is an Economist with the Poverty Reduction and Economic Management network of the World Bank, Washington D.C.

Sheldon Danziger is Henry J. Meyer Collegiate Professor of Social Work and Public Policy, and Director of the Center on Poverty, Risk and Mental Health, at the University of Michigan.

Mark Foley is a post-doctoral Fellow at the University of North Carolina, Chapel Hill.

Svetlana Gerassimova is a scientific Researcher at the Institute of Sociology, Russian Academy of Sciences, Moscow.

Jeni Klugman is a Senior Economist with the Poverty Reduction and Economic Management network of the World Bank, and an associate Fellow of UNICEF Innocenti Research Centre, Florence.

Alexandre Kolev is an Economist at the UNICEF Innocenti Research Centre, Florence.

Alastair McAuley is Reader in Economics and Director of European Programmes at the University of Essex, Colchester, England.

Albert Motivans is a Programme Specialist with the UNESCO Institute for Statistics, Paris.

Michael Swafford is a Fellow of the Institute of Sociology of the Russian Academy of Sciences and President of Paragon Research International, Inc.

List of Tables

2.1 Changes in Family Trends in Four Countries, 1970 and 1990   29
2.2 Distribution of Families/Households with Children by Type in Russia   35
2.3 Prevalence of Single-Parent Households by Type and
    Custodial Parent, 1994   36
2.4 First Marriage Rates among Women by Age, 1990-1996   42
2.5 Age-Specific Birth Rates by Marital Status, 1989-1997   47
2.6 Age-Specific Mortality Rates by Gender, 1989-1997   48
3.1 Children's Living Arrangements with Parents and Their Partners,
    RLMS 1994-1996   61
3.2 Typology of Child Living Arrangements with Parents and Other Adults,
    RLMS 1996   64
3.3 Child Living Arrangements with Parents and Other Adults
    by Location, RLMS 1996   68
3.4 Education, Occupation, and Age of Parents by Living Arrangements,
    RLMS 1996   73
3.5 Transitions in Living Arrangements with Parents between 1995
    and 1996, RLMS   75
3.6 Transitions in Living Arrangements between 1995 and 1996, RLMS   77
4.1 Single-Parent Families as a Percentage of All Families
    with Dependent Children   90
4.2 Marriage and Divorce Rates in Selected Industrialized Countries   92
4.3 Fertility Rates in Selected Western Industrialized Countries   96
4.4 Labour Force Participation Rates of Women under Age 60,
    by Presence and Age of Children in Eight Countries, 1986 and 1988   99
4.5 Mean Total Transfers as a Percentage of Median Equivalent Income   101
4.6 Expenditures on Social Protection as a Proportion of GDP   103
4.7 Poverty Rates for Children in Single-Mother Families before
    and after Government Programmes   104
4.8 Female-Headed Households as a Percentage of All Households
    with Children   120
5.1 State Expenditures on Family Benefits in the USSR, 1975-1989   130
5.2 Changes in the Value of Child Allowances in Russia, 1991-1996   140
5.3 Changes in Benefits, Amounts and Administrative Responsibility   141
5.4 Coverage and Significance of Public Transfers, 1994-1995   144
5.5 Parental Leave Benefit in Central and Eastern Europe   145
6.1 Severe Poverty and Family Types, RLMS 1994-1996   160
6.2 Individual Poverty Incidence by Demographic Group and Family Type,
    RLMS 1994-1996   161

6.3   Education Characteristics by Family Type, RLMS 1995   163
6.4   Labour Market Characteristics by Family Type, RLMS 1995   165
6.5   Within-Group and Between-Group Inequality, RLMS 1994-1996   170
6.6   Between Group Inequalities in Per Capita Family Labour Earnings,
       RLMS 1994-1996   172
6.7   Impact of Transfers on the Poverty Head Count, RLMS 1994-1996   174
Appendix
6.2   Family Characteristics, RLMS 1996   184
6.3   Income Sources for Families with Children, RLMS 1994-1996   185
6.4   Components of Real Family Earnings, RLMS 1996   186
6.6   Significance of Public Transfers in Household Income
       for Recipient Families with Children, RLMS 1994 and 1996   187
6.7   Errors of Exclusion for Specific Public Transfers   188
6.8   Significance of Private Transfers in Household Income
       for Recipients   189
7.1   Distribution of Children by Family Type and Age Group,
       RLMS 1996   202
7.2   Educational Attainment by Family Type and Gender, RLMS 1996   217
7.3   Welfare Outcomes among Young Children, RLMS 1996   221
7.4   Health and Education Outcomes among Children, RLMS 1996   222
7.5   Welfare Outcomes of Adolescents and Young Adults by Family Type,
       RLMS 1996   223

List of Figures

1.1 Child Poverty by Family Type in the Early 1990s 8
1.2 Share of Single-Parent Households, 1970 and 1989 10
1.3 Trends in Real GDP Growth and Real Wage Growth in Russia, 1990-1998 14
1.4 Childcare, Kindergartens and Female Employment, 1989 and 1996-97 17
2.1 Distribution of Single-Parent Households by Age Group of Child 37
2.2 Number of Children in Public Care, 1989-1997 39
2.3 First Marriage, Remarriage and Divorce Rates, 1985-1998 41
2.4 Annual Number of Divorces by the Presence of Children 45
2.5 Share of Non-Marital Births by Age of Mother, 1989 and 1997 46
3.1 Presence of Other Adults in Household by Number of Parents, RLMS 1996 65
3.2 Presence of Other Children and Relatives, RLMS 1996 66
3.3 Parental Configurations by Age of Child, RLMS 1996 70
5.1 Trends in Social Protection Spending, 1992-1997 134
5.2 Kindergarten and Nursery Gross Enrolment Rate, 1989-1997 146
6.1 Distribution of Households by Type, RLMS 1996 156
6.2 Distribution of Children in Single-Parent Families by Type, RLMS 1996 156
6.3 Poverty Status and Family Structure, RLMS 1994-1996 159
6.4 Real Household Income Per Capita by Household Type, RLMS 1994-1996 167
6.5 Lorenz Curves for Real Family Income Per Capita, RLMS 1996 171
6.6 Poor Households Receiving Public Transfers by Family Type, 1994 and 1996 174
6.7 Errors of Exclusion of Poor Single Parents, RLMS 1994 and 1996 177
7.1 Trends in Child Welfare Indicators: Education Enrolment Rates, 1989-1996 192
7.2 Trends in Child Welfare Outcomes: Criminal Sentencing and Sexually Transmitted Disease, 1989-1996 193
7.3 Welfare Outcomes by Family Type, RLMS 1996 208
7.4 Welfare Outcomes by Family Type: Children Aged 7-14, RLMS 1996 212
7.5 Activities of Young Adults by Age, Gender and Family Type, RLMS 1996 216
7.6 Health Behaviours of Young Adults by Family Type, RLMS 1996 218

Chapter 1: Single Parents and Child Welfare in the New Russia

Albert Motivans and Jeni Klugman

In Russia, as in the West, the form and role of the family as a social and economic unit have changed dramatically during the post-war period. The changes have continued and accelerated during the period of transition which followed the break-up of the USSR in the early 1990s; a transition which has been associated with massive economic disruption and considerable changes in daily life. This book aims first to draw attention to and document one of the most striking manifestations of these changes in family structure, namely the increasing number of children growing up in single-parent families; second, to examine the welfare implications of these changes for children; and third, to investigate the social policy responses of the Russian government with respect to families and children, especially single-parent families.

In 1989, one in seven children (i.e., under 18 years-old) in Russia lived with only one parent; in 1994, by including single-parent sub-families, this figure had risen to one in five children. This has also meant large absolute increases in the number of children living in a single-parent household in the 1990s. In 1994, one and a half million more children in Russia were living in single-parent households than in 1989. As in the West, the vast majority (over 90 per cent) of single-parent households are headed by a woman.

The phenomenon of single-parenthood in the West has generated a large academic literature across several disciplines, as well as widespread popular media and political interest. It has not yet received the same attention in Russia. Both international and domestic analysis in the 1990s has focused on other striking demographic trends in Russia, such as increased mortality, especially among adult males,[1] and the plummeting fertility rate.[2] The links between these demographic changes and the

1

trends related to single parents and family structure have attracted less attention and are less well understood. Official statistics show, for example, that while birth rates fell to an unprecedented low, an increasing proportion of children are born out-of-wedlock. At the same time, the ratio of divorces to total number of marriages has increased by a third during the transition period. The net result of increased divorce, non-marital childbearing and premature mortality during the 1990s has been a greater number of children living in single-parent families. While many of these trends were evident prior to the transition, the pace of change has greatly accelerated since the late 1980s.

This book provides new evidence and analysis of the effects of single-parenthood on child welfare in Russia. The shifts in demographic trends have taken place during a period of massive changes in household welfare. Several studies have documented the growing inequality in Russia, and increases in the incidence and depth of poverty (Klugman, 1997; Klugman and Braithwaite, 1998), and analysis of individual and household-level data has consistently indicated that families with children have been particularly adversely affected (ibid.). In the West, cross-national studies based on household income and budget surveys have documented that the economic status of single-parent families is lower than that of two-parent families (Bradbury and Jännti, 1998, Wong et al., 1993, Bradshaw et al., 1996). We use new statistical data to analyse the welfare of children in single-parent families in Russia during the transition period.

The third main aim of the book is to examine how policy responses in Russia have, or have failed to contribute to protecting the welfare of children in single-parent families. The importance of the welfare system in explaining differences in the economic conditions of single-parent households in Western countries has been documented (Wong et al., 1993; McLanahan et al., 1995; Kamerman and Kahn, 1989) and suggests that public policy can play a key role in alleviating the potential hardship faced by such families. In Russia significant institutional and fiscal obstacles have conditioned and constrained the policy responses to growing welfare needs. The declining role of the state in social protection and service provision has meant that costs and responsibilities have increasingly been borne by households and communities. The role of women in society and the economy also appears to be moving towards more traditional patterns, as levels of female employment and state child-care provision have receded. All this would be expected to have direct implications for the welfare of the vast majority of single-parent families.

While existing analysis of single-parenthood in the West is of relevance to this study, the situation in the 'new Russia' is unique for several reasons, and calls for detailed country-level analysis. More than fifty years of a centrally-planned economy and state ideology created specific social norms and expectations, and these condition both the behaviour of the population and the response of policy makers to the phenomenon. Thus Russia can draw from the Western experience, but it cannot divorce itself entirely from its own historical experience. Social values are changing with a marked but gradual swing towards those associated with Western-style individualism, but these are still mixed with the norms and values of pre-transition Russian and Soviet culture. The shift away from central planning in the 1990s has, moreover, been accompanied by considerable economic dislocation. There have been dramatic falls in average household income alongside rising poverty and inequality, making the need for appropriate policy responses to protect child welfare more urgent.

Despite the prevalence of single-parent families in Russia, very little is known about the routes into single-parenthood, the correlates of family well-being and family structure, the welfare characteristics of children in single-parent families, particularly indicators reflecting educational achievement, health status etc., and the way in which state policies have affected and been affected by this phenomenon.[3] Access to new sources of national data allows detailed empirical investigation of these issues. In particular, the detailed micro-level analyses in this volume draw upon the Russian Longitudinal Monitoring Survey (RLMS) and unpublished data from the 1994 Russian micro-census. The nationally-representative RLMS surveys used in this book were conducted between October 1993 and December 1996. The micro-census, which covered five per cent of the population, was conducted in February 1994, in all regions of Russia (excluding the Chechenya republic). Both sources are described in greater detail later in this chapter. These new data sources allow the authors, coming from a diverse range of disciplines, to make a significant contribution to filling the gap in knowledge about single parents and child welfare in Russia.

The transition period, which began at the outset of the 1990s, could be argued to be too short a time for which to study changes in family structure, which is generally a long-term process. However, international experience suggests that change may unfold quite rapidly. In the United States, for example, the share of children living in single-parent families almost doubled (from 12.8 per cent to 21.5 per cent) in the 1970s, a period which was also characterised by an economic recession, growing inequality and a sharp decline in fertility (Bianchi and Spain, 1996). The fact that Russia has experienced demographic shifts in a similar context of economic and social change in the 1990s provides additional interest from a comparative perspective.

This introductory chapter is structured as follows. The next section reviews the main concepts and data sources. Section 1.2 sets out the relevant conceptual background and a framework for examining alternative policy approaches, before highlighting some key findings from Western research on single parents and child welfare. Section 1.3 summarises historical trends with respect to single parents in Soviet Russia and the wider policy context in the period leading up to the transition. The task of section 1.4 is to set out those economic and social developments of the 1990s that are most salient to analysing trends in family formation and dissolution, and to the welfare of single-parent families. The final section sets out the overall structure of the book and briefly describes the contents of each of the individual chapters.

1.1 Definitions and Data Sources

Classifying a family or a household is as problematic in Russia as it is in Western Europe, if not more so. In this volume we follow the accepted international definition of the household as a single individual or a group of individuals who are sharing a common dwelling unit and household budget (Burch, 1995).

There are many ways to define family relationships within a household. A single-parent family can be defined narrowly, that is households comprising only one adult with co-resident dependent children. Alternatively, a single-parent family may be defined in broader terms, which includes sub-families, or households with the presence of a single parent. This distinction was always recognised in the Russian literature, and corresponded respectively to the terms "incomplete" and "complex" families, although official reporting practices created problems, as noted below, due to failure to consistently differentiate between the two concepts.

All the chapters in this volume employ a definition of single-parent households that includes those in which children under 18 years of age live with less than two parents (father and mother), whether or not with anyone else. The definition also includes cases where children are living in a household with a single adult who is not their biological father/mother. This approach, based on the broader of the two definitions offered above, is consistent with that adopted in much of the Western literature and by the OECD, for example (Ermisch, 1990).

Much of the analysis presented in this volume takes advantage of two new data sources, namely the Russian Longitudinal Monitoring survey (RLMS) and the 1994 Russian micro-census. The RLMS is a multi-purpose panel survey based on a probability sample of individual dwelling units, excluding the institutionalised population, which began in 1994.[4] The household questionnaire contains a wide range of questions on living conditions, income, expenditures, and household composition. In addition, face-to-face interviews were conducted with every member of the household 14 years of age and older, and data were gathered on those younger using an adult interviewee. Adult or child questionnaires were obtained for 97 per cent of all individuals in participating households. The individual questionnaires cover a wide range of topics, ranging from work and school to migration, health, diet, time-use and physical measurements. In subsequent years, interviewers returned to dwelling units in the sample to administer virtually the same questionnaire irrespective of whether interviews were with the households that had participated in the first round in 1994. The relevant fieldwork dates were October-January 1993 (Round IV), November 1994-January 1995 (Round V), October-December 1995 (Round VI), and October-December 1996 (Round VII). Response rates were 84 per cent, 80 per cent and 76 per cent, respectively.

The micro-census was conducted by the Russian state statistical agency, Goskomstat, between 14-23 February 1994. It covered 7.3 million individuals or about five per cent of the population. The survey comprised 49 questions on household structure, education, employment, housing, and other characteristics of the population. Some of the topics (e.g., cohabitation, unemployment) were included for the first time in the history of state surveys in Russia. The survey was also unique in that it marked the return to household-based sampling units rather than the family-based definition used in earlier censuses. Prior to 1994, the Russian (Soviet) practice for censuses used families as the unit of observation. This meant that only individuals related by blood or marriage (including common-law spouses), were counted as households, disregarding any unrelated individuals in the household. Since 1994, the introduction of the new concept defines a household as one sharing a common residence and budget. However, there is evidence that this has not affected comparisons over time because the presence of an unrelated individual in a household was quite rare (see Chapter 3).

We now turn to a brief overview of the Western literature about single-parenthood, before presenting evidence about the pre-transition situation in Soviet Russia.

1.2 Single Parents and Child Welfare in the West

The prevalence of single-parenthood in Western countries has been rising since the 1960s. This has attracted much attention in academic circles and also in broader society. The phenomenon has led to a rich literature in the disciplines of economics, sociology and demography which provides evidence not only on the determinants underlying the increase, but also on the links between family structure, welfare and outcomes. While Chapter 4 is devoted to an analysis of Western experience, it is appropriate here to provide background on the paradigms that have emerged in the Western literature which help set the stage for the analysis that follows.

In the 1980s Western economic theorists began to explain marital behaviour and family formation in terms of economic incentives (see, for example, the so-called 'New Home Economics' associated with work of Gary Becker[5]). They interpreted marriage as the outcome of bargaining by utility maximising agents, and argued that anything that alters the payoffs to the union affects the incentives to enter into marriage and/or stay together. This has the advantage of drawing attention to the trade-offs and constraints which could affect family structure, and does seem to cast some light on observed patterns of behaviour.[6]

The Western literature also points out that private decisions about family formation and dissolution are strongly affected by government policies. Relevant state policies range from rules which govern decisions about marriage and the ease of divorce, to provision of services like child-care, and differential treatment of family types by the tax and benefit system. In particular, the stance of state policy can either encourage or discourage reliance on a male breadwinner (Lewis, 1992). Within this framework, we can see that some states – like Ireland, for example – have encouraged the strong breadwinner (mostly men) model, whereas the Scandinavian countries have adopted a weak breadwinner model (Paci, 1998). The latter approach has included strong support for working mothers (including maternity leave entitlements and subsidisation of childcare) and high levels of financial support for children (Bradshaw et al., 1993).

Western research has also established significant relationships between single-parenthood and economic well-being. Single-parent families have generally been shown to be at greater risk of poverty or poor living conditions, as shown in Figure 1.1. The causes of poverty are related to several factors: the loss of income and economic instability following a divorce, the relatively low earning capacity of the custodial parent (normally the mother), and low levels of child support and public transfers (Garfinkel and McLanahan, 1986). In all European Union countries, for example, the average woman contributes less than half of the total household income – the net result of fewer hours in paid work and lower rates of pay (Paci, 1998). A substantial gender gap in earnings has persisted through the mid-1990s, even if the trend shows some narrowing over time. It is therefore not surprising that households dependent solely on female earnings tend to be worse off.

Growing up in a single-parent home has also been shown to be associated with lower adolescent and later adult achievements. Some

Figure 1.1: Child Poverty by Family Type in the Early1990s
(percentage of children)

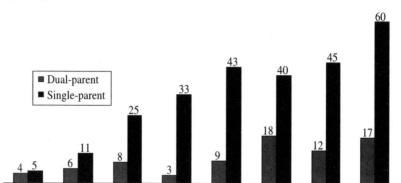

Source: Bradbury and Jännti (1998).
Note: Poverty is measured as a child's having equivalent disposable income less than 50 per cent of
the overall median. Data refer to: Austria, 1987; France, 1989; Sweden, Denmark, 1992; Germany,
Canada, United States, 1994; United Kingdom, 1995.

studies have shown that children from single-parent households fare
worse than those from dual-parent households in terms of educational,
occupational and economic achievement, health status and family formation behaviours. For example, children and adolescents from single-
parent households were found to have lower levels of educational
attainment due to discontinuation of their studies (Entwisle and
Alexander, 1995). In the United States, the probability of high school
graduation by children who have lived in single-parent households is
reported to be up to 16 per cent lower than that of children in dual-parent families (Sandefur, McLanahan and Wojtkiewicz, 1992). Studies
have also shown that living in a single-parent household may have a
greater effect on boys' educational attainment than girls (Ermisch,
1997; Ni Broclchain et al., 1994). Adolescent girls living in single-parent households and especially those having experienced family disruption may be at higher risk of having a non-marital birth or experiencing
a dissolved marriage themselves (Bumpass and McLanahan, 1989;
Plotnick, 1992).

    However, living in a single-parent family is obviously not a
direct indicator of welfare; single parents encompass a range of demo-

graphic profiles and are found across different age, education and income groups. The Western literature on the impact of family structure on child welfare outcomes often distinguishes between those effects due primarily to family structure and those related to household economic resources. Several studies suggest that many of the adverse effects of having lived in a single-parent household depend on income levels (Bane, 1986; Duncan and Rodgers, 1990). The implication is that policy emphasis could be better focused on poverty alleviation, rather than on developing specific policies towards single-parent families. Other studies have shown that changes in family structure have an effect independent of income level (Lerman, 1996). Here, the lower level of total parental "resources", i.e., time spent with children due to maternal employment or lack of parental involvement, is an important factor (Sandefur, 1996), suggesting that specific policy measures aimed at children in single-parent households are both necessary and desirable.

1.3 Single Parents before the Transition

Single-parent families are not a new phenomenon in Russia. Indeed, the prevalence of single-parent families grew rapidly in the 1960s and 1970s. According to 1970 census data, Russia (and other former USSR countries, such as Estonia) had among the highest rates of single-parenthood in the world, at around 12 per cent of all families with children. By comparison, the rate was 10 per cent in Sweden and 8 per cent in the United Kingdom (see Figure 1.2). From 1970 to 1990, however, many countries experienced rapid growth in prevalence. Rates more than doubled in the U.S. and U.K. during this period while rates in Russia remained relatively unchanged over the two decades.

The factors underlying the rapid post-war growth of single-parent families in Russia were broadly similar to those in the West, and can be found in the labour market, social norms and social policies. At the same time, however, the unique characteristics of Soviet Russia played a specific role in family structure developments.

The most oft-cited explanation for changes in family dissolution in

Western countries has been the growing participation of women/mothers in paid labour (Becker, 1981; McLanahan, 1991) and changes in social norms (Thornton, 1989). In Russia, the number of single parents grew, though not as fast as labour market opportunities widened for women.[7] The perceived labour shortages which characterised Soviet central planning led to a range of measures designed to facilitate female employment, which succeeded in the sense that Russian women joined the labour force in large numbers in the late 1960s and early 1970s (McAuley, 1981). According to Soviet data, female employment (as a share of the working age cohort) stood at 87 per cent in 1975 (ibid.).

Rising female employment during the Soviet period can be seen as a rational response at the individual and household level to state subsidies which facilitated labour force participation. This included extensive kindergarten provision, and other services which were linked to the employer (like housing), or linked to work history (like labour pensions). It was also a reflection of social norms and the ideological pressure that was placed on Soviet citizens to work and contribute to the construction of a socialist society. Increasing female participation was, however, also

Figure 1.2: Share of Single-Parent Households, 1970 and 1989
(percentage of all households with children)

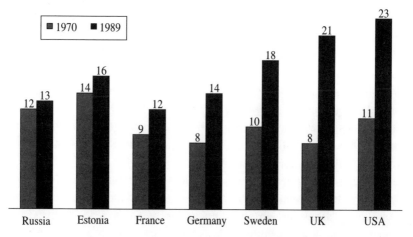

Sources: Goskomstat (1993), McLanahan and Casper (1995), Bradshaw et al. (1996), Sorrentino (1990).
Notes: Data refer to, France=1968 and 1990; Germany=1972 and 1988, Sweden=1990, UK=1971 and 1992, USA=1990. Country specific definitions of age of children may differ.

a response to the simple need to provide for the family: the Soviet system of planning was premised on the assumption of dual-earner households, so that deviations from that norm were less likely to be able to afford to purchase basic subsistence requirements (Braithwaite, 1997).

Viewed in an economic framework, there were competing factors which affected decisions about marital formation and dissolution during the Soviet period. In a number of respects the Soviet approach encouraged economic equality and female independence in ways which typify the so-called weak breadwinner model, e.g., where all adults not in full-time education are assumed to be in employment. As already noted, female employment rates were high and the infrastructure to enable paid work existed in the form of enterprise-based childcare and relatively generous provisions for maternity and parental leave.

On the other hand, state wage policies meant that men tended to be the main breadwinner in the household, which tended to increase dependency among women even if they were working. There was a persistent gender wage gap of the order of about 30 per cent (McAuley, 1981; Oxenstierna, 1990). Given the fact that all earnings were set centrally by the state, and the general awareness of the high degree of occupational segregation of women into certain economic sectors and occupations – in particular, social services and administrative roles – the gender wage gap was at least partially attributable to the stance adopted by state planners.

Some authors have attributed the rise in single-parenthood in Western societies to growing social acceptance of the phenomenon and increasingly individualistic values (Casterline et al., 1996; see also Chapter 4 in this volume). In Russia, social norms regarding single-parenthood are mixed. Marriage is widely practised and has remained a very strong tradition. Moreover, people tend to marry at a relatively young age. In 1989, over 67 per cent of Russian women in the age group 20-24 years had married compared to 25 per cent in Germany or 14 per cent in Denmark (UN, 1995). Ideological norms that stressed collective needs over individual ones represented a strong element of the Soviet social system, and favoured the maintenance of a marriage over individual preferences. On the other hand, the first (1918) Marriage Code introduced at the beginning of the Soviet state was based on the ideological premise that marriage should be a free union based on the mutual consensus of the two partners (see Chapter 5), although under Stalin this approach was abandoned. Some remnants of this original revolutionary ideology survived, and have arguably contributed to the high divorce rates and the resulting single-parent families that have been a feature of Russian society for several decades. While there is anecdotal evidence of stigma attached to non-marital child-bearing, there is general acceptance of divorce and the resulting single-parent family. The ideological norms stressing collective needs became weaker and more superficial with each new generation, especially in the post-war period, and could not in any case compete with the stress placed on marital union by the realities of Soviet life (for example, cramped and difficult living conditions) which also contributed to high divorce rates.[8]

In terms of concerns about the welfare of children in single-parent families, some modest support appeared in the 1980s. For example, from 1981, single mothers were given priority in pre-school placements over married mothers. A modest cash benefit was introduced at about the same time. However, housing shortages were pervasive. For example, a 1984 study showed that many young couples still lived with their parents even following marriage (Lutz et al., 1994). One would have expected the housing situation to have created strong disincentives to single-parenthood through the route of a non-marital birth. The priority given to married couples in the housing queue ahead of others influenced decisions about family formation (Elizarov, 1996), and the tendency toward early marriage noted above.

Data regarding the welfare of single-parent families in the pre-transition period are sparse, as is information about living standards generally (Atkinson and Micklewright, 1992). Nonetheless some recognition of the material needs of low-income families was given in 1974, with the introduction of a targeted cash benefit for "under-provisioned" families.[9] Single-parent families were also recognised as a socially vulnerable group around that time, and became a target of social policy, when special benefits were introduced for families "at high risk". (This category also extended to families with four or more children, and to families with the head of the household in military service.) Not until the outset of the transition, however, was a new broad range of family-related benefits introduced, as detailed in Chapter 5.

1.4 Changing Macro-Economic and Labour Market Trends in the Transition

The macro-economic and structural difficulties associated with the transition from a centrally planned system are by now well-known. It is nonetheless worth highlighting those trends which have had a direct impact on household welfare in general, and more specifically on the welfare of children in single-parent families.

The economic impact of transition is most dramatically reflected in the large falls in production over a succession of years, which were most severe in 1992 and 1994. In terms of measured output, real GDP was down by 42 per cent in 1998 over the 1989 level (see Figure 1.3). Declines in output, reduced administrative capacity of the state and the growing importance of informal sector activity have translated into lower government revenues. This has created significant downward pressure on public spending, given the government's objective to stabilise inflation and the commensurate need to limit budget deficits. Tax revenue as a share of GDP dropped from over 40 per cent at the start of the 1990s to under 30 per cent by 1995-96 (Hemming et al., 1995) and down to just over 20 per cent in 1997 (RECEP, 1998). The decline in revenues has put downward pressure on social expenditure, which dropped, as a share of GDP, from 10.1 per cent in 1989 to 8.0 per cent in 1995.[10]

Another important characteristic which has shaped social policy is the decentralisation of social expenditures. Over 80 per cent of expenditure on education and health is the responsibility of regional governments, which vary greatly in terms of their own fiscal capacity. Measured in terms of expenditure responsibilities, Russia is now a more decentralised country than the United States (IMF, 1998). The system of re-distribution from richer to poorer regions within the Federation is notably weak (Stewart, 1997). Thus not only is there overall a shortage of revenue with which to finance social expenditure; there are growing discrepancies in the ability of the various regions of the country to finance social programmes. This situation looks unlikely to improve in the immediate future.

Real wage levels have fallen substantially (Figure 1.3). This has been associated with labour market adjustment which, for several years at least, involved only limited adjustment on the quantity side; that is, overall unemployment levels are low relative to the scale of output decline. As a result, levels of labour productivity and earnings have fallen significantly (Commander and Yemtsov, 1997). The sharp wage reduction which followed the price liberalisation of January 1992 had not yet been recovered by early 1999. By 1998, the real wage was still only half of its 1990 level. The official wage figures even understate the actual extent of decline, insofar as a substantial portion of wages go unpaid, often for months, and are not indexed for inflation if and when payment is made (Standing, 1997). Thus, coupled with the lack of revenue to finance state social policy expenditure, there is a decreasing ability of households and private individuals to cover costs themselves.

As output fell and economic restructuring proceeded, the distribution of income became increasingly polarised. According to Russian household budget surveys the top income quintile of the population received 38 per cent of income in 1992 and 47 per cent in 1997 (Frolova,

Figure 1.3: Trends in Real GDP Growth and Real Wage Growth in Russia, 1990-1998 (1990=100)

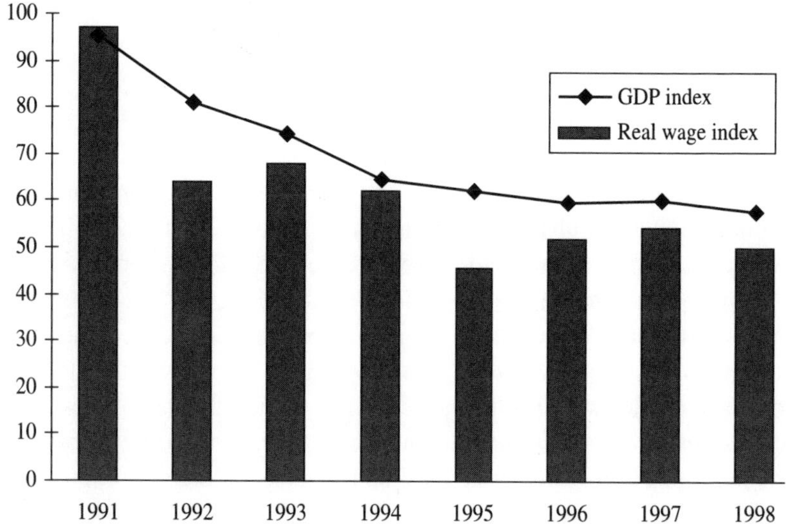

Source: EBRD (1999).

1998). The bottom 20 per cent received only 6 per cent of income in 1997. Households with children were more concentrated in the lower income quintiles (ibid.). The Gini coefficient of per capita income, another way to the show the level of equality in the income distribution (where zero equals a perfectly equal distribution), increased in Russia from 0.24 in 1985 to 0.375 in 1996 (UNICEF, 1998; Fleming and Micklewright, 1999). Thus, in terms of income inequality, the trend in Russia is moving closer towards the United States (0.38) than Sweden (0.24) (ibid.).

The net effect of income declines and higher inequality has been a sharp increase in the prevalence and depth of poverty (Klugman and Braithwaite, 1998). Household level surveys have shown that the risk of poverty has been correlated with the number of children or dependants in a household (Frolova, 1998; Mroz and Popkin, 1996). Families with more children run a greater risk of poverty than smaller families (ibid.). And households with fewer wage-earners, particularly single-parent families, face a higher risk of poverty.

The conceptualisation of state attitudes toward women's roles in the family and in the economy in terms of the weak and strong breadwinner states set out in Section 1.2, is a useful framework for understanding recent developments. The transition has seen several trends, a number of which have reinforced the strong breadwinner model and the assumption that men are the main providers for the family, with women being treated as dependent wives. The overall tendencies are mixed however, as shown below.

A key dimension of the breadwinner model is the extent to which childcare support is offered. During the transition, the supply of childcare and similar services aimed at supervising school-aged children while the parent(s) were working (e.g., extended day schools, summer camps and extra-curricular activities) has been cut sharply or subject to cost-recovery, which has created barriers for parents with lower incomes. Childcare provision by the state has fallen, with coverage dropping to one in five under-3 year olds and just over three in five in the 3-6 year-old age group (Figure 1.4). This has been related to both a decline in supply (27,000 kindergartens closed between 1989-1997), but also to a decline in demand due to higher fees. Alternatives to formal state institutions are rare, as private childcare has been forbidden by law since 1995.

It has been noted that over 90 per cent of single-parent households are headed by women. This makes the employment and earning opportunities of women particularly relevant to the welfare of children in single-parent households. How has female employment been affected by transition? On the one hand, one would expect diminished access to childcare to reduce the extent of female participation. This would be compounded by the fact that the reduction in real wages noted earlier has reduced the attractiveness of market work outside the home. On the other hand, general reductions in labour earnings of men and women and the liberalisation of prices of basic goods and services would be expected to increase the incentive to find paid work to try and maintain, or at least protect, the living standards of the family. It might also be expected that relative wage adjustments associated with economic liberalisation would serve to benefit women, who traditionally entered the labour market with higher levels of education than men.[11] Finally, it might be expected that greater flexibility in the labour market would allow women to take advantage of emerging private sector opportunities, and also engage in paid work on a part-time basis. The latter is a common practice in Europe, where almost one-third of female employees work part-time (CEC, 1994).

In fact, the available evidence shows that labour market developments have been, overall, quite detrimental to women (UNICEF, 1999). There have been large declines in what was previously one of the highest female labour force participation rates in the world. As shown in Figure 1.4, during the transition period participation rates have dropped by 12 percentage points among young women, aged 15-59 years. While there is evidence that women on the whole are freely choosing to withdraw from the labour market, the majority are involuntarily unemployed or discouraged job-seekers who would prefer to maintain their labour market activity. Levels of employment among women aged 15-29 years fell by about 17 percentage points over the period 1989-1996 (OECD-CCET database; ILO, 1992, 1997).

An examination of average gender pay ratios shows that the historically disadvantaged position of women has not improved during the transition. This experience has been shared by women throughout the

Figure 1.4: Childcare, Kindergartens and Female Employment, 1989 and 1996-97
(percentage of relevant age group)

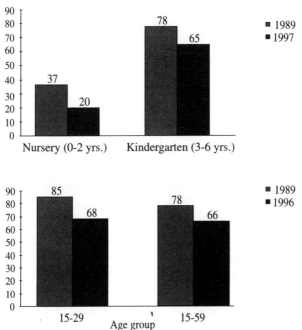

Source: ILO (1992, 1997), MONEE Project database, UNICEF IRC.
Note: Gross enrolment rates of 0-2 and 3-6 year-olds.

formerly planned economies.[12] This can be traced, at least in part, to the concentration of women into the relatively lower paid jobs, a legacy that has continued in the transition. The gender segregation of the workforce could thus be taken to explain a significant part of their wage disadvantage relative to men.

Undoubtedly, there are a number of Russian women for whom the transition has meant new opportunities and choices, however, for the majority of women, this has not been the case. Privatization has had an uneven effect in gender terms with the rate of female relocation from the public to the private sector being lower in comparison to men. Although the service sector has witnessed significant growth in most transitional economies, men appear to have been the main beneficiaries of the rapid development of this sector (UNICEF, 1999). Female employment remains heavily concentrated in the public or state sector and this is partly attributable to the occupational skills they possess, a legacy of central planning. Gimpleson and Lippoldt (1998), for example, find that in five regions of Russia examined in March 1996, between 55 and 60 per cent of private sector employees were men. The share of self- employment among women remains fairly low at around 10 per cent (OECD, 1997).

The foregoing sheds some useful light on the economic context facing current and potential single parents. It should be considered alongside the evidence, detailed in Chapter 6, suggesting a sharp withdrawal of state support for the family, including children in single-parent families. While this has been at least partly forced by the dire fiscal circumstances faced by the Russian government during the transition, it does have serious implications for the well-being of families and single-parent families, as we show below.

The overall impression of the transition period reveals contradictory tendencies with respect to the breadwinner model. While the transition has adversely affected most breadwinners and potential breadwinners, in the form of falling wages and rising unemployment, women have generally also failed to gain in relative terms. Coupled with limited and declining public support for families, this would tend to reinforce their dependency on men. In this sense the empirical point from which this volume embarks – that is the rising prevalence of single-parenthood – is somewhat surprising. The next two chapters serve to shed light on this question. It also leads to heightened concern about the welfare implications of single-parenthood, which is a major focus of this volume.

1.5 The Structure of the Book

How did the massive economic changes associated with transition and the broader shifts in society impact on demographic trends, social policies and child welfare? The book examines these issues in three parts, each comprised of two chapters.

Demographic Trends Underlying the Growth in Single-Parent Households

Part I sets the demographic context for understanding how the situation of single parents has evolved in Russia. The two chapters examine change from different perspectives: the first analysing national trends since 1970 and the second focusing on individual behaviour during the transition.

In Chapter 2, Albert Motivans places post-1970 trends in household structure in Russia within the demographic processes unfolding in Western countries. He examines current levels of prevalence of single-parent families and explores the main demographic determinants of the rise in such households – marital instability, non-marital births and parental mortality – since 1970. Before the transition, demographic trends in Russia differed from western or other European countries mainly in the virtual universality of registered marriage and the tendency to marry at increasingly younger ages. During the transition, the growing number of children in single-parent households was due to increased marital instability, non-marital births and, particularly disturbing, high rates of premature parental death. Another transition-related development has been the increased number of extended families, as more single parents are compelled to move in with their grandparents or other relatives, mainly due to economic reasons.

In Chapter 3, Michael Swafford analyses changes in household structure at the micro-level during the transition based on results from several rounds of the Russian Longitudinal Monitoring Study (RLMS). He reviews the context of social norms and perceptions integral to understanding household structure and family types in Russia. He also examines the nature of different types (co-residence, kinship) of single-parent households, the factors which mediated their entry into single-parent status and the characteristics of the sole parent. He finds that the premature death of the father has emerged as an important cause of single-parenthood. The chapter analyses family-cycle events such as entries into and exits from single-parent status, complex families and incomplete families confirming a tendency toward consolidation of households, usually through a single parent and child(ren) relocating with her parents or in-laws. The author also takes advantage of the panel data available through the RLMS to look at evidence of growing instability in the living arrangements of children in the transition period.

Social Policy and the Single Parent

The aim of Part II is to evaluate the social policy framework for dual and single-parent families in the context of historical and international experience and of the evolution of Russian social policy approaches toward families with children, especially single parents. Both chapters assess current social policy and discuss options through analyses of the underlying political and economic dimensions of Soviet and current Russian policies, and the lessons of Western experiences.

Sheldon Danziger and Marcia Carlson examine Western experiences in Chapter 4. While the U.S. case has been most extensively studied in the literature, the chapter includes analysis of relevant experience and perspectives arising in OECD countries. The authors explore the factors driving observed changes, in particular female labour force participation, changing societal attitudes and norms, and the legal and regulatory framework. Attention is drawn to areas of consensus as well as continuing controversy with regard to the nature and impact of alternative policies. The chapter goes on to investigate the poverty status of single parents in the West, highlighting cross-national variation in trends and possible explanations. A typology of state policy approaches is used to highlight the choices facing policy-makers in Russia.

In Chapter 5, Jeni Klugman and Alastair McAuley analyse the social policy context for dual and single-parent families in Russia. Social policy is examined in the broad sense of state attitudes toward different marital and reproductive behaviour, as well the social protection dimension and the linkages among different policies. While the primary interest is the transition period, (i.e., post-1991), a long-term perspective enables the reader to put the current system and recent changes into context. The chapter provides an overview of the evolution of Soviet policy towards the single-parent family and how this has influenced the current debate. It shows how the Russian government's policies to support the needs of single parents have been influenced and constrained by the circumstances of transition from a command economy. Among the main findings is that single-parent households were protected and supported by the collectivist welfare system that characterised the planned economy, insofar as prices for basic goods and services were kept low and employment opportunities were relatively abundant. However state support was based primarily on the fact that the family contained children, and that the household was poor, rather than on the absence of a second parent, as the problem of poverty gained official recognition during the late Soviet period. There was little support for single-parent households as such.

The transition to a market economy has also seen a further relaxation of the already liberal rules governing divorce, and some attempt to tighten financial support from non-custodial parents, although the latter remains very problematic. More importantly, however, the transition has undermined the rationale of the collectivist welfare system. The nature and extent of support provided for single-parent households has been altered, not least because of the economic crisis and the collapse of state revenues. The transition to a market economy has intensified the economic disadvantage traditionally faced by single-parent families, a topic which is addressed in depth in the next part of the book.

Single-Parenthood and Measures of Welfare

Part III investigates welfare outcomes of different family types, focusing on poverty among children in single-parent households and direct measures of child well-being in the transition. The chapters focus on the status of children living in single-parent households in an overall context where poverty has been rising. This extends to an analysis of the factors influencing the risk of poverty for single-parent families as compared to other family types and an investigation of the welfare impact on children in terms of their education and health. The analysis in both chapters is based on micro-data from the RLMS.

In Chapter 6, Jeni Klugman and Alexandre Kolev highlight several developments regarding poverty and single-parent families in Russia during the transition, based on the analysis of national survey data between 1994-96. In the context of increasing aggregate poverty there has been a widening dispersion in poverty rates between family types. Most striking has been the surge in poverty among single-parent families, whose poverty rate has almost tripled over a three-year period. This chapter represents the first detailed study of poverty among single-parent families in the transition based on nationally-representative micro-data.

The authors investigate the causes of poverty among single parents and find that many of the poverty risk factors confronting single parents are similar to those facing families generally, including the number and age of children, the effect of unemployment, and so on. Specific to single parents, however, they find that divorce and the number of wage earners in the household both have an impact on the risk of poverty. Moreover typical coping mechanisms in the face of vulnerability (i.e., home production and informal sector employment), are less open to single parents presumably because of time and other domestic constraints. They also conclude that there are unobserved characteristics that affect the welfare status of single parents. In particular, single-parenthood *per se*, even after controlling for observed variables like marital and employment status, significantly heightens the probability of the family being in poverty. Public transfers, which make an important contribution to the income of single-parent families, have exhibited sharp changes during the transition. The authors show that single parents are especially vulnerable to changes in public transfers.

Extending the analysis of welfare and poverty across family types using consumption-based indicators, Aline Coudouel and Mark Foley look in Chapter 7 at other indicators of child welfare. Although economic security is an important underlying determinant of welfare, it is not a direct measure of child welfare outcomes. To this end, Chapter 7 turns to other direct indicators, including health and nutritional status, and educational participation and attainment.

The main contribution of this chapter is to elaborate child welfare outcomes among those children living in single-parent families compared to other children. The analysis is based on a distinction between children of different ages (pre-school, compulsory school and extending up to 22 years), and also by gender of the child. The authors find that both direct and indirect measures of child welfare outcomes differ systematically by family type. These differences are most evident in terms of school enrolment and the health status of children under 6 years and in terms of educational and occupational achievements among post-compulsory school graduates. Although the differences are generally not large with respect to individual indicators, the cumulative effect is nonetheless important. The authors suggest, however, that household income levels are a stronger influence on child outcomes than family structure, including particular single-parent status.

NOTES

1 See for example, UNICEF (1993, 1994), Kingkade (1994), Cornia and Paniccià (1995), Anderson and Silver (1995), Shapiro (1995), Shkolnikov (1996), Chen, et al. (1996), Paniccià (1997).

2 See Haub (1994), Ivanova (1996), Heleniak (1997), Vyshnevskiy (1997).

3 Recently, however, studies have begun to examine demographic changes: Sinel'nikov (1997), Institute of Family Studies (1997), Borisov and Sinel'nikov (1996); and household welfare by family type, see for example, Rimashevskaya (1996) and Mozhina and Prokofieva (1997).

4 Earlier rounds of the RLMS were based on a different sample.

5 See Paci (1999) for a useful overview of the theory and its implications regarding family policy.

6 Most obviously, it is rational in this framework for the partners with lower outside earning capacity to specialize in home production.

7 Note that in terms of levels of educational attainment, women first moved ahead of men in the 1970s, in that higher shares of female cohorts were completing university. However, the private returns to education were relatively higher for young men who left school early to enter industrial occupations.

8 Chapter 5 investigates official attitudes toward marriage as reflected in legislation about divorce and child support.

9 The level at which the threshold for "under-provisioned" was set was based on expert assessment of minimal subsistence needs; at that time, 50 roubles (see Braithwaite 1997). This was used as an unofficial poverty line.

10 Based on unpublished World Bank staff estimates.

11 There is evidence that returns to educational qualifications have risen during the transition (see Rutkowski, 1996, Klugman 1997, Reilly, 1999).

12 For example, the average monthly female earnings in the mid-1990s in Latvia, Lithuania, Estonia, the Ukraine and Uzbekistan range from two-thirds to just over three quarters of male earnings, and suggest little movement in this gap since the period of central planning (UNICEF, 1999).

PART I

THE DEMOGRAPHIC CONTEXT

Chapter 2: Family Formation, Stability and Structure in Russia

Albert Motivans[*]

Patterns of family formation, dissolution and the resulting family structure in Russia have changed considerably in post-war period. Changing demographic patterns have also characterised most Western countries. In Russia, however, these changes have been accelerated in the context of the massive economic and social change in the 1990s, leading to shifts in the living arrangements of children, particularly the increase of single-parent households.

This chapter has three important aims: first, to place post-1970 demographic trends related to family formation in a broader historical and comparative context. This overview will draw attention to important pre-transition differences between trends in Russia and those in other industrialized countries that have implications for household structure and the single-parent phenomenon. The second section examines changes in household structure and child living arrangements during the transition, especially single-parent families. The third section explores the main routes into single-parenthood in the 1990s – marital instability, non-marital births and parental mortality – and how these trends have contributed to changes in living arrangements. In conclusion, these analyses provide the basis for hypotheses about the future development of demographic trends and convergence and the single-parent phenomenon in Russia.

2.1 An Overview of Demographic Trends: East and West

Comparative research on changing demographic behaviour in Western and Eastern Europe is rather limited. Several studies have examined the determinants of both long- and short-term change in family formation in

Central and Eastern Europe in comparison to European and North American countries, some expressing more potential for convergence in trends than others.[1] In Russia, however, the study of family structure and factors influencing its change has been limited due to ideological concerns.[2] This section will compare patterns in fertility, marriage and divorce in Russia and other developed countries, highlighting the trends and factors that differentiate the Russian case.

Patterns of Fertility, Marriage and Divorce

While post-1970 demographic trends in Russia have followed a pattern similar to other Western countries, it should be noted that trends in Russia have been strongly affected by historical events. In particular, the large population losses due to the Second World War created significant gender and age imbalances in the structure of the Russian population. These imbalances, for example, have influenced trends in family formation and, although diminished by time, their echoes were still felt through the 1990s.

As in other industrialized countries, fertility has been steadily declining in Russia (Table 2.1), although retaining its unique characteristics (young age at first birth, short intervals between births) more comparable to other middle-income per capita countries (Latin America, Southeast Asia). As elsewhere, this has led to both declining levels of desired and actual family size.

While birth rates declined following the war, rates suddenly increased in the 1980s. The increase in fertility was notable in that the largest increase in births was among second and higher parity births. Thus, the share of women who had given birth to their second child rose from 26 per cent in 1979 to 32 per cent in 1989.

The rise in fertility during the 1980s subsequently abated, however, and fell to below population-replacement levels by 1990. Despite general similarities in this trend, certain characteristics of fertility have sharply contrasted with those found in Europe and North America.

The demographic trends that distinguished Russia from other industrialized countries and other countries of the former socialist bloc (e.g., Hungary) during the 1970-1990 period are:

● An increasingly young profile to family formation. The mean age of

Table 2.1: Changes in Family Trends in Four Countries, 1970 and 1990

	1990 level				**Per cent change: 1970 and 1990**			
	Russia	**Hungary**	**Sweden**	**USA**	**Russia**	**Hungary**	**Sweden**	**USA**
Total fertility rate [a]	1.89	1.84	2.14	2.01	- 6	- 7	**10**	- 18
Teen birth rate [b]	55.6	39.5	14.1	53.6	**87**	- 21	- 59	- 21
Non-marital birth share [c]	14.6	13.1	47.0	28.0	**38**	143	153	162
Crude marriage rate [d]	8.9	6.4	4.7	9.8	- 12	-31	-13	- 7
Mean age of women at first marriage [e]	22.6	22.2	27.6	24.4	- 7	5	15	18
Crude divorce rate [d]	3.8	2.4	2.3	4.7	27	9	44	34
General divorce rate [f]	42.2	46.5	47.9	48.6	41	86	60	49
Share of single parents [g]	13	16	18	23	**8**	60	90	109

Sources: Ch. 1, p. 10, Figure 1.2; Council of Europe (1998); MONEE Project database, UNICEF IRC; Eurostat (1993).
Notes: [a] children per woman; [b] births per 1,000 women aged 15-19 years; [c] percentage of live births; [d] per 1,000 population; [e] years; [f] divorces per 100 registered marriages; [g] share of single-parent households among all households with children; Russia=1989, U.S.=1988.

women and men at first marriage and of women at first birth became increasingly younger, contrary to western countries, where family formation was delayed.

• A low and stable share of childbearing outside marriage and presumably low levels of cohabitation; the prevalence of single-parent households remained stable, whereas in western countries all three measures increased markedly during the period, although the scope of change varied widely by country.

To some extent these trends may reflect the links between sexual activity and pregnancy and between pregnancy and marriage. As these links weakened in western countries, they remained strong in Russia. Family formation at a young age is an important characteristic differentiating Russia and the rest of Europe. More importantly, the tendency has been towards increasingly youthful family formation since 1970. For example, the mean age at first marriage for both men and women in Russia declined steadily during the period. As shown in Table 2.1, the mean age of women fell by 7 per cent in Russia, while showing a modest increase in Hungary (5 per cent) and quite large gains in the U.S. (18 per cent) and Sweden (15 per cent).

Moreover, an overwhelming majority of women were married by their early-20s. In 1990, the percentage of women aged 20-24 years who were not married was 34 per cent in Russia, which was substantially below, for example, 56 per cent in Hungary, 67 per cent in the United States and 91 per cent in Sweden. This trend also influenced childbearing patterns. Whereas in every western country the level of adolescent childbearing had steadily decreased in the 1970-1990 period, rates in Russia increased by 87 per cent (Table 2.1). By 1990 the adolescent birth rate was several times higher than in neighbouring European countries at, for example, 55.6 in Russia compared to 14.1 in Sweden (Table 2.1), 9.1 in France, 8.0 in Italy and 6.9 in the Netherlands (UN, 1997).

In terms of marital behaviour, Russia was characterized by the universal practice of civil-registered marriages and low levels of childbearing outside marriage. The available evidence on cohabitation in Russia shows relatively low rates that are strikingly similar across age groups suggesting relative stability over time. In the early postwar period the share of non-marital births was 2-5 times higher in Russia than in most other European countries, but subsequently fell. Since 1970, however, the share has remained quite low (Table 2.1) in comparison to western countries. By comparison, shares in Hungary, Sweden and the United States rose four times more rapidly during the same period.

A common feature has been the increase in divorce and separation. Along with the United States, Russia has one of the highest divorce rates in the world, almost 50-90 per cent higher than rates in neighbouring European countries (Table 2.1). A ratio based on the annual number of marriages and divorces – the general divorce rate – shows similar levels across the four countries. The effect of divorce rates has been somewhat mediated by remarriage. Remarriage rates in Russia have grown as a share of total marriages, from 8 per cent in 1960 to 25 per cent in 1985, though at the outset this was due to sharp declines in any type of marriage. Since 1985 the share has remained stable, so that about one in four marriages is the second for either or both partners.

These demographic patterns also help to explain comparative changes in household structure over the period. The share of children living in single-parent households in Russia was quite high by international standards in the 1960s, though the level remained stable in the following several decades. In 1970, for example, in Russia the share was similar to that in most European countries, although comparisons should be made cautiously, as there are cross national differences in definitions of family types (Table 2.1). In Russia, 13 per cent of households with children were headed by a single parent, compared to 11 per cent in the United States, 10 per cent in Sweden, 8 per cent in Germany and the United Kingdom. Over the next 20 years, the Russian level remained practically unchanged, while prevalence rose by 60 per cent in Hungary and 109 per cent in the United States.

Implications of the Pre-Transition Legacy

What accounts for the differences in family formation trends as compared to other industrialized countries? The factors which contributed to the universality and youthful profile of marriage in Russia are related to social norms and behaviours and the characteristics of the socialist system, namely the paternalistic role of the state. As both the system and social norms are in a state of great flux during transition, this has begun to impact on demographic processes. However, it will be difficult to distinguish these effects until the economic and social environment becomes more stable.

The universality of marriage is based partly on its strength as a traditional social institution. This is reflected in the extremely high share of pre-nuptial conceptions, that is, the share of births which were conceived out-of-wedlock and precipitated marriage. According to regional studies, they represented 30-40 per cent of all first births and 50-60 per cent of adolescent births (Zakharova, Ivanovna, 1996). The link between pregnancy and marriage, which has weakened in the European countries, has remained strong in Russia.

At the same time, the act of registering a marriage was also a bureaucratic hurdle to access a number of important state benefits. For example, the opportunity to obtain housing separate from one's parents, although access to housing still entailed a substantial waiting period. In a national opinion poll, three quarters of young married couples stated their preference to live in a residence separate from their parents (Goskomstat, 1990), but there were also considerable constraints in the supply of housing. According to another survey, most young couples continued to live with their parents (Volkov, 1991).

It has also been suggested that there are health reasons underlying the high rate of adolescent childbearing and consequent marriages. Young women tend to complete childbearing at a young age and reduced birth intervals (Zakharov, Ivanovna, 1996), while many took early pregnancies to term for fear that heavy dependence on abortion as a means of family planning would lead to birth complications later in life (DaVanzo, 1996). There are grounds for this perception, as two in three women suffer from health problems caused by abortions, according to Health Ministry statistics. One of the resulting health problems, infertility, has been estimated to affect 15 to 20 per cent of Russian couples (AFP, 1998). In more than half the cases, this sterility is due to abortions carried out too early, or to untreated venereal disease in the man (ibid).

The elaboration of state policies had an instrumental affect on demographic processes. The relationship between the family and state has undergone considerable change during the post-war period in Russia. In many ways these changes reflected general demographic and institutional processes across the industrialized world: declining fertility, new family forms and the emergence of the welfare state. Nevertheless, the timing and character of these changes, as well as the role of the state in the process, was markedly different to that in the West. For example, evidence of progress in terms of women's empowerment and independence, especially from the late 1950s, was considerable, and presaged similar developments in the West in the following decades.

While social policies in some Western European countries have often been seen as a means of keeping women at home as housewives and mothers, those in Russia have played a major role in sustaining mothers as workers. Such policies achieved high levels of women's employment, but still bore significant costs in terms of workload and lower levels of pay while the attachment of benefits to employment brought a higher risk of poverty to lone mothers and children. Still, in the context of full employment, a relatively flat wage distribution, and significant non-cash transfers, family benefits were relatively liberal. This had important implications for single-parents as they were facilitated in balancing household tasks and employment by having access to child care facilities, after-school care, summer camps and so on.

Entering marriage or bearing a child at a young age in other developed countries is often interpreted as a reaction to a lack of opportunity. In formerly socialist countries, this behaviour could also be interpreted as a reaction to the lack of risks (employment, state benefits, even child care were guaranteed by the state). Thus, young adults were penalised much less in terms of potential earnings by an early marriage or an early birth. It was also made easier to enter marriage because family law made it easier to divorce.

2.2 Trends in Family Structure and Child Living Arrangements

According to the 1994 micro-census, the population (148 million) of Russia consisted of 52 million households with an average size of 2.84 persons. The most common family type is that of a married couple with or without children. The share of households with children (children refers to the population under 18 years old) was 59% with an average of 1.6 children per household. Of these households a majority (53 per cent) had a single child, 37 per cent had two children and the remaining 10 per cent had three or more. Large families of three and more children are relatively rare in Russia and are primarily found in rural regions.

The regions of Russia reflect considerable differentiation in family size and family structure. This is due to differences in birth rates related to socio-economic and cultural factors. Higher fertility rates, large family size and extended households are characteristic across the primarily agricultural southern autonomous regions (North Caucasus and Siberia), especially Chechenya-Ingushetia, Dagestan, Kalmykia, Tuva, Buryatia and Yakutia. Households that are much smaller in size and seldom comprise three generations are found in the more industrialized North-West and Central regions. The variation in family size is even greater when comparing rural areas: from over five members in rural Chechenya-Ingushetia to under three in regions bordering Eastern Europe. The share of large families (seven or more persons) varies from 18 per cent in Chechenya-Ingushetia to one per cent in the industrial region of Ivanovo, northwest of Moscow.

While the term family structure can refer to a group of individuals linked by blood relation, as noted in the previous chapter, here it follows the accepted UN definition where a household is a single individual or a group of individuals sharing a common dwelling unit and household budget (Burch, 1995). This concept was employed in the 1994 microcensus. It is important to note that earlier censuses were based on a concept of the family which counted only those household members who were blood relations. According to Russian statistical specialists, this definitional change has only a minor effect on comparisons between groups of households, such as the distribution of children across households, as the practice of non-relatives living in a household was extremely rare (Zbarskaya, 1998).

A single-parent household can be defined either narrowly, that is as a household comprised of one adult with co-resident dependent children, or in broader terms, which includes sub-families, or households with the presence of a single parent.

A common approach to measuring the prevalence of single-parent families is by using the household as the unit of analysis, for example, the share of single-parent households over the total number of households with children under 18 years (as noted above, three in five of all households in 1994). Here, the category of single-parent households is broken down into three categories, each with different implications for the children living in them: 1) single-parent households where the custodial parent is the only adult in the household; 2) single-parent households that include another adult, typically a grandparent, and since the 1994 microcensus a third category; 3) single parents who are defined as sub-families. In census tabulations, single-parent families living with a married couple (typically the grandparents) were included in the total for the *married couple* category. The children living in single-parent sub-families could be considered potentially less at risk than other types, although this depends largely on the number of wage-earners in the household.

According to this measure, the trend in Russia has been towards the declining prevalence of dual-parent households and increasing numbers of single-parent households. Moreover, these figures show slow change over time, especially in comparison to other European countries. In the last period, 1989-94, the figures reflect the consolidation of households – particularly in extending households across families or across family generations. As Table 2.2 shows, the household categories "two or more married couples" and "single parents and related single adults" showed a marked increase in the 1990s. The increase in the number of extended families reflects the economic difficulties during the transition and the low supply and high cost of housing, particularly in the light of privatization.

However, this measure is not sufficient because these data represent households rather than children. With respect to child welfare, an alternative approach is to analyse child living arrangements from the perspective of the child – i.e., the share of children under 18 years-old living in single-parent households. Using this measure, the results of the 1994 micro-census show that the proportion of children living in single-parent families has grown from 4.5 million in 1989 to 5.3 million in

Table 2.2: Distribution of Families/Households with Children by Type in Russia (percentages)

	Share of families/households		
	1979	1989	1994
All households with dependent children	**100**	**100**	**100**
Dual-parent	**84.0**	**83.5**	**82.2**
One married couple	79.7	78.8	76.0
- of which, with single parent	*na*	*2.9*	4.9
Two or more married couples	4.3	4.7	6.2
Single-parent	**13.8**	**14.1**	**15.8**
Single parent only	11.1	11.3	10.9
Single parent/related adult	2.7	2.8	4.9
Other households	**2.2**	**2.4**	**1.9**

Source: Goskomstat (1996); and unpublished data provided by Goskomstat.
Note: na=not available. Concept of family/household differs in 1994.

1994. Perhaps more importantly, for the first time the number of children living in different types of single-parent families and sub-families has been reported. Together, they represent a considerable share of children in Russia – almost one in five live with a single parent. Based on the population in January 1994, this share translates to 7.65 million children.

The differences in the prevalence of children living in single-parent households varied widely across by urban/rural categories and across Russia's regions. The highest rates of single parents were found in Moscow and St Petersburg and other urban, industrial *oblasts* in the northwest. Rates were also high along the southern Siberian *oblasts* (Irkutsk, Tuva) and the Far East (Magadan). Rates were lowest in the autonomous ethnic regions (Dagestan, Tatarstan) and throughout parts of Russia that are predominantly agricultural.

As shown in Table 2.3, slightly more single-parent households are headed by a parent on their own, i.e., with no other adults, such as grandparents, in the household. The remainder was divided across the three other types of households. The implications, as noted earlier, are significant in terms of the potential welfare of the child. Almost all children living in single-parent families were female-headed (94 per cent). The remaining 6 per cent lived with their father. In terms of other characteristics, an analysis of the composition of single-parents in the Russian

Table 2.3: Prevalence of Single-Parent Households by Type and Custodial Parent, 1994 (percentages of all households with dependent children)

| | | Parent | |
	Total	Mother	Father
Total	**19.7**	**18.5**	**1.2**
Alone	**10.9**	**10.3**	**0.6**
Single parent living with			
other adults	**8.8**	**8.2**	**0.6**
Grandparent	2.9	2.7	0.2
Non-relatives	2.0	1.9	0.1
Grandparents	3.9	3.6	0.3

Source: Goskomstat (1995).

Longitudinal Monitoring Study panel survey[4] shows a fair degree of heterogeneity among single parents – they do not fit the preconception of being predominantly young and poor (see Chapter 3).

Generally, single-parent households have only one child. Of all households with one child, 25 per cent are with a single parent; those with two children represent 14 per cent, and of all households with three or more children, 13 per cent are single-parent households. The same pattern holds true across urban and rural households though with different levels. The distribution of children by household type and age shows that children under six years are more likely to be found in extended families than with a lone mother (Figure 2.1). Sharing the household with her parents reflects a number of factors, such as the young age of the mother, economic vulnerability as a young mother, the need for child-care, etc. Older children, especially those who have already entered basic schooling, are more likely to be living with a parent who is the sole adult in the household. More than two in three children over ten years old live in such a household. This can be linked to the fact that mothers who become single parents as the result of a divorce have older children.

Figure 2.1: Distribution of Single-Parent Households by Age Group of Child
(percentage of relevant age group)

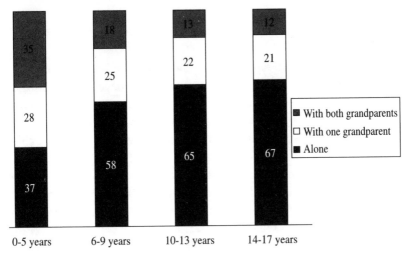

Source: Unpublished data, Goskomstat, 1994 micro-census.

Of course, there are many difficulties faced in categorizing households and categories may not accurately reflect different family situations. Thus, another approach to classifying households is based on the presence of parents in the household. In fact, the share of children living with only one parent (regardless of household classification) is 17.3 per cent and when adding children living without a natural parent, the share increases to 20.1 per cent.

In total, almost 2 per cent of all children were living with neither parent – in these cases children were placed with substitute caretakers (usually relatives) or entered the institutional system, though the majority are living with relatives. Moreover, among all 14-17 year-olds, 6 per cent were living without a natural parent. The increase in the annual number of children classified as *social orphans* (a child whose parent or parents are still alive, but are no longer legally responsible for him or her) has more than doubled during the 1990s (MSP, 1996). In 1995, the total number of social orphans was 533,000 (ibid). As shown in Figure 2.2, both the number of children in foster families (though this is more akin to guardianship, as the caretaker has no legal authority over the child), and of orphans in public care have increased sharply over the period. These trends have been characteristic of several other transition countries and reflect a growing family instability (see UNICEF, 1997).

2.3 Demographic Trends Underlying Changes in Family Structure

The prevalence of single-parent households is basically determined by changes in family formation: marriage and remarriage, family dissolution (divorce and separation), non-marital child-bearing and parental mortality. However, from the perspective of child welfare, the prevalence at a given time is less telling about the duration of time a child spends in a single-parent household.

How have demographic trends contributed to the rising prevalence of children living in single-parent households during the transition? Estimates show that the share of children who experience living in a single-parent household, regardless of duration, grew from 45 per cent to 64 per cent between 1988-1993 (Borisov and Sinel'nikov, 1996). This share of children may be overstated in that the three routes are not discrete – a child may have both a divorced and deceased father. Divorce was the most important contributing factor, accounting for roughly half of all cases, followed by non-marital births and parental mortality. While the frequency of these events has increased over time, the contribution of parental mortality rose disproportionately. Parental mortality in this context involves primarily to the loss of the father (78 per cent of cases in 1993), which almost doubled over pre-transition levels (ibid). This reflects the consequences of the male mortality crisis of the 1990s.

Decomposition of routes into single-parent or incomplete families in the United States have shown a similar overall level to that of Russia and it has likewise increased over time. Estimates of the percentage of children experiencing the absence of a parent or parents have ranged from 46 per cent in 1970, 53 per cent in 1980 and 59 per cent in 1983 (Hernandez, 1993). However, in comparison to Russia, there are important differences. Parental mortality plays far less of a role in the United States than non-marital births. Divorce accounts for a larger share in the

Figure 2.2: Number of Children in Public Care, 1989-1997 (thousands)

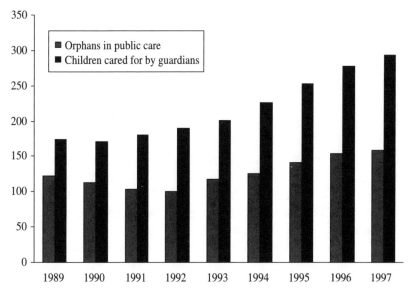

Source: MONEE Project database, UNICEF IRC; Ministry of Social Protection (1996).

United States as well as in other countries, such as the United Kingdom, where two-thirds of single parents are divorced (Jenkins, 1997).

Fertility in Transition

The drop in birth rates has been exacerbated during the transition. The birth rate fell from 14.6 in 1989 to 8.9 in 1996, and the absolute number of births was the lowest recorded level in Russian history. The total fertility rate declined from a peak of 2.194 in 1986-87 to 1.887 in 1990 and 1.281 in 1996. Russia occupies 187th position in the world relative to the total fertility rate (followed by Germany, Spain and Italy).

Changes in fertility have been linked to several factors. First, to falling household incomes and pessimistic economic expectations (Elizarov, 1996). In a poll conducted in 1992, when asked about factors influencing women's decisions on childbearing three in four women cited insufficient income as a factor in discouraging childbirth (Haub, 1994). Second, the decline is connected to the demographic 'echo' of the small post-war birth cohort. In 1998, the number of women aged 25-29 and 30-34 years was 77 and 79 per cent of 1989 levels. This compares larger younger (20-24 year-olds represented 108 per cent of 1989 levels) to older cohorts. As this larger young cohort enters into historically the most active child-bearing years, the birth rate is likely to increase. Finally, it has been shown that a large share of couples achieved their desired family size in the 1980s by shortening the interval between first and second births as a result of the introduction of new policies in maternity and other child-related benefits (Zakharov and Ivanovna, 1996). One reflection of this phenomenon has been the steep decline in second or higher parity births in the 1990s.

The birth rate actually increased at the outset of the transition against a backdrop of steeply falling fertility rates among other age groups. By mid-transition, however, rates stabilised and began to decline. Finally, adolescent births are mostly marital but are increasingly becoming non-marital.

Abortion remains the primary measure of family planning. Rates far exceed those in other industrialized countries (Table 2.1) where access to modern contraceptives is wider. According to the VTsIOM survey in early 1994, it is still widely used: 13 per cent of respondents intended to keep a child in the case of unexpected pregnancy, 40 per cent intended to have an abortion, while 47 per cent had no answer. The number of abortions declined during the transition, from 4.43 million in 1989 to 2.50 million in 1997, but still exceeded the number of births by almost twice (205 abortions per 100 births in 1989 and 198 in 1997).

The drop in fertility in the 1990s has been linked to the decline in marriages during the same period. In absolute terms, the number of marriages dropped from 1.38 million in 1989 to 866 thousand in 1996, before increasing to 928 thousand in 1997.

Marriage and Divorce in the Transition

As noted earlier, marriage has been a strong tradition in Russia. Has this changed during the transition? Do we see a reversal of the trend towards marriage at an increasingly younger age? During the 1990s, first marriage rates have declined considerably, while remarriage rates have remained generally stable (Figure 2.3). In comparison to the 1980 rate,

Figure 2.3: First Marriage, Remarriage and Divorce Rates, 1985-1998
(per 1,000 population)

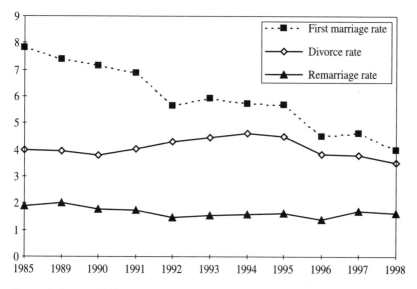

Source: Goskomstat (1998); Avdeev and Monnier (1996).

in 1998 the first marriage rate was halved – almost equalling the divorce rate and while it had already been declining pre-transition, the decrease was accelerated in the 1990s. The determinants of this decline are similar to those noted earlier regarding the decline in fertility. First, the economic difficulties experienced by a majority of the population, particularly potential young families, were formidable. In addition, part of this decline is due to a smaller cohort of women at the typical age of marriage (20-24 years).

Does the sharp decline in marriages signal a postponement of marriage or a shift towards cohabitation? Several indicators show that this is difficult to determine. First, the overall mean age at first marriage has remained constant over the 1989-96 period, from 22.7 to 22.9 years for women and from 24.9 to 25.0 years for men. First marriage rates show mixed results (Table 2.4). On the one hand, first-marriage rates have dropped sharply among 20-24 year-olds. At the same time, rates of first marriage have actually increased among adolescents. In fact, the adolescent birth rate remained relatively stable during this period, from 52 births per 1,000 women under 20 years in 1989 to 48 in 1994.

Other evidence on cohabitation from the 1994 micro-census shows a great deal of uniformity across age groups and gender. Levels of cohabitation show stable patterns across all age groups, on average about

Table 2.4: First Marriage Rates among Women by Age, 1990-1996
(first marriages per 1,000 women in relevant age group)

Age group	1990	1991	1992	1993	1994	1995	1996	% change 1990-1996
15-19 years	99.5	98.2	81.4	84.2	77.5	72.0	53.2	-47
20-24 years	89.0	84.1	68.5	73.0	69.8	69.2	56.4	-37
25-29 years	18.3	17.7	13.8	14.6	14.9	15.7	13.7	-25
30-34 years	6.0	5.7	4.4	4.5	4.5	4.6	3.9	-35
First marriage rate [a]	1.09	1.05	0.86	0.90	0.85	0.73	0.65	-40

Source: Council of Europe (1998).
Notes: [a] The first marriage rate is calculated as the number of first marriages among 1,000 women in relevant age group.

6-7 per cent. The youngest age groups showed high levels of cohabitation: 26 per cent of 16-17 year-old boys and 30 per cent of girls (Goskomstat, (1995a). These rates may be partly due to the fact that the legal age of marriage is 18 years, although authorities may grant permission in the case of a birth (Sinel'nikov, 1996).

As one would expect, public acceptance of cohabitation is strongly linked to age – in a 1989 national poll, one in two respondents aged over 60 disapproved of cohabitation compared to one in seven respondents under 20 years (Vyshnevskiy, 1996). As noted earlier, historically there have been significant disincentives to cohabitation, and there seems to be little evidence pointing towards increased levels of cohabitation.

In the West, divorce and separation are the main routes into single-parenthood (Ermisch, 1990). Thus, the steady increase in divorce rates during the 1990s (and little change in remarriage rates) has increased the prevalence of single-parent households. For the first time, the micro-census queried respondents about separation and found relatively low rates. The share of females separated (almost all from their first marriage) was just under 2 per cent. Likewise, among males, about 1.5 per cent had separated (Goskomstat, 1995b). Divorce rates are higher in urban areas, and generally correlate to the level of urbanization of a region. Divorce rates have also increased in rural areas, although not as rapidly as in urban areas.

After stable trends in the 1980s, the 1990s have witnessed large increases in marriage instability. Moreover, remarriage rates have also decreased, suggesting that a larger share of the population is divorced. The determinants of divorce during the transition are related to economic and social conditions, characteristics of marital behaviour in Russia, and changes in family code legislation. The link between falling living standards and increased marital instability has been shown in the United States. Studies have shown that the consequences of economic downturns, such as rising unemployment and falling real incomes, can lead to increased marital conflict and the risk of divorce (Conger, 1990). Given economic trends during the transition – rapid inflation, falling real incomes, rising unemployment and mounting wages arrears – the economic pressures and social stress were obviously quite substantial.

Another hypothesis regarding high rates of divorce is that many marriages in Russia are 'forced' marriages, that is, the conception of a child precipitated the marriage, and are therefore more vulnerable to breakdown (Cartwright, 1997). The identical average age at first marriage and births for females suggests this. As noted in Section 2.1, premarital conceptions are considered to represent an important factor in the young age at first marriage and birth, and the subsequent instability of marriages formed under such circumstances.

At the same time there has been a general liberalization in family legislation that has allowed for relatively streamlined divorce procedures. The introduction of a new family code in March 1996 may affect divorce trends, as earlier social leglisation influenced other trends (see Chapter 5).

The new family code shortens the period for granting marriage and divorces, eliminates the need to provide a justification for the divorce and introduces new concepts such as the marriage contract and foster families (Sinel'nikov, 1997). The reporting of divorces is likely to be subject to opposing forces related to the administrative and economic implications. An innovation of the family code is that courts, rather than the individuals, are now responsible for informing administrative authorities (who often delayed reporting). At the same time, however, the fee for processing divorce papers has increased substantially, from a purely symbolic 100-200 rubles (USD1=4,500 rubles) to several times the minimum wage (ibid).

The number of divorces both with and without the presence of children decreased between 1988-1990 before rising sharply during the transition period (Figure 2.4). The divorce rates among adults with children increased much faster than those without children. About two in three divorces (60-65 per cent) in the 1990s involved children. The rate of children in divorce rose by almost a third from 1990 (11.6) to 1995 (15.4) among 1,000 children aged 0-17 years.

The absolute number of children involved in divorce increased from 479,000 in 1989 to peak in 1994 at 613,000 (a 28 per cent increase) before falling to 455,000 in 1997. The increase in the number of children has been primarily among families with two or more children. While divorce among couples with a single child stayed relatively stable dur-

Figure 2.4: Annual Number of Divorces by the Presence of Children
(Index 1980=100)

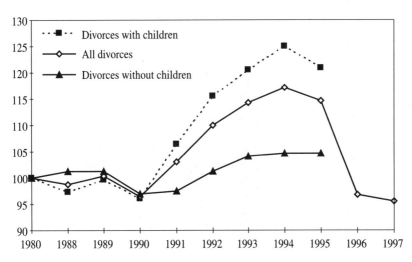

Source: Goskomstat (1996).

ing the 1990s, the number of children/siblings involved increased by 43 per cent between 1990-94 before declining from 1995 on. This suggests that the presence of children, especially more than one, increased the probability of divorce during the transition.

Non-Marital Fertility

In the 1990s, much attention has been directed at the rapidly increasing share of non-marital births. In fact, since 1965, the number of non-marital births has risen along with the number of marital births. However, from the onset of the transition, trends in non-marital births have diverged. While marital births have continued their downward plunge, non-marital births declined somewhat mid-transition and recovered.

The underlying factors could be rather contradictory. On the one hand, the non-marital birth in the context of the economic deprivations of the transition, could mean that the parent(s) were in a better financial situation than most of the population or had a more optimistic outlook on the future. On the other hand, it could have quite a contrary

Figure 2.5: Share of Non-Marital Births by Age of Mother, 1989 and 1997
(in percentage of live births)

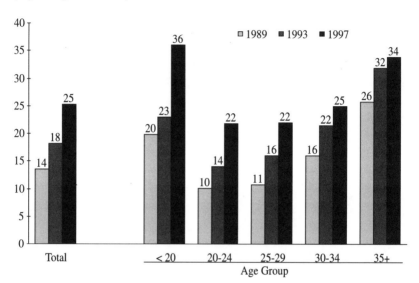

Source: MONEE Project database, UNICEF IRC.

meaning if the birth was to a young woman just leaving school. Without more detailed data on living standards, it is difficult to make such conclusions, although there is some evidence regarding age and family stability.

The distribution of non-marital births echoes the findings of the 1994 Micro-census in that, like consensual unions, non-marital births are found in large numbers across the age distribution, although they follow more of a U-distribution. Cohort-specific shares are highest among the under-20 years and the over 35 years cohorts (Figure 2.5). At the same time, the greatest absolute number of non-marital births is among the 20-24 year-old cohort. The growth of non-marital births across age groups might suggest changing social norms. However, the share of non-marital births is heavily influenced by the sharp decline in overall births.

The rates of non-marital and marital births across different age groups show several important aspects. First, marital birth rates are still considerably higher than non-marital rates in the same age group (Table 2.5). Second, marital rates declined much more steeply, by almost half in most age groups, during the 1990s. Finally, while non-marital rates are low, they are growing among women under 30 years.

Table 2.5: Age-Specific Birth Rates by Marital Status, 1989-1997
(births per 1,000 population; percentage change)

Age group	1997 rate		% change 1989/1997	
	Unmarried	**Married**	**Unmarried**	**Married**
15-19 years	13	23	26	-45
20-24 years	22	77	30	-48
25-29 years	14	51	30	-44
30-34 years	8	23	-11	-49
35+ years	2	4	-42	-60

Source: MONEE Project database, UNICEF IRC.

An important aspect is whether non-marital births represent non-union births (i.e., without the paternity established). Another source of information which is useful in assessing the family stability of non-marital births is the actual birth registration at the local administrative office. The share of joint registrations of a birth – two adults signing the birth certificate – may be indicative of consensual unions and therefore greater stability in the household. Joint registration of non-marital births has represented two in five births, consistently over time in Russia (Avdeev and Monnier, 1995).

Parental Mortality

The rates of premature adult mortality rose sharply during the 1990s, particularly among working-age males (UNICEF, 1993, Eberstadt, 1994). While much attention has been focused on elaborating the determinants of this sudden rise (UNICEF, 1994, Shapiro, 1995, Chen, 1996, Cornia and Paniccià, 1999), far less effort has been made in assessing the impact on family structure and welfare. The rise in mortality is reflected by the decline of more than six years in male life expectancy between 1990-1994. While in absolute terms, the largest number of deaths took place in the over 60 age group, relative increases among male cohorts in their prime family formation years were much higher. For example the age-specific mortality rate for men in the 40-44 year-old age group doubled during the period (Table 2.6). Rates of premature female mortality also increased, but from significantly lower starting points than men. Age-specific mortality rates declined somewhat in subsequent years, but mortality rates remained at significantly higher levels compared to 1990.

In constructing a crude measure of the impact of the mortality crisis on family structure and routes into single-parenthood, several assumptions regarding the distribution of fathers with dependent children by age group, with age-specific male and female mortality rates adjusted for probability differentials related to marital status, were made to calculate the cumulative number of children losing a parent during the period. The cumulative number of children estimated to have lost a parent in excess of 1989 levels was roughly 400,000 and the greatest increase relative to 1989 levels took place during 1994-1995.

In order to test these estimates of parental mortality, administrative records of survivor and social pensions, which are awarded to the sole remaining parent or to the children of the deceased, should reflect this

Table 2.6: Age-Specific Mortality Rates by Gender, 1989-1997
(deaths per 1,000 relevant age group)

Age group	Male				Female			
	1989	1994	1997	% change 1989/94	1989	1994	1997	% change 1989/94
20-29 years	3.0	4.7	4.2	157	0.8	1.0	1.1	133
30-39 years	4.6	9.1	6.8	198	1.3	2.2	1.8	176
40-49 years	8.9	17.3	12.4	196	2.9	5.0	2.5	172
50-59 years	18.5	32.9	25.7	178	14.6	18.7	3.7	128
Life expectancy at birth (years)	63.8	57.6	59.9	90	74.3	71.2	72.6	94

Source: MONEE Project database, UNICEF IRC.

increase. However, no sizeable increases were noted in the take-up of either survivor or social pensions. According to official data, there were 2.64 million recipients in 1989 and 2.53 in 1997. Although the number of social pensions awarded to children rose rapidly in the 1990s, it was primarily due to the large inflow of children with disabilities. As the organization of pensions remained in the hands of the central authorities, there is less reason to believe that under-reporting due to the changes in central/local responsibilities has affected these data. Moreover, the levels of the benefits are not inconsequential and would supplement falling incomes, thus disincentives to registering for the benefit would be minimized. Thus the evidence on the extent of parental mortality, a seemingly important transition route into single parenthood in Russia, remains mixed.

2.4 Conclusions: Will Russia Catch Up with the West?

We have seen that in Russia since 1970, specific historical, cultural and policy features have influenced changes in family formation and household structure. For example, policies aimed at encouraging women to join the workforce and at promoting pre-school facilities meant that, in practical terms, women were in a better position to opt for single-parent status than their western counterparts. However, economic changes created pressures that slowed the growth of single-parent households.

The evolution of trends in family behaviour in Russia has been subject to unique circumstances. In the transition, Russia is undergoing massive social and economic change. As the state withdraws from its previously paternalistic approach and social spending dwindles due to fiscal constraints, it could be argued that a new social contract is emerging. Relevant to family formation and stability, and in particular the formation of single-parent households, is the new set of policy incentives which includes less social support for women, new sets of values (oriented more towards individualism) and new technological innovations (greater prevalence of modern methods of contraception).

Despite the fact that these processes and their implications differ in many ways from those in most western countries, Russian demographers have interpreted changes in family trends during the transition as "catching up" with the West (Zakharov and Ivanova, 1996) or as "adopting western models" (Vishnevsky, 1996). The changes in family trends will be articulated in terms of changing incentives and opportunities (one part of which is conditioned by social policy) for young families. In the longer term, as more individualistic values prevail, as living standards rise, it is likely that cohabitation and non-marital births will be more prevalent. And as methods of family planning are more widely accessible, the link between sexual activity and pregnancy will be weakened.

While this is a possible long-term scenario, it is less likely in a transition context. In Western countries the growing prevalence of single-parent families takes place in relatively stable economies, with flexible labour markets adapted to women's work needs (availability of part-time work, for example) and alternative forms of childcare provision. In the short term, economic recession will continue to be the dominant influence on family behaviour. Western experience suggests that the number of single-parent families usually rises during economic recession (Hernandez, 1996).

In terms of family structure and child living arrangements, this means that divorce remains the key route into single parenthood. The introduction of a new family code in 1996 has further eased the process of divorce (see Chapter 5), non-marital births also remain an important route into single parenthood, and evidence shows increasing rates among younger women. Perhaps most unsettling is the rapid growth of premature adult mortality.

The receding state role in the economy and in assuring social protection raises concern for single parents. Without these safeguards, they are more likely to be marginalized. These issues are discussed in detail in subsequent chapters and reveal a disheartening picture. Policy initiatives may not be responding to the changes in the routes into single parenthood, nor to the changing economic circumstances of single parents.

* The author wishes to thank John Micklewright, Jeni Klugman and Sheila Marnie for useful comments. The author is particularly grateful to Leonid Sokolin and Irina Zbarskaya of the State Statistical Committee of the Russian Federation and Olga Remenets of UNICEF for facilitating the processing of micro-census data.

NOTES

1 See Coleman (1991), Council of Europe (1993), Kuijsten (1995), Vishnevsky (1993, 1996), Zakharov and Ivanovna (1996).

2 Sinel'nikov (1996) claims that the terminology for the study of household structure does not appear in the dictionary of social science terms. Elizarov (1996) notes that neglect in the area of economic studies of family behaviours is probably due to an ideological perspective of the family/household as a social structure whose economic function was disappearing under socialism.

3 Round VII of the Russian Longitidinal Monitoring Study was conducted in October 1996. The single-parent subsample comprised 313 individuals.

Chapter 3: The Living Arrangements of Russian Children

Michael Swafford, Elena Artamonova and Svetlana Gerassimova

Concern for the well-being of children leads inexorably to consideration of their living arrangements. Each child requires the nurture of adults to achieve socialisation into the ways of society. Much of this occurs within the context of the household in which a child lives. Less obviously, the household also serves as an economic production unit that takes goods from outside the household and transforms them to serve the child's needs, for example by preparing nutritious meals or administering medicine.

Of course, in modern societies other institutions such as schools and polyclinics assume some of these functions in rearing the young. Indeed, the Bolsheviks' revolutionary goals explicitly envisioned the State assuming the family's economic and educational functions. Taking inspiration from the writings of Engels,[1] one extreme faction even mounted a wholesale campaign against the institutions of marriage and the family. However, starting with Lenin, those actually in power never advocated abolishing the family, and the importance of the family has for many decades been virtually unquestioned by Russian authorities (Liegle, 1975).

No doubt it is the altruistic nature of households that ultimately renders them irreplaceable by other social institutions. As a by-product of duty and love for their children, parents and other adult relatives perform essential social and economic child-rearing functions. Without these services, the State would have to pay other institutions dearly, while achieving less effect than parents usually achieve, if only because of the deficit of affection in other institutions. Admittedly, parents' concern for their young is by no means entirely altruistic. Children may provide essential workers on the family farm, or security for parents in their old age, and failure to produce offspring may constitute grave financial misfortune. However, affection and altruism remain salutary ingredients in a healthy household, giving both the child and society advantages that no other institution can provide.

Thus, the living arrangements of children constitute a worthy concern in any society. In the Russian Federation, however, the topic is particularly important at this time. As Chapter 1 demonstrated, all manner of indicators point to dramatic social trauma during the transition to a market economy. To what extent has the social strain revealed by these trends also affected the stability of Russian households? Alternatively, to what extent has the Russian household remained a stable refuge amidst all the turmoil?

Chapter 2 addressed this question by employing cross-sectional data from official sources to reveal changes in family formation and dissolution, as well as in fertility trends. This chapter endeavours to answer these questions by employing both panel and cross-sectional data from the Russian Longitudinal Monitoring Survey (RLMS) to draw a more detailed picture of the living arrangements of children than official sources permit.

The first section sets the stage by reviewing the demographic, economic, and cultural factors that have likely conditioned household structure in Russia during the past three decades, thereby placing changes during the 1990s into perspective. The second section turns to an empirical analysis of the living arrangements of children, using survey data to produce a special typology of living arrangements that differs considerably from census classifications. Trends in children's living arrangements are then examined, giving special attention to those in single-parent households. The third section uses panel data to measure the instability of children's living arrangements by calculating the transition probabilities into and out of various types of household from year to year, highlighting not only the presence or absence of parents, but of other significant adults. We also examine whether these transition probabilities are conditioned by factors such as the attributes and circumstances of parents. The concluding section returns to the broader questions raised about the stability of Russian households, discussing the viability of Russian households as a source of succour for Russia's children during the transition. The implications of household composition for the material well-being and personal outcomes of children are discussed in Chapters 6 and 7.

3.1 Factors Influencing Russian Household Composition

Our concern with household composition lies ultimately in its relevance to the welfare of children and society. However, in the larger scheme of things, household composition is actually an intervening variable which is itself determined by other variables before in turn transmitting its own effect to children. In this section, then, we focus on the forces acting upon household composition in Russia rather than on its function as an explanatory variable.

Demographic, Economic and Sociocultural Factors

Consider the demographic trends as set out in the previous chapter.[2] First, the Russian mortality rate increased while fertility decreased, and both trends accelerated during the 1990s. Holding other factors constant, both trends likely augured for smaller and less complex households. On the other hand, the rising differential in male and female mortality rates probably lengthened widowhood, encouraging the formation of extended households, since single grandparents are more likely to join their children than elderly couples are. In other words, while rising mortality may have decreased household complexity somewhat, the rising differential may have had just the opposite effect. Second, the rising divorce rate would have generated smaller households were it not for a high rate of remarriage. The net effect was likely to increase the number of blended households and step-relatives. Finally, the early age at first marriage and first birth would be expected to increase the number of households. However, in light of housing constraints discussed below, this trend probably contributed instead to the complexity of households.

Various economic factors have also left their mark on household composition in recent decades. Some factors probably militated for reduced size and complexity in Russian households: all else being equal, high job security and social security prior to the reforms should have reduced the need for maintaining multiple workers in the household to offset the risk of unemployment. Moreover, relatively widespread and inexpensive day care should have also reduced the need for extended families. Most other economic factors, on the other hand, would have tended to augment household size and complexity. Women's high rate of employment created what was popularly called their 'double burden' of labour and homemaking, and having their parents reside in the household often eased this burden. Furthermore, pension eligibility at the relatively young ages of 55 years for women and 60 years for men gave them time to assist children and grandchildren.

The housing shortage, combined with the fact that housing was administratively allocated by municipal governments and enterprises, rendered separate housing exceedingly rare for newlyweds. Waits of ten to fifteen years were commonplace, as were situations in which one spouse was allocated housing by one employer, while the other was issued additional housing from another employer. Lack of housing per se tended to depress the number of households, while increasing their size and complexity markedly. As noted in Chapter 2, it may have also influenced demographic processes by reducing fertility, increasing pressure to divorce in response to conflicts with in-laws and crowded conditions, and constraining geographic mobility.

Much has transpired in the economic reforms of the 1990s that could affect household composition. About half of housing has been privatized and housing is often distributed through market mechanisms. Furthermore, whereas young people formerly could rarely get ahead quickly (being required to work up slowly through one bureaucracy or another), nowadays they are much freer to exercise initiative to get ahead. To the extent that young couples are more likely to be able to afford separate housing, these developments should be simplifying household structure. However, affordability cannot be taken for granted. As described in Chapter 1, and investigated further below in Chapter 6, the available evidence suggests that mean incomes have fallen and inequality has risen during the 1990s, and the percentage of households in poverty has increased (Braithewaite, 1997; Goskomstat, 1997; Mroz et al., 1999). Meanwhile, job security and social security have declined. These trends could work instead in the direction of complex household structures, as people move in with other relatives in the effort to cope with financial duress and uncertainty.

Finally, in this overview of factors impinging on Russian household composition, we move from demographic and economic factors to the third set of factors: tradition, value and preference. Household composition in two societies with similar demographic and economic characteristics might nevertheless differ by virtue of disparate values and preferences. For instance, all else being equal, veneration of the elderly and antipathy towards individualism would give rise to larger and more complex households, while desire for privacy and independence would work in the opposite direction.

Looking to Russian history for cultural legacies, we note that the peasant *dvor* (household) of previous centuries was marked by certain peculiarities in comparison to households in other European countries. Peasant households were characterised by their large size as well as by their inclusion of an extraordinary number of kin in addition to household heads, their wives, and children. More than half of household members consisted of other more distant kin according to one estimate (Hajnal, 1983; Czap, 1983). By the same token, peasant households rarely included unrelated individuals, unlike households in some other European locales that routinely included unrelated farm hands or servants. There was even a formal means for adopting unrelated adults and sons-in-law into the Russian *dvor* to maintain some semblance of patrilineage in the absence of sons. All this is to say that there is a long tradition of complex household structure and communal living in Russia. In the absence of opinion data, we cannot automatically attribute this to peasants' preference for large, complex households – though some historical commentators have done so colourfully.[3] The large, complex households were also in some measure a response to ill-conceived Tsarist taxation policies directed at serf-holders.

Despite the legacy of communal living, and despite decades of indoctrination on the virtues of collectivism, Russians in the 1990s seem far more inclined towards Western individualism than towards Eastern communalism, let alone Soviet communism. As leading Russian demographers have surmised, we can expect a further rise "in the role of values such as the liberty of individual choice, self-actualisation, hedonism, etc." (Kuijsten, 1995). In general, within the strictures of demographic and economic forces, these values and preferences may already be lessening the tendency for Russians to adopt complex household arrangements – although, as was pointed out in Chapter 2, it is too early to see any concrete evidence of this.

Methodological Preliminaries

The aim of this chapter is to describe the actual living arrangements of Russian children, not to dwell on methodology. Nevertheless, we must first describe our source of data in sufficient detail that readers can easily follow the cross-sectional and panel analyses presented below.

Many authors have bemoaned the inadequacy of census data and vital statistics for detailed study of living arrangements (Bartlema and Vossen, 1988; Hill, 1995). Census data typically include only demographic variables, rendering it impossible to develop adequate models incorporating other relevant psychological, social, and economic variables. Moreover, since census data are cross-sectional, they only permit us to describe 'stocks' of various kinds of households, not dynamic 'flows' of people from one kind of household to another. Stability in the percentage of households with, say, two parents might mask tremendous change as some children suddenly find themselves in broken homes while an equal number from broken homes re-enter reconstituted homes through a parent's remarriage.

The data analysed here are drawn from the Russian Longitudinal Monitoring Survey (RLMS), introduced in Chapter 1 and described in the Appendix.[4] For present purposes we wish to highlight some features directly relevant to this analysis. First, the questionnaire asked about the relationship of every household member to every other member, so that we could avoid the ambiguities that inevitably arise when relationships are defined solely in reference to a putative household head (Watts, 1985; Duncan and Hill, 1985). Second, the survey was conducted so as to permit both cross-sectional and panel analyses. Individual and household data were gathered in dwelling units in the cross-sectional sample during the last quarters of 1994, 1995 and 1996. Interviewers returned to every dwelling unit in the sample, endeavouring to administer virtually the same questionnaires irrespective of whether interviews were obtained in the dwelling units in the past (i.e. not just to those with participating households in 1994). Cross-sectional response rates ranged from 84 per cent in 1994 to 76 per cent in 1996. This yielded the three cross-sectional surveys used below (referred to by year, e.g. RLMS 1996). In addition, data from all individuals who participated in more than one round have been linked across rounds, rendering panel analysis possible. Whenever possible we followed those who moved out of the dwelling sample in 1996 (excluding them from cross-sectional results, however, so as not to bias that sample). Attrition over the three panels was only 20 per cent, less than in many ideally designed panel surveys (Swafford and Kosolapov, 1999). Naturally, the integrity of all panel surveys is threatened by attrition. We return to this issue below and present reassuring results.

It is extremely important to bear in mind that the analysis here utilizes individual children, not households, as the unit of analysis. This is deemed essential in panel analyses (Duncan and Hill 1985; Keilman and Keyfitz 1988; Willekens 1988; Richards et al., 1987). Each child provides one data record; that record includes data not only on that child (e.g. age, sex, schooling), but on the household in which that child lived (e.g. household expenditure, number of parents, and other details on household composition), as well as characteristics of all other members of the household (e.g. their occupations and education levels). For example, a household with three children provides three records, not one; the fields pertaining to the children vary across the three records because they describe three different children; however, since all three children lived in the same household, the fields pertaining to the household in which they lived are identical in all three records (except as they pertain to the other two children in the household).

Since children constitute the unit of analysis, readers should use caution in comparing statistics in this chapter directly with statistics based on households as the unit of analysis (e.g. Chapter 6 and most relevant tables in census publications).

3.2 Typology of Russian Children's Living Arrangements

Developing a typology of living arrangements might seem unproblematic. In everyday conversation, people routinely employ such adjectives as 'single-parent,' 'extended,' 'blended,' 'nuclear' and the like. Unfortunately, however, there is no unified typology used by governments, let alone by individual researchers (Keilman, 1995).

Recent Russian censuses have taken families as the unit of observation and placed them into one of only five categories: married couple, two or more related married couples, single parent, single parent living with one of his or her own parents, and other. Unfortunately, these five categories mask distinctions that Russian officials themselves consider increasingly important. The category 'married couple,' for example, includes extended families consisting of one couple and their children, plus one parent of a spouse – often a grandparent. It also subsumes married parents living with their divorced or single adult child, as well as her (or his) minor children. Hence, it is impossible to count completely the number of 'incomplete families' on the basis of published statistics.

This inadequacy has been corrected in reports based on the 1994 mid-term micro-census. Goskomstat switched to using households as the unit of observation, including individuals unrelated by blood and marriage in the household if they were sharing in the household economy. In addition, however, Goskomstat introduced a new typology of households with seventeen categories in its fully-fledged manifestation. This eliminated the ambiguities mentioned above, but the all-purpose typology nevertheless retains categories that lack the desired precision in describing children's living arrangements – for example, "married couple with or without children, with or without one parent of one of the spouses, and with or without other related or unrelated individuals" (Goskomstat, 1995).

A Refined Typology

Fortunately, the RLMS data set allows us to escape the shortcomings of official categories to develop a typology well-suited to the study of children's circumstances. Since their well-being is primarily contingent on the configuration of adults in their households, we distinguish between three categories of adults: (i) natural parents and (if they are remarried or cohabiting) their partners; (ii) other adults of working age who could contribute to the financial support of the child or provide childcare; and (iii) other adults who would not be expected to contribute substantial earnings to the household, but who might provide childcare.

As a first step, Table 3.1 distinguishes between unmarried children under 18 years old by the number of natural parents with whom they resided (see the rows in boldface). In all three cross-sectional surveys of the RLMS, approximately 75 per cent of children lived with both natural parents; 6 per cent, with a parent and step-parent; 14 to 16 per cent with only one parent; and about 3 to 4 per cent with no natural parent. The

Table 3.1: Children's Living Arrangements with Parents and Their Partners, RLMS 1994-1996 (percentage distribution of unmarried children under 18 years)

Number of child's parents and step-parents (partners) in household	1994	1995	1996
Two natural parents	**75.8**	**75.2**	**74.4**
Married	73.6	73.3	72.6
Cohabiting	2.2	1.9	1.8
One natural parent with partner	**6.4**	**6.2**	**6.2**
Mother	6.0	5.7	5.7
married to stepfather	*5.2*	*4.7*	*4.7*
cohabiting	*0.8*	*1.0*	*1.0*
Father	0.4	0.5	0.5
married to stepmother	*0.4*	*0.4*	*0.5*
cohabiting	*0.0*	*0.1*	*0.0*
One natural parent without partner	**14.2**	**15.4**	**16.3**
Mother	13.7	14.9	15.8
Father	0.5	0.5	0.5
No natural parent present	**3.7**	**3.2**	**3.1**
Step-parents (only)	0.2	0.2	0.2
Alone	0.1	0.0	0.0
Other (subcategories are not mutually exclusive)	3.4	3.0	2.9
grandparent(s) present	*2.6*	*2.4*	*2.6*
adult sibling present	*0.3*	*0.2*	*0.2*
other adult relatives present	*1.2*	*1.1*	*0.8*
Total	**100.1**	**100.0**	**100.0**
Number of child respondents in sample (unweighted)	*2,982*	*2,789*	*2,587*

table further distinguishes between natural fathers and mothers, when only one was present. As would be expected, fathers were more than ten times as likely as mothers to be the absent parent.

When no natural parent was present, at least one grandparent was present in more than 70 per cent of cases (Table 3.1, 2.6/3.7 per cent under '1994'); however, other relatives such as aunts and older siblings were present in more than 35 per cent of cases. A couple of seventeen-year-olds were found to be living alone, and several children were being raised only by step-parents.

The table also records our effort to identify cohabiting parents. As in Russian censuses through 1989, the RLMS surveys did not explicitly ask about cohabitation, relying on the person who answered the household questionnaire to report which couples were spouses by their own definition, whether registered or common-law spouses. However, all adult respondents were individually asked for their marital status. In a small percentage of cases, neither of the spouses was married; in other cases, one or the other was not married – implying that one partner was married to someone else, perhaps in the process of getting a divorce. When at least one of the spouses was identified as being unmarried, they were both treated as cohabiting. It appears that two percent of children were living with cohabiting natural parents, and somewhat less than one percent with cohabiting mothers.[5]

Focusing on trends between 1994 and 1996, we find only the hint of increased single parenthood in all forms (i.e. with or without other adults in the household), from 14.2 to 16.3 per cent. This was accompanied by corresponding decreases in other parental configurations. The two percentage-point increase seems small, but such a trend sustained for several years would make a big difference. Unfortunately, given the size and design of the sample, we cannot say with assurance that the trend is real.[6]

Thus far, our typology has dealt only with the configuration of parents. It is important to take into account other adults in the household as well. Unlike most government agencies depending on census data, we prefer not to focus on kinship in describing other adults members of the household. An aunt or great aunt, for example, can serve the same role as a grandparent, so we decline to build a system which confines aunts and uncles to a residual category. Instead, we distinguish between two classes of adults in addition to parents and their partners: 1) those 18 years of age to retirement age (55 years for women; 60 years for men), as well as pensioners through age 65 who continue working; and 2) retirement-aged people who are not working, as well as all individuals 65 and older. We exclude full-time students from 18 to 22 years of age from both classes of extra adults, since they may still be dependants. For shorthand, the term 'work-aged' below refers to the first class; 'retirement-aged' refers to the second – even though those two terms fail to capture fully the contents of the classes. The presence and absence of these two classes of 'extra' adults, when cross-classified, yields four combinations of adults other than parent figures: neither class present (no adults other than parent figures); only work-aged present (as defined above); only retirement-aged present; and both work-aged and retirement-aged adults present in the household. These four combinations are then cross-classified with the main four parental settings enumerated in Table 3.1: two natural parents; one natural parent plus step-parent; one natural parent only; and no natural parent. This yields a total of sixteen different household living arrangements in which Russian children might find themselves.[7]

3.3 Living Arrangements According to the RLMS

Table 3.2 reports the results of this cross-classification (see the sixteen shaded cells). To simplify the presentation, only results from RLMS 1996 are presented since no appreciable differences in results from the three surveys were observed. The '52.7' in the first column means that 52.7 per cent of all children lived in households with two natural parents and no other adults (with the possible exception of students from 18 to 22 years of age). That is, only about half of all children lived in stereo-typical nuclear families consisting of only natural fathers, mothers, and their children. We see only that 7.7 per cent of all children lived in one-parent households with no other adults. The totals (bottom row) show that about 35 per cent of all children lived in homes with some adult in addition to parents present; 65 per cent did not.

Table 3.2: Typology of Child Living Arrangements with Parents and Other Adults, RLMS 1996

(percentage distribution of unmarried children under 18 years)

Number of child's parents and step-parents (partners) in household	(1) No other adults present	(2) Work-aged, or working pensioners < 66 years	(3) Retirement aged & not working; or disabled	(4) At least one adult of both classes	(5) Total row percent	(6) Number of children (N)
		Two classes of adults in household in addition to parents and partners (disregarding students)				
Two natural parents	52.7	9.4	9.4	2.8	74.4	1,925
One natural parent with partner	4.6	1.0	0.6	0.1	6.2	160
One natural parent w/o partner	7.7	3.5	3.1	2.0	16.3	422
No natural parent present	0.2	0.8	1.0	1.1	3.1	80
Total column percentages	65.2	14.7	14.1	6.0	100.0	2,587

It is also instructive to examine the relationship between parental configurations and the presence of other adults in households. In Figure 3.1, the percentages in Table 3.2 have been recalculated to make this evident. For instance, according to the left-hand column in Figure 3.1, 71 per cent of children with two natural parents lived without any other adults in their households; 13 per cent lived with other work-aged adults; 13 per cent with other retirement-aged adults; and 4 per cent with work-aged and retirement-aged adults. By contrast, among children with single parents, only 47 per cent lived without any other adults in their households; 22 per cent with other work-aged adults; 19 per cent with other retirement-aged adults; and 12 per cent with both.

The effect of parental configurations on the presence of other adults is best revealed by comparing the size of the column segments moving from left to right in the chart. As one would expect, the fewer the parents, the greater the likelihood of living with other adults in the households.

One might ask why we did not distinguish between adults in the household who were actually earning wages and non-working adults, rather than between work-aged and retirement-aged adults. The RLMS data would easily permit this approach. To our way of thinking, how-

Figure 3.1: Presence of Other Adults in Household by Number of Parents, RLMS 1996 (percentage of children under 18 years by parental configuration)

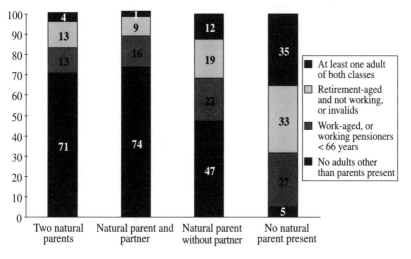

ever, this would be construing household structure too narrowly. Failing to work cannot be interpreted easily: it may merely reflect a collective decision that the person does not need to work in view of another members' generous income. Of course, earnings are ultimately a big issue. However, they are best calculated directly (as in Chapter 6) rather than using the number of workers as a proxy. In any case, published data on earners based on the 1994 micro-census show that 4.1 per cent of children under 18 years lived in households with no individual bringing in earnings (not to be confused with income from transfer payments, gifts and the like), 11.2 per cent with one earner, 58.2 per cent with two earners, and 26.5 per cent with three or more earners.[8]

A Digression on Other Kin in the Household

Given our focus on child welfare, we eschewed kinship other than parenthood for classifying living arrangements. It is nevertheless interesting

Figure 3.2: Presence of Other Children and Relatives, RLMS 1996
(percentage of children under 18 years with 1, 2, or 3+ of certain relatives in household)

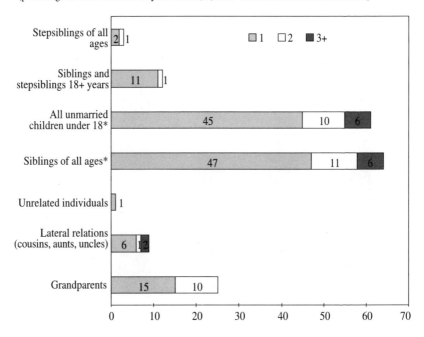

to take brief note of the presence of other kin in children's living arrangements. As Figure 3.2 indicates, in 1996 15 per cent of children lived in households with one grandparent and another 10 per cent lived with two or more grandparents; almost 9 per cent lived in households with lateral relations such as uncles and cousins; and less than one per cent lived with unrelated individuals, disregarding cohabitors who were considered step-parents. About 64 per cent lived in homes with other natural siblings of any age, which of course implies that 36 per cent did not;[9] 60 per cent lived with other unmarried children under 18 years of age. Approximately 12 per cent lived with siblings or stepsiblings 18 years of age and older in the household, but a remarkably low 3 per cent lived with any stepsiblings.

Urban-Rural Differences

Urban-rural differences are generally quite salient in sociological analyses of Russia. They are equally salient in the perceptions of the populace – not just because the Communist Party preached incessantly for decades that the arrival of Communism would somehow eradicate the differences between the city and countryside, but because in fact the drastic disparity in life-styles is still baldly obvious. Thus it comes as a surprise that urban-rural differences in children's living arrangements per se are only modest. In Table 3.3, living arrangements according to our typology in Table 3.2 have been broken down by location, following Goskomstat's practice of grouping 'villages of the city type' (PGTs) with cities in defining the urban population. Comparing the italicized figures under each bold-faced row reveals small percentage differences which, even if statistically significant, speak mostly to the similarity of household structures experienced by children in the two environments. For instance, 53.2 per cent of urban children with two natural parents lived in households with no additional adults (column 1), while 51.6 per cent of their rural counterparts did. Some 8.5 per cent of urban children lived in lone single-parent households, as did 6 per cent of rural children. Both are statistically non-significant in this sample.

In a similar vein, Goskomstat's figures on the number of earners in children's households, given above, differ only slightly for urban and rural locations. The percentage of children living in households with no

Table 3.3: Child Living Arrangements with Parents and Other Adults by Location, RLMS 1996
(percentage distribution of unmarried children under 18 years)

	(1)	(2)	(3)	(4)	(5)
		Two classes of adults in household in addition to parents and partners (disregarding students)			
Number of child's parents and step-parents (partners) in household	No other adults present	Work-aged, or working pensioners < 66 years	Pension-aged and not working; disabled	At least one adult of both classes	Total row percent
Two natural parents	**52.7**	**9.4**	**9.4**	**2.8**	**74.4**
Urban	*53.2*	*8.8*	*8.9*	*2.3*	*73.2*
Rural	*51.6*	*10.9*	*10.5*	*3.9*	*76.9*
One natural parent with partner	**4.6**	**1.0**	**0.6**	**0.1**	**6.2**
Urban	*4.4*	*0.8*	*0.7*	*0.1*	*6.0*
Rural	*5.0*	*1.3*	*0.4*	*0.1*	*6.8*
One natural parent without partner	**7.7**	**3.5**	**3.1**	**2.0**	**16.3**
Urban	*8.5*	*3.8*	*3.3*	*1.8*	*17.4*
Rural	*6.0*	*2.9*	*2.7*	*2.3*	*13.9*
No natural parent present	**0.2**	**0.8**	**1.0**	**1.1**	**3.1**
Urban	*0.2*	*1.1*	*0.8*	*1.2*	*3.3*
Rural	*0.0*	*0.2*	*1.3*	*0.9*	*2.4*
Total	**65.2**	**14.7**	**14.1**	**6.0**	**100.0**
Urban	*66.3*	*14.5*	*13.7*	*5.4*	*99.9*
Rural	*62.6*	*15.3*	*14.9*	*7.2*	*100.0*

earners equalled 4 per cent in both locations, while the percentage with only one earner was 10.1 per cent in rural locations and 11.7 per cent in urban ones. This is not to say that differences were entirely absent. In column 5 of Table 3.3, we find that the percentage of rural children living in two-parent households (with or without step-parents) was 4.5 percentage points higher than among urban children, while the percentage living with a single parent was 3.5 percentage points lower than among urban children.

The other disparity worthy of mention concerns household size, a dimension captured only indirectly by our typology. According to the 1994 micro-census, overall mean household size was virtually identical in urban and rural locations (about 2.84).[10] However, the mean number of children under 18 in households with such children was approximately 1.5 in urban areas, but 1.9 in rural areas (Goskomstat 1995). If instead we take individual children as the unit of observation, in RLMS 1996, children in urban areas had on average 0.7 siblings, while rural children had 1.3 – a result consistent with the micro-census, given the different units of observation. In other words, in comparison with urban children, rural children lived on average with more children, but with correspondingly fewer adults.

Age Differences in Living Arrangements

Next, we turn to children's living arrangements by age. Not surprisingly, the older children get, the less likely they are to live with both natural parents. Figure 3.3, which groups unmarried children into three-year cohorts to smooth the curve, shows that the percentage living with both natural parents drops steadily from 82.6 per cent in the youngest cohort to 68.1 per cent in the oldest. Naturally, the percentage living in other arrangements increases: among those with one parent and one step-parent, from about 0.9 to 11.2 per cent; among those with no natural parent, from 0.3 to 3.9 per cent. Interestingly, however, the percentage living with one natural parent (and perhaps other non-parent figures) manifests no trend. It fluctuates around 16 per cent across all age cohorts.

In the previous chapter we saw that the percentage of births to mothers outside registered marriages rose from 14 to 25 per cent

Figure 3.3: Parental Configurations by Age of Child, RLMS 1996
(percentage of unmarried children under 18 years)

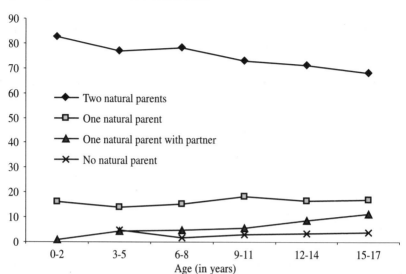

Age (in years)

between 1989 and 1997 (Figure 2.4). On this basis, one might expect the percentage of children under one year of age living with only one parent to approximate 25 per cent, rather than the 15.6 per cent in RLMS 1996. However, the birth registry of about 43 per cent of out-of-wedlock children names both the father and the mother, indicating at least some attachment between the unmarried parents (Karelova, 1997). Some of these parents of children under one year of age born out-of-wedlock perhaps began marriage or cohabitation after the registration of their child but prior to the date of our survey. Furthermore, there is anecdotal evidence that Russian women are beginning to take into account government benefits to children in deciding whether or not to formally marry their partners, and this could affect 'illegitimacy' rates.

Status of Parents in Various Living Arrangements

The primary reason for examining variation in children's living arrangements is that different arrangements potentially represent different resources available to children. It is quite interesting to examine the social resources typically available to children as embodied in their parents' educational and occupational attainment. Specifically, does the plight of children in single-parent households lie primarily in the absence of one parent, or is it compounded by the fact that single mothers are more poorly educated or employed than mothers in two-parent households – delivering a double blow to children's welfare?

The evidence contradicts expectations. The cross-classification of children by their mother's education level and parental configuration reveals no association between the two variables. Among children with two parents, 18.4 per cent had mothers with higher education; 29.8 per cent with specialized secondary; 45.3 per cent with secondary diplomas; 6.5 per cent with less than a secondary diploma. The corresponding figures for children with single mothers are 19.3, 27.9, 44.3 and 8.6 per cent, respectively.

Precisely the same is true for occupational standing. Among both groups of children about 22 per cent had mothers working as professionals; 21 per cent as technical workers; 20 per cent as clerical or skilled manual workers; and 37 per cent as personal service or unskilled labour. Here, however, the analysis is complicated by the fact that some mothers were not gainfully employed and were therefore omitted in the calculation of the above statistics – 28 per cent of married mothers and 35 per cent of single mothers.

To get around this problem and expand the analysis beyond mothers, we created four other variables: mean parental education and occupation, as well as 'maximum' parental education and occupation. If no parents were present, the education and occupation levels of other work-aged or retirement-aged adults were substituted. (For stylistic simplicity, however, the term 'parent' is still used below in naming the variables.) Although we examined frequency tables using log-linear analysis to avoid violating statistical assumptions, in Table 3.4 we present our results in terms of means as if our education and occupation variables were metric, since doing so simplifies the presentation without doing injustice to reality in this particular case.

First, we focus solely on the figures in bold in Table 3.4. Columns 1 and 4 restate the results on mothers' education and occupation that were presented above – in terms of means rather than percentages. Comparing children living with single versus married mothers, we found no appreciable difference in these variables: 2.60 versus 2.58 for education (column 1) and 1.30 versus 1.20 for occupation (column 4).[11] However, mean parent education and occupation (columns 2 and 5, figures in bold) were somewhat lower in two-parent households than in those with one or no parent. This is not surprising given the equality between mothers' figures just noted, since men tend to have somewhat lower education and occupation levels than women (as coded here). Even with the slightly lower means, however, children in two-parent households were better off than others, since two parents with a given education or occupation level constitute a greater resource than one.

Not surprisingly, maximum parents' education was higher for children in two-parent households (columns 3 and 6, figures in bold). This, too, was a mathematical inevitability given the equality between mothers' figures: the maximum function recorded the father's education or occupation only when it exceeded the mother's. On average, then, children in two-parent households had access to greater social resources than other children. Even so, the differences were modest: less than 0.3 on a four-point scale.

The other notable feature of Table 3.4 is that it breaks down the above figures in terms of our typology, albeit collapsed to avoid unreliable estimates due to small cell sizes.[12] Here, the essential point is that the education and occupation levels of parents in households with other work-aged adults were lower than in other configurations, with one minor exception. (That is, the figures in row 2 are lower than those in rows 1 and 3, and the figures in row 5 are lower than those in rows 4 and 6.) One possible explanation is that parents with lower education and occupation levels were more prone to join other work-aged adults to cope with their circumstances, a theme to which we return in the conclusion.

Table 3.4 also provides summary information on the age of mothers (column 7). Again, we are struck not by differences across categories, but by similarities in the means (as well as in the variances, which are not reported). Among children with only one parent, mother's age was only somewhat higher than among those with two parents (35.1 versus 34.4 years, a statistically significant difference). Evidently, remarriage compensated for the cumulative increase in the likelihood of experiencing divorce with increasing age. This claim is consistent with

Table 3.4: Education, Occupation, and Age of Parents by Living Arrangements, RLMS 1996 (unmarried children under 18)

1996 living arrangements	(1) Mother's education	(2) Education		(4) Mother's occupation	(5) Occupation	(6)	(7) Age
		Mean parents' education	Maximum parents' education		Mean parents' occupation	Maximum parents' occupation	Mother's mean age
Two parents	**2.60**	**2.51**	**2.81**	**1.30**	**1.05**	**1.38**	**34.4**
1. No other adults	*2.65*	*2.55*	*2.84*	*1.32*	*1.09*	*1.42*	*34.4*
2. Work-aged adults with or without pension-aged	*2.35*	*2.32*	*2.62*	*1.09*	*0.85*	*1.15*	*34.5*
3. Pension-aged without work-aged adults	*2.60*	*2.60*	*2.87*	*1.40*	*1.10*	*1.45*	*33.8*
One parent (or none)	**2.58**	**2.58**	**2.58**	**1.20**	**1.19**	**1.18**	**35.1**
4. No other adults	*2.60*	*2.66*	*2.67*	*1.27*	*1.27*	*1.28*	*37.0*
5. Work-aged adults with or without pension-aged	*2.30*	*2.49*	*2.49*	*1.16*	*1.14*	*1.11*	*32.5*
6. Pension-aged without work-aged adults	*2.90*	*2.60*	*2.60*	*1.26*	*1.10*	*1.12*	*34.9*
Children (N)	*2477*	*2578*	*2578*	*1829*	*2364*	*2371*	*2492*

Notes: Maximum standard error for each row of education and occupation figures reading from top to bottom: .03, .04, .07, .09, .06, .09, .11, .15. Coding of education: 4=higher; 3=specialized secondary; 2=secondary; 1=less than secondary. Coding of occupation: 4= professional; 3=technical; 2=clerical and skilled manual; 1=unskilled manual and personal service. We first employed log-linear analysis to avoid undue assumptions about the metric of ordinal variables. In our view, this simplified table reveals precisely the same conclusions.

the discussion of Figure 3.3 above, in which children's probability of living with only one natural parent showed no trend related to age. Interestingly, however, among children with single mothers and other work-aged adults, the average mother's age was only 32.5 years (s.e. 0.79), considerably less than among children with single mothers and no other adults (37.0, s.e. 0. 49). Perhaps younger single mothers were less established and therefore more likely to draw other work-aged adults into their homes, to repeat a point introduced in the previous paragraph.

Finally, it is possible to take mothers as the unit of analysis (rather than children, as in all other analyses in this chapter), and attempt to develop a function that discriminates between single mothers and mothers with partners. In doing so, we employed age as a metric variable, education as a four-category nominal variable, and occupation as a five-category nominal variable (including 'no occupation' as a legitimate category). Given the above results, it comes as little surprise that none of the variables manifested a statistically significant effect in a logistic regression equation. In Russia during the mid-1990s, then, single mothers were not distinguished from married mothers as expected.

3.4 Stability in the Living Arrangements of Russian Children

As was explained above, relative stability in aggregate statistics based on cross-sectional surveys proves little about stability in the living arrangements of individual children. Are the 'stocks' of children in particular household configurations fairly stable because the same children remain in a given situation year after year, or because children are exchanging places with children in other configurations in equal numbers?[13]

We begin by examining the transitions in children's living arrangements with parents irrespective of other adults in the household (Table 3.5, shaded area). Though we have computed the four-by-four transition matrices for both 1994-1995 and 1995-1996, because they were found to be so similar, we present only the latter matrix. The bold-faced percentages in the diagonals represent children whose living arrangements with parents remained the same for the year between 1995 and 1996. Among those living with only one natural parent or with none, 83 to 88 per cent remained in the same state after one year (Table 3.5, bottom two rows).

By contrast, among those living with two parents, perhaps including a step-parent, over 95 per cent remained in the same arrangement, implying of course that 4 to 5 per cent experienced the loss of a parent from their households during the year (see top two rows).

Given the lack of any panel data gathered previous to the RLMS, we cannot write definitively about changes in transition rates. However, there is some evidence that the annual rate of losing one natural parent (3.8 per cent in 1995-1996, based on Table 3.5, row 1) has probably increased considerably from the 2 per cent rate implied in Figure 3.3.[14]

It is also interesting to notice that the rate with which children with two parents in the RLMS lost parents from their households exceeds the rate implied by official statistics on divorces. In 1995 and 1996, according to official statistics, 1.2 to 1.6 per cent of children under 18 were affected by divorce.[15] After this figure is adjusted to apply only to children eligible to experience parents' divorce (i.e. children with two parents), the percentage of eligible children actually experiencing divorce still falls a bit short of two percent, considerably shy of the 4 to 5 per cent instability observed in Table 3.5. Of course, losing a parent from the household may result from separation rather than divorce, a loss detected by RLMS but seemingly not by divorce statistics. This, however, does not ulti-

Table 3.5: Transitions in Living Arrangements with Parents between 1995 and 1996, RLMS (percentage distribution of unmarried children under 18)

Transition matrix 1995 living arrangements	1995 N	1995 %	1996 living arrangements				1996 row totals
			Two natural parents	One natural parent with partner	One natural parent	No parent	
Two natural parents	1,698	76.9	**96.2**	0.5	3.0	0.3	*100*
One natural parent with partner	131	5.9	0.0	**95.4**	4.6	0.0	*100*
One natural parent	327	14.8	4.9	5.5	**88.4**	1.2	*100*
No natural parent	53	2.4	3.8	5.7	7.5	**83.0**	*100*
Column totals	2,209	100.0	*1,662*	*144*	*350*	*53*	*2,209*
Column percentages			*75.2*	*6.5*	*15.8*	*2.4*	*100*

mately explain the discrepancy. Though official divorce statistics in 1996 missed separations in 1996, they did presumably include a roughly equal number of separations from previous years which were converted to official divorces in 1996. We return to discuss the unexplained gap below.

In Table 3.6, we look instead at transitions in terms of our more detailed typology of parents and other adults. Since this six-by-six cell transition matrix also takes into account changes in the configuration of adults other than parents, it naturally reflects less stability in the boldface figures in the diagonal. Interpreting every cell of the matrix would make for very tedious reading, so we instead emphasize here the main findings that relate to the coming and going of work-aged and retirement-aged adults in children's households. First, among children with 'extra' adults in their households as of 1995 (rows 2, 3, 5 and 6), those in two-parent households were about three times as likely as others to lose those extra adults by 1996. (Compare the 17.0 and 20.5 per cent in column 1 with the 4.9 and 6.9 per cent in column 4.) Second, among children with no extra adults in the household as of 1995 (rows 1 and 4), those with two parents were only half as likely as others to see the addition of extra work-aged or retirement-aged adults by 1996. (Compare the 4.1 and 2.1 per cent in row 1 to the 9.0 and 3.0 per cent in row 4.) Both of these findings indicate the greater functional importance of extra adults in broken homes as a coping mechanism, a theme to which we return in the conclusion.

Factors Conditioning the Transition Rates

The ideal approach to modelling the movement of children from one living arrangement to another is to employ a hazard model, in which the amount of time to an event (changing from one living arrangement to another) is treated as a function of relevant explanatory variables. Given the issues raised in this chapter, the events of particular interest include: 1) changing from a living arrangement (state) of having two natural parents to having less than two; 2) from having two parents (including a step-parent) to having less than two; 3) from having one natural parent to having both a parent and step-parent; and 4) from having no extra work-aged adults in the household to having at least one. Numerous other transitions could be listed, but it would be foolhardy to take on more complexity without first tackling the most salient transitions.

Table 3.6: Transitions in Living Arrangements between 1995 and 1996, RLMS
(percentage distribution of unmarried children under 18)

Transition matrix			(1)	(2)	(3)	(4)	(5)	(6)	(7)
						1996 living arrangements			
			Two parents			**One parent or none**			
1995 living arrangements	1995 N	1995 %	No other adults	Other work-aged with-w/o retirement-aged	Retirement-aged and not working; disabled	No other adults	Other work-aged with-w/o retirement-aged	Retirement-aged and not working; disabled	1996 row totals
Two parents									
1. No other adults	1,325	59.9	**90.9**	4.1	2.1	2.0	0.5	0.4	100
2. Other work-aged with or without pension-aged	273	12.3	20.5	**65.6**	9.2	1.1	3.7	0.0	100
3. Retirement-aged without other work-aged adults	230	10.4	17.0	5.2	**73.0**	1.7	0.4	2.6	100
One parent or none									
4. No other adults	167	7.6	4.8	1.8	0.0	**81.4**	9.0	3.0	100
5. Other work-aged with or without pension-aged	144	6.5	8.3	9.0	0.7	4.9	**70.1**	6.9	100
6. Retirement-aged without other work-aged adults	72	3.3	2.8	0.0	1.4	6.9	5.6	**83.3**	100
Column totals (N)	2,211	100.0	1321	261	223	182	138	86	2,211
Column percentages			59.7	11.8	10.1	8.2	6.2	3.9	100

For technical reasons, developing a hazard model of these events using the RLMS data is premature and unjustified in our view.[16] Instead, we have contented ourselves with estimating logistic regressions in which the above dichotomous variables (change versus no change between Time 1 and Time 2) were taken as functions of several explanatory variables: maximum education of parents, maximum occupation of parents, discrepancy between spouses' education levels, discrepancy between spouses' occupational levels, age of mother, age of oldest child in the household (as a surrogate for length of marriage between natural parents), and urban versus rural location. Furthermore, reasoning that changes in living arrangements are often a response to financial stress, we examined the effect of financial standing at Time 1 on changes in living arrangements recorded at Time 2.[17]

In view of the large number of dependent and explanatory variables, it was almost inevitable that some seemingly statistically significant findings would surface due to Type 1 statistical error. To reduce the chances of being misled, we therefore conducted all analyses separately for both the 1994-1995 and the 1995-1996 periods. Since there were no theoretical reasons to expect drastically different results during these two successive years, we insisted on consistent results within the range of sampling error.

The results are remarkably simple (if somewhat disappointing) to summarise. Despite double-checking our work painstakingly, we found no theoretically intelligible and statistically significant results that held up in both time periods, even when each explanatory variable was entered singly into the logistic regression. This finding mirrors the results of the cross-sectional analysis presented above, in which children in various living arrangements were found to have parents with remarkably similar education and occupation levels.

We did, however, unearth one particularly interesting finding when examining children's paths into single-parent homes. Of course, divorce and separation constituted the primary cause of such transitions. However, in the 1994-1995 period, 16 of the 67 children making the transition from two- to single-parent households did so by virtue of a parent's death (almost always the father's death); in the 1995-1996 period, 16 of 61 such children did. Thus, about a quarter of the transition rate was explained by fathers' mortality rate, confirming the discussion of premature adult mortality in Chapter 2. The absolute number of children entering single-parent living arrangements in this manner actually approximated the number entering via out-of-wedlock birth.[18] Parent's mortality, then, accounts for much of the unexplained gap between figures in Table 3.5 and official statistics on divorce, discussed above.

3.5 Conclusions

We return now to the question that motivated this analysis of children's living arrangements: amidst all the turmoil of the 1990s, to what extent has Russian household structure managed to hold its own, enabling it to fulfil its function in the socialization and support of children?

We began our analysis with ample reason for expecting dramatic change as a result of the maelstrom of forces playing on the Russian household. Several demographic trends have intensified during the 1990s: increasing rates of mortality, divorce, and out-of-wedlock births, along with a decreasing fertility rate. Moreover, the rules of the economic game have changed spectacularly, replacing administrative edicts with market forces. Particularly during the first half of the 1990s, Russians completely lost their economic bearings while inflation obliterated savings and wreaked havoc with prices: a loaf of bread for 2,900 rubles rather than 60 kopecks; a wheelbarrow of cash for a car; or 300 kilograms of sunflower seeds for a washing machine. Now, more households than in the 1980s find themselves in poverty, but a class of wealthy 'new Russians' has also emerged, largely replacing politicians as the target of resentful jokes. Young people can get ahead now unless they live in the particularly depressed regions around the many one-factory cities concocted years ago by Soviet planners. They can acquire anything for which they have the money – including privacy, autonomy, and separate housing from parents.

Cultural values are seemingly in flux, too – free of the steady drone of Soviet propaganda, but buffeted by insipid Western-style commercial advertisements and B-grade foreign movies. No doubt the most significant cultural fact of all is the sheer anomie that set in during the early

1990s: elderly people concluding that their lives had come to naught; war heroes demoralised by accepting foreign aid from vanquished foes of yesteryear; automobile drivers spontaneously ganging up to take over the lanes of on-coming traffic, turning two-way streets into one-way streets until other drivers staged a counter-revolution – or just driving down sidewalks with impunity. Many a Russian has bemoaned the loss of sensibility in personal relations, and it is easy to believe that this loss has told on households.

It is possible to adduce alarming statistics on the morbidity of Russian households – to wit, the increasing rates of divorce and out-of-wedlock births just mentioned, and the 68 per cent increase in the annual incidence of child abandonment or court-ordered removal from parental custody between 1992 and 1996 (Karelova, 1997). However, these statistics must be put in proper perspective. By Western European standards, the divorce and out-of-wedlock birth rates are not extraordinary. The total percentage of institutionalized children is still less than 0.5 per cent, which is admittedly little consolation given the wretched condition of the institutions.

In view of all the change surrounding Russian households, we are more struck by the stability reflected in the cross-sectional data in Tables 3.1 (and Chapter 2) than by the fragility of household structure. There is no evidence of precipitous change. This optimistic note, however, must be tempered somewhat by the results of the panel analysis of transitions in the lives of individual children, presented in Tables 3.5 and 3.6. It is difficult to put the transition rates into perspective since no comparable baseline transition rates exist. However, by placing the transition rates in the context of indirect evidence in Figure 3.3, we deduced that the rate at which minor children lose natural parents from their households has increased appreciably over the past two decades, from about 2.0 to 3.8 per cent. Increased divorce rates account for much of this increase in transition rates; however, death of parents accounts for about one-quarter of transitions from two-parent households in 1995-1996, generating as many children in single-parent households as out-of-wedlock births have – a finding which sets the Russian Federation in stark contrast to Western Europe and the United States.

Another surprising finding is that the processes associated with living arrangements operated rather equally across the social board, whether viewed in light of cross-sectional or panel data. The metamorphosis of the social stratification system, still very much underway, has not to date coalesced with living arrangements. Social class differences are not obvious (Table 3.4). Neither are urban-rural differences (Table 3.3). The beloved social indicators of the West seem strangely ineffectual in explaining either stocks or flows in the living arrangements of Russian children during the mid-1990s.

Finally, perhaps the single most salient impression based on our analysis is the fact that the living arrangements of Russian children are implicated in a quintessential sociological feedback loop. Yes, changes in living arrangements impinge on material well-being, and living arrangements therefore by definition constitute a traditional explanatory variable. However, at the same time, material well-being explains living arrangements to some extent. People confronted by poverty might cope with it by attempting to earn more money; however, they can – and do – also cope with it by reconfiguring their households. Surveying their circumstances, Russian people (like people in all societies) negotiate living arrangements that suit their purposes within the confines of demographic, economic and cultural reality.

Admittedly, our effort to explain transitions directly by using poverty status bore no fruit. However, this can be explained away by methodological considerations. People in poverty in 1995 could not change their living arrangements as of 1996 in response to their poverty unless eligible and willing relatives outside the household existed whose inclusion would actually assist them. Faced with years of financial strain and uncertainty between 1991 and 1995, it is quite possible that most households by 1996 had long since exercised their options in using household configuration to cope with financial circumstances, in which case regression analysis would be misleading. In any case, we had no data on the existence or absence of eligible people to use in a sophisticated analysis.

Certainly, several pieces of other evidence suggest that living arrangements have been employed as a coping mechanism: the increase in the percentage of children living with grandparents and in multiple-couple households between 1989 and 1994 (Chapter 2, Table 2.2), the higher percentage of children living with extra work-aged adults among those whose parents had relatively low education and occupation levels in 1994 to 1996 (Table 3.4); and the higher annual rate with which single-parent households attracted and kept work-aged adults (Table 3.6).

It seems, then, that Russian household structure has served as a social flywheel, maintaining its momentum reasonably well despite the fits and starts of the social order around it. However, a strong word of caution is warranted here. Demonstrating the robustness of Russian household structure in the face of adversity does not prove that all is well within Russian households – a topic beyond the scope of this chapter. Indeed, even official Russian sources provide a daunting litany of woes related to families, confirming the government's awareness of the problems and appreciation of their significance. Despite salutary legislation, however, the government's difficulties in raising taxes severely hamstring its ability to deal with the problems, with only 10 to 15 per cent of the demand for family-related social services met (Karelova, 1997). Unfortunately, then, it would seem that Russian households are implicated in yet a second feedback loop – this one, a vicious cycle: households contribute too little tax to government coffers, and the government in turn is ostensibly left with insufficient financial resources to assist the ailing families.

NOTES

1 As Engels wrote more than a century ago in *The Origin of the Family, Private Property and the State*: "With the passage of the means of production into common property, the individual family ceases to be the economic unit of society. Private housekeeping is transformed into a social industry. The care and education of the children becomes a public matter. Society takes care of all children equally, irrespective of whether they are born in wedlock or not." Translated in Marx and Engels, 1962.

2 Many hypotheses about the likely effect of factors on household composition in general (not in Russia specifically) are suggested in Imhoff et al., 1995: Chapters 2-4.

3 As early as 1847, August von Haxthausen wrote: "No one considers a large family a greater blessing than the Russian farmer," and "In West Europe it is the greatest burden for the lower classes to have many children; in Russia children form the greatest wealth!" Quoted in Mitterauer and Kagan 1982: 108.

4 Funding for Rounds V-VII of the RLMS (1994-1996) was provided by the United States Agency for International Development, the National Institutes of Health (Grant # RO1HD30880), the National Science Foundation (Grant #SES92-23326), and the

University of North Carolina at Chapel Hill (UNC). The UNC team includes Professor Barry Popkin and co-investigators Namvar Zohoori, Barbara Entwisle, Thomas Mroz, and Lenore Kohlmeier. The Institute of Sociology team at the Russian Academy of Sciences is headed by Drs. Polina Kozyreva, Mikhail Kosolapov, and Michael Swafford. The Institute of Nutrition team is headed by Drs. Alexander Baturin and Arseni Martinchik.

5 Calculating on the basis of the 1994 micro-census, among married people 24-59 years of age, about 6 per cent were in common-law marriages. These results, however, apply to many people without minor children, who may be more likely to cohabit (Goskomstat, 1996, p. 46).

6 Nearly all conventional tests of significance assume the independence of observations. Because of clustering, this assumption is rarely justified in any national sample. Swafford and Kosolapov (1999) demonstrate that the standard errors calculated by conventional statistical packages would often be wrong by a non-negligible factor of 2 to 4 in the RLMS data. In this particular study, the problem is exacerbated by the fact that the observations on children from the same household were not independent of one another (since they all lived within the same household); furthermore, since the same dwellings were used in each round, and households within a given dwelling usually participated in more than one round, independence did not hold over time either. Therefore, the assumption of independence is wholly unjustified, and the apparent statistical significance of the upward trend is called into question.

7 We would be remiss not to remind readers that our typology, based on a survey of the non-institutionalized population, misses children in orphanages, as well as any homeless children. This topic is considered in Chapter 2 of this volume. Suffice it to say, 0.4 per cent of children between 0 and 17 years of age were wards of the State in half a dozen different type of institutions, ranging from children's homes and orphanages to boarding schools for children with serious mental and physical handicaps (Karelova, 1997, p. 107).

8 As always, the data are transformed to make individual children the unit of observation (Goskomstat, 1995).

9 According to the 1994 micro-census, of households with children under 18 years of age, 53 per cent had only one such child; 37 per cent had two; and 10 per cent had three or more (Goskomstat, 1995, p. 83). These figures might seem to contradict ours, but they are not contradictory if one takes into account the disparate units of observation. Consider a hypothetical society with two households – one with only one child, the other with three. Half the households have only one child, but only one-quarter of the children have no siblings in their households.

10 Furthermore, the variances are very similar. Bear in mind that seemingly inconsistent figures based on previous censuses were based on families, not households, and that single-person households were excluded from calculations because they were not considered families (Goskomstat, 1996 pp. 29-31).

11 As was noted above, in the category 'one parent or none,' a small proportion of nat-

ural parents were fathers rather than mothers. Due to small cell size, they are excluded from the analysis here. Also, in all figures presented below, calculations for mothers by definition eliminate children in households with no natural parents. However, references to mean and maximum parent levels do not exclude them since, as the text explains, figures from other adults were substituted in the absence of all parents.

12 To avoid examining unreliable percentages based òn small numbers, we merged all two-parent households into one category, and joined those living with no natural parents to those living with one. Furthermore, we reduced the four categories of other adults in Table 3.2 to three categories by joining the small number with both work-aged and retirement-aged adults to the category of work-aged only (i.e. columns 2 and 4 in Table 3.2).

13 Bias due to loss-to-follow-up is a big issue in any panel survey. Two tests directly relevant to this chapter were performed (Swafford and Kosolapov, 1999). First, children in the 1994 RLMS were separated into two groups: those who were still participating in 1996 and those lost to follow-up as of 1996. Those lost to follow-up were only 5.5 percentage points less likely than those retained to have lived with two natural parents in 1994, and 3.6 percentage points more likely to have lived without any natural parents. These differences seem modest, and other differences were even more modest. In the second test, we compared children who had not moved out of the sample of dwellings with those who had moved out of the cross-sectional sample by 1996, but whose households were nevertheless located and interviewed to maintain the panel. This test attempted to answer the question, "Were movers much more likely than non-movers to have experienced a change in living arrangements?" Approximately 69 per cent of movers were still with two natural parents, only some 5 percentage points less than among non-movers. In other words, bias seems modest.

14 Compounding (not subtracting) the annual 3.8 per cent loss over 18 years for children born in 1995 would result in an expected percentage below 45 per cent living with two natural parents at age 18 in the year 2013 (taking into account that only 85 per cent started out with two natural parents in their households). By contrast, according to the figures underlying Figure 3.3, which reflect the cumulative effect of historical rates over the past two decades, about 68 per cent of children born in 1978 were still living with two natural parents as of 1996. Assuming that approximately 94 per cent started out with two natural parents in their households in 1978, an annual loss of under 2 per cent would have yielded the 68 per cent observed in 1996 – a much lower rate than the 3.8 per cent in 1995-1996.

15 Calculated based on figures published in *Sem'ya v Rossii* 1997, pp. 171 and 174; Goskomstat 1997, p. 35; Goskomstat 1996, p. 80, with minor interpolation for the 1990 figure.

16 First, the time scale of the panel survey is still short (three rounds in two chronological years), and that in itself hampers the study of demographic processes (Ott, 1995). Second, the events enumerated were measured at the time of the survey, without specification of when precisely the change took place during the year, yielding a crude

measure of time to event. Finally, the data are heavily left-censored: we do not have the marital histories of parents since the study was not designed for this analysis. We are aware of various approaches to getting around this (Rendall, 1992), and in fact constructed a surrogate for length of marriage. However, given the other shortcomings, it proved to be an academic exercise in the pejorative sense. See also Richards et al., 1987.

17 Financial standing was measured as reported monthly household expenditures at Time 1 as a proportion of a carefully constructed poverty threshold for each household, taking into account regional market baskets and regional price variations (Popkin et al., 1996). Monthly income rather than expenditures was also utilized. The dichotomous variables 'spending less than half the poverty threshold or not' and 'spending less than the full poverty threshold or not' were also used in addition to the metric variable mentioned above.

18 The number entering via out-of-wedlock births was approximately 15 in 1996. Bear in mind that the total number of children eligible to make the transition exceeded 1,600 (Table 3.5), and this is a key figure to use in judging the reliability of the percentages. The percentage of all children experiencing the death of a parent was about 1 per cent. Note, too, that these transition rates exclude children born into single-parent homes, since by definition such children were not in the data set in 1995.

PART II

SOCIAL POLICY
AND THE SINGLE PARENT

Chapter 4: Single Parents, Poverty and Social Welfare Policies in the West

Sheldon Danziger and Marcia Carlson*

Most Western countries have experienced a rapid increase in the number of single-parent families since the 1960s. This demographic trend, regardless of its causes, has consequences for the poverty and economic well-being of children, because single-parent families have higher poverty rates and less economic security than other family types. In this chapter, we review the levels and trends of single-parenthood and related demographic trends in Western industrialized countries and discuss the causal factors driving these trends. We then compare and contrast the economic status of single-parent families and how social policies in the various countries contribute to their well-being. We conclude by discussing the implications for the development of social policies focused on single-parent families in Russia.

4.1 Levels and Trends in Single-Parenthood

Although the extent of single-parenthood varies across countries, the trend has been remarkably similar – single-parent families as a percentage of all families with children have increased rapidly in most Western industrialized nations in recent years (Table 4.1).[2] The United States has the highest proportion of single-parent families of all countries shown and has experienced a significant increase in the last two decades, rising to 27.1 per cent in 1996. Other countries with at least twenty per cent of families with children that are single-parent families include Belgium, Canada, Iceland, New Zealand and the United Kingdom. Little change has been observed in the Scandinavian countries between the 1980s and the 1990s.[3] For every country, all of the numbers shown in Table 4.1, however, are substantially greater than they were in the 1960s (earlier numbers are not shown).

Single-parent families are not a homogenous group. Although there are differences across countries at any point, the trends in different types are similar in most Western nations, and most single parents are single

Table 4.1: Single-Parent Families as a Percentage of All Families with Dependent Children

Country	(reference years)	1981-86	1991-96
Australia	(1983,1993)	13.6	17.2
Austria	(1981,1991)	19.3	19.7
Belgium	(1981,1991)	14.6	20.0
Canada	(1981,1991)	—	20.0
Denmark	(1981,1991)	18.0	18.0
Finland	(1983,1993)	13.0	11.9
France	(1981,1991)	9.9	15.6
Germany	(1981,1991)	14.6	16.4
Iceland	(1984,1993)	23.1	21.1
Ireland	(1981,1991)	15.8	17.9
Italy	(1981,1991)	13.6	14.9
Japan	(1980,1995)	8.9	12.8
Luxembourg	(1981,1991)	14.1	15.7
Netherlands	(1981,1991)	11.9	15.9
New Zealand	(1981,1996)	—	25.5
Norway	(1983,1993)	17.8	19.7
Portugal	(1981,1991)	14.5	13.1
Spain	(1981,1991)	—	12.8
Sweden	(1983,1993)	19.0	18.0
Switzerland	(1981,1991)	12.1	13.7
United Kingdom	(1981,1991)	17.8	20.7
United States	(1986,1996)	22.7	27.1

—: Not available.
Source: Table provided by Sheila Kamerman. Based on data from the OECD (1998).

mothers. As male life expectancy has increased, widows and separated wives have declined as a proportion of single family heads. Divorced women now represent the largest group of single mothers in Austria, Finland, France, the United Kingdom, the United States and West Germany (Kamerman, 1995).

The number of single-parent families at any point in time depends on the rates of inflow and outflow from the state of single-parenthood (Ermisch, 1990). As discussed in the previous chapters, the pathways into single-parenthood include: marriage and childbirth with subsequent separation, divorce or widowhood, or childbirth outside of marriage. We now discuss several of the underlying demographic trends that have contributed to increased single-parenthood in the West.

Changes in Marital Behaviours

Several major changes have occurred vis-à-vis marriage in recent decades. First, there has been an overall decline in marriage rates, especially since the 1960s, due to increasing age at first marriage and rising proportions of persons who never marry. Table 4.2 shows a decline since 1970 in the crude marriage rate (marriages per 1,000 inhabitants) in 23 countries. In 1995, the average crude marriage rate among the industrialized nations shown was 5.5; the United States had the highest crude marriage rate, at 8.9, and France (4.4), Ireland (4.3) and Sweden (3.8) had the lowest. The marriage rate for Japan also declined over the period, from 10.1 to 6.3.

The second major change in marital behaviour has been the separation of sexual experience from marriage. During the 1950s and 1960s, sexual activity increased among teenagers, especially outside marriage, even before oral contraceptives became widely available. Greater non-marital sexual activity increased the likelihood of non-marital birth. For example, in Great Britain in the mid-1960s, 16 per cent of adolescents ages 15 to 19 had engaged in sexual intercourse at least once; one decade later, the figure for teens ages 16 to 19 was 51 per cent (Schofield, 1968 and Farrell, 1978, cited in Land and Lewis, 1997). In the United States, more than half of young women and nearly two-thirds of young men have had sexual intercourse by age 18 (Moore et al., 1998). During the mid-1960s, a premarital conception was typically 'legitimized' via marriage before the birth of the child, but by the 1980s, it was more likely to result in a non-marital birth. Similarly, in Great Britain, most births that were conceived outside marriage in the 1950s and 1960s still occurred within marriage, while as of the early 1970s, young unmarried women who became pregnant increasingly chose to have an abortion or a non-marital birth (Land and Lewis, 1997).

Table 4.2: Marriage and Divorce Rates in Selected Industrialized Countries

	Crude marriage rate (marriages per 1,000 persons)			Crude divorce rate (divorces per 1,000 persons)			Total divorce rate[c]	
	1970	1985	1995	1970	1985	1995	1970	1995
Australia	9.3	7.3	6.1	1.0	2.5	2.8	—	—
Austria	7.1	5.9	5.3	1.4	2.1	2.3	.18	.38
Belgium	7.6	5.8	5.1	0.7	1.9	3.5	.10	.55
Canada	8.8	7.3	5.4	1.4	2.5	2.6	—	—
Denmark	7.4	5.7	6.6	1.9	2.8	2.5	.25	.42
Finland	8.8	5.3	4.6	1.3	1.9	2.7	.17	.49
France	7.8	4.9	4.4[a]	0.8	2.0	2.0	.12	.37[c]
Germany (West)	7.3	6.0	5.3	1.2	2.1	2.1	.21	.33
Greece	7.7	6.4	6.1	0.4	0.8	1.1	.05	.15
Iceland	7.8	5.2	4.6	1.2	2.2	1.8	.18	.34
Ireland	7.1	5.3	4.3	[b]	[b]	[b]	[b]	[b]
Italy	7.4	5.2	4.9	0.3[g]	0.3	0.5[c]	.05	.08[c]
Japan[h]	10.1	6.1	6.3	0.9	1.4	1.6.	.11[d]	.26[d]
Luxembourg	6.4	5.3	5.1	0.6	1.8	1.8	.10	.33
Netherlands	9.5	5.7	5.3	0.8	2.4	2.2	.10	.32
New Zealand	9.2	7.6	6.3[c]	1.1	2.6	2.7[f]	—	—
Norway	7.6	4.9	4.6[a,c]	0.9	2.0	2.5[c]	.13	.44
Portugal	9.4	6.7	6.6	0.1	0.9	1.2	—	.16
Spain	7.4	5.0	5.0	[b]	[b]	0.8	[b]	.12[d]
Sweden	5.4	4.6	3.8	1.6	2.4	2.5	.23	.50
Switzerland	7.5	6.0	5.8	1.0	1.8	2.2	.15	.38
United Kingdom	8.5	6.9	5.7	1.2	3.1	3.0[c]	.16[i]	.45[a,i]
United States	10.6	10.1	8.9[a]	3.5	5.0	4.4	—	.55[d]

—: Not available.
[a]Data are provisional. [b]Divorce not allowed. [c]Average number of divorces per marriage assuming current-year divorce rates were to continue. [d]Eurostat estimate. [e]1994 data. [f]1992 data. [g]1971 data. [h]Crude marriage and divorce rates are for Japanese nationals only. [i]England and Wales only.
Source: Eurostat (1997), United Nations (1974), (1989), (1995).

Third, non-marital cohabitation has blurred the boundaries of 'marriage'. One implication of this trend, beyond its contribution to the decline in marriage rates, is that cohabiting couples now account for many non-marital births (Bumpass and Sweet, 1989). Cohabitation has long been an accepted union type in Scandinavia, and it has become increasingly common in other countries either before marriage, or as a substitute for marriage. In the United States, more than half of all non-marital births now occur within a consensual union (Bumpass and Raley, 1995; Bumpass and Sweet, 1989); in England and Wales, 54 per cent of all births outside marriage in 1991 were jointly recognized by parents living at the same address, presumably cohabiting (Clarke and Henwood, 1997). In France, seven out of ten children born outside marriage in 1982 were formally recognized by both parents (Muller-Escoda and Vogt, 1997). Also, a large proportion of all cohabiting couples have children present – approximately 40 per cent in the U.S. (Bumpass, Sweet and Cherlin, 1991), and 47 per cent in Canada in 1996 (Statistics Canada, 1996).

In the United States, an unmarried, cohabiting woman with a child is classified in official statistics as a single mother; this is not the case in Europe. Thus, because of the rise in cohabitation, the measured growth in single-parent families in the U.S.A. (as shown in Table 4.1), and the number of children therein, is overstated, because two-parent unmarried families are classified as single-parent families (Ermisch, 1990). According to Bumpass and Raley (1995), 17 per cent of the 'single-parent' time of children (as classified by marriage) in the early 1980s in the United States was actually spent living with cohabiting parents. Further, cohabiting parents often marry at some point, as has become the norm in Scandinavia, further blurring the definition of 'marriage' (Hoem and Hoem, 1988).

Increases in Divorce

Increased marital instability has also contributed to the prevalence of single-parent families. In most Western countries, divorce rates have risen dramatically since 1960. As the middle columns in Table 4.2 indicate, the crude divorce rate (divorces per 1,000 marriages) increased in almost every country shown between 1970 and 1995. In 1995, the

United States had the highest rate, at 4.4 divorces per 1,000 persons, and over half of all marriages begun in the 1980s were projected to end in divorce (Castro-Martin and Bumpass, 1989). Although the divorce rate has levelled off in the mid-1980s, this was not due to increased marital stability, but to other factors: increased cohabitation, an increase in the age at first marriage, and the ageing of the baby boom cohort (McLanahan and Casper, 1995; Bumpass and Sweet, 1989). Most European nations have divorce rates between 2.0 and 3.0 per 1,000 inhabitants, with other European nations having somewhat lower rates (except for Belgium, where the rate is 3.5 per 1,000). Of the countries shown in Table 4.2, Italy and Spain have the lowest divorce rates at 0.5 and 0.8, respectively. The divorce rate has also increased in Japan in recent decades, from 0.9 to 1.6.

The total divorce rate (the proportion of marriages that are expected to end in divorce) provides a better indicator of the prevalence of divorce because it controls for the number of persons who enter marriages in the first place. The last column of Table 4.2 shows that the United States and Belgium have the highest total divorce rates, with 55 per cent of marriages expected to end in divorce, followed by Sweden (50 per cent), Finland (49 per cent), the United Kingdom (45 per cent), Norway (44 per cent), and Denmark (42 per cent). Continental European countries have total divorce rates ranging from 30 to 40 per cent, while rates in the Catholic countries are much lower (8 per cent in Italy and 12 per cent in Spain). The 1995 rate was higher than the 1970 rate for every country for which data are shown.

As attitudes toward marriage and divorce – and observed demographic trends – changed in the 1950s and 1960s, legal provisions related to marriage and divorce were re-evaluated by many Western governments. Between 1960 and the mid-1980s, most Western countries implemented some reform or complete revision of divorce legislation, so that obtaining a divorce became easier (Phillips, 1988). Prior to the 1960s, divorces were granted only for specific reasons; by the 1980s, 'no fault' divorce was common, so couples could decide that their relationship had changed and that they no longer wished to remain married (ibid.). This change represented an historic shift from marriage being closely regulated by the church and/or state toward recognising marriage as a free-will commitment between individuals. A civil divorce was legalised in Catholic countries, such as Italy (1970), Spain (1981), Portugal (1985), and Ireland (1997); in other Western countries, the grounds for divorce were relaxed, and no-fault divorce was introduced and/or simplified (Kamerman, 1995).

Changes in Fertility

Overall declines in fertility and differential trends in marital and non-marital fertility represent the third major change in family demographics. Total fertility rates have steadily declined since the early 1960s. As Table 4.3 indicates, most Western countries had rates above 2.5 in 1965, but by 1995, most ranged from 1.4 to 1.9 – below replacement level. As a point of comparison, figures for Japan are shown; the total fertility rate there was lower in 1965 than rates in all Western countries; and in 1995, Japan had a fertility rate in the mid-range of countries shown.

While overall fertility has fallen for at least three decades, non-marital fertility has increased as a proportion of total fertility. As marriage rates declined and divorce rates increased, the number of single women 'available' to have a child outside of marriage increased. In the United States, the average length of time between first intercourse and marriage is now seven years for women and ten years for men (Moore et al., 1998). Increased non-marital sexual activity has raised the likelihood of a non-marital conception and birth, and thus increased the ratio of non-marital births to all births. As the right-hand section of Table 4.3 shows, between 1965 and 1995, this ratio, in both the United States and the United Kingdom, increased from 5.2 to 8.0 per cent to about one third. The levels and trends are similar in Finland and France. In the Netherlands and Italy, the proportion was only 1.4 and 2.4 per cent in 1965, and rose to 15.5 and 8.1 per cent, respectively, by 1995. Denmark, Norway and Sweden have experienced the greatest increase in the proportion of births outside marriage; in Denmark the proportion rose from 7.8 to 46.5 per cent, in Norway from 3.7 to 47.6 per cent, and in Sweden from 11.3 to 53.0 per cent, between 1965 and 1995. Again, many non-marital births in Scandinavia are to cohabiting couples and not to single mothers. In Greece, only 3.0 per cent of all births take place outside of marriage and in Switzerland only 6.8 per cent.

Table 4.3: Fertility Rates in Selected Western Industrialized Countries

	Total fertility rate[b]				Non-marital births: proportion of total			
	1965	1975	1985	1995	1965	1975	1985	1995
Australia[c]	2.88	2.06	1.87	1.82	5.1	9.3	13.2	26.6
Austria	2.70	1.82	1.47	1.40	13.0	12.8	22.4	27.4
Belgium	2.62	1.74	1.51	1.55[a]	2.1	2.8	7.1	15.0[e]
Canada	3.15	—	1.66	1.61	—	—	—	—
Denmark	2.61	1.92	1.45	1.80	7.8	11.0	43.0	46.5
Finland	2.48	1.68	1.65	1.81	4.0	5.8	16.4	33.1
France	2.84	1.93	1.81	1.70[a]	6.1	6.9	19.6	37.2[a]
Germany	2.50	1.48	1.37	1.25	7.6	7.2	16.2	16.1
Greece	2.30	2.38	1.68	1.32	1.2	1.1	1.8	3.0
Ireland	4.03	3.40	2.50	1.86[a]	1.6	2.7	8.5	22.7
Italy	2.66	2.20	1.42	1.17[e]	2.4	2.2	5.4	8.1[a]
Japan	2.14	1.91	1.76	1.50[f]	—	—	—	—
Luxembourg	2.42	1.55	1.38	1.69	3.2	4.0	8.7	13.1
Netherlands	3.04	1.66	1.51	1.53	1.4	2.1	8.3	15.5
New Zealand[c]	3.41	2.27	1.96	2.04	—	—	—	—
Norway	2.95	1.98	1.68	1.87	3.7	4.5	25.8	47.6
Portugal	3.14	2.58	1.40	1.72	9.5	7.3	12.3	18.7
Spain	2.94	2.80	1.64	1.18[e]	2.3	1.4	8.0	10.8[a]
Sweden	2.42	1.77	1.74	1.73	11.3	18.6	46.4	53.0
Switzerland	2.61	1.61	1.52	1.48	3.8	3.8	5.6	6.8
United Kingdom	2.89	1.81	1.79	1.70[a]	5.2	8.0	18.9	33.6
United States	2.91	1.77	1.84	2.02[f]	7.7	14.3	22.0	31.0[d]

—: Not available.
a Data are provisional.
b Average number of children born to a woman throughout her childbearing years (ages 15-44).
c Figures for Australia and New Zealand are for 1966, 1976, 1986 and 1995.
d This figure is for 1993.
e Eurostat estimate.
f This figure is for 1992.
Sources: Total fertility rates for European countries are from Eurostat, Demographic Yearbook, 1997. Figures for Australia are from Australian Bureau of Statistics (1998), for New Zealand from Statistics New Zealand (1998), for Canada and Japan from Coleman (1996), and for the United States from U.S. National Center for Health Statistics (1996) and U.S. Department of Health and Human Services (1995).

4.2 Causal Factors Accounting for the Rise in Single-Parenthood

Despite differences in economic circumstances and public policy regimes (as described below), the similarity in demographic trends across these two dozen Western countries is remarkable. We now discuss three causal factors that help to account for the changing patterns of marriage, divorce and fertility and the consequent rise in single-parent families. These causal factors are operative in most nations, although their relative importance varies from country to country.

Changes in Societal Values and Norms

Single-parenthood has increased, in part because of changes in norms, values and attitudes; a cultural shift has occurred in most Western societies with regard to societal views about marriage, divorce, and childbearing. Since the beginning of the twentieth century, marriage has evolved from an institution characterized by its public role and duties (primarily the care of children) to a largely private relationship between two persons who can freely choose the course of that relationship (Morgan, 1985, cited in Land and Lewis, 1997).

Particularly since the 1960s, attitudes have changed dramatically. Following the conservatism of the 1950s, authorities and institutions were challenged by a large, youthful post-war generation, and a 'sexual revolution' brought more permissive attitudes and practices, greater individualism and acceptance of ideas about personal fulfilment (Phillips, 1988). This included shifts in views about the primacy of dual-parent models of the family. For example, in the United States, in 1962 about half of mothers surveyed said that parents with children present should not stay together if they do not get along; by 1980, more than 80 per cent said parents should not stay together in such a situation (Thornton, 1985).

The pressures and reforms that ensued as attitudes changed varied across societies. The Scandinavian countries (especially Denmark and Sweden) witnessed the greatest changes, while some of the Catholic countries (such as Spain and Ireland) lagged behind (Phillips, 1988). Overall, changes in attitudes and values led to greater public acceptance of sex and childbearing outside marriage, and thus contributed to the increased prevalence of single-parent families. Kristin Moore (1995) writes:

"In sum, the data paint a clear picture of increasing and substantial tolerance for non marital childbearing and the behaviors leading up to non marital childbearing. Even if these tolerant attitudes and values do not actively encourage parenthood outside of marriage for a given individual, they may increase its prevalence by reducing the personal, social and familial pressures that have discouraged non marital parenthood in previous generations."

Although there is little cross-national data about changes in attitudes, one study of several European countries notes that "in general, there seems to be an ideological shift in the direction of more egalitarian roles for men and women" (Alwin et al., 1992). Overall, there has been a shift in attitudes toward greater autonomy and individualism with respect to personal and family relationships (Kiernan, Land and Lewis, 1998).

Increases in Women's Economic Independence

A second causal factor, women's growing economic independence, derives from an economic analysis of marriage posited by Becker (1991). As noted in Chapter 1, this approach implies that labour market changes that increased women's employment and earnings prospects reduced their economic benefits from marriage and increased the appeal of being single (either through divorce or never marrying). Because women are now better able to support themselves financially, they have less incentive to enter into a marital or other union. Women's increasing economic independence – proxied by increases in real wages and increases in labour force participation, both absolutely and relative to those of men – has been associated with declines in marriage and increases in marital disruption (McLanahan and Casper, 1995).

The rise in female labour force participation, especially among married women with children, represents one of the most dramatic socio-economic changes in the West in the latter half of the twentieth century. Around 1970, participation rates among women ages 25 to 34 ranged from 24 per cent in the Netherlands to 61 per cent in Sweden (McLanahan and Casper, 1995). In 1994, the overall female labour force participation rate ranged from a low of 43 to 47 per cent in the Catholic countries (Ireland, Italy and Spain) to a high of 70 to 74 per cent in the U.S. and the Scandinavian countries (OECD, 1996).

Table 4.4 shows labour force participation rates in the late 1980s for all women under the age of 60, women with children, and single mothers with children in selected countries (Kamerman, 1995).

Denmark and Sweden have the highest rates of labour force participation for all categories of women, 80.0 per cent or more; Italy and Germany, the lowest at 43.3 and 55.8 per cent, respectively. Even in the last two countries, however, over half of lone mothers with children under three years of age are employed.

An extension of the women's economic independence hypothesis attributes increased single-parenthood to the declining economic status of men relative to women (McLanahan and Casper, 1995). Deindustrialization, economic restructuring, labour-saving technological changes, and the globalisation of markets beginning in the 1970s and accelerating in the 1980s, resulted in increased rates of joblessness and/or low earnings, especially for less-skilled workers in many industrialized countries (Gottschalk and Smeeding, 1997). For example, between the early 1970s and 1997 in Australia, the number of full-time

Table 4.4: Labour Force Participation Rates of Women under Age 60[a], by Presence and Age of Children in Eight Countries, 1986 and 1988[b] (percentages)

	All women	All mothers with children		Lone mothers with children	
		Under 18 years-old	Under 3 years-old	Under 18 years-old	Under 3 years-old
Canada	66.8	67.0	58.4	63.6 [c]	41.3
Denmark	79.2	86.1	83.9	85.9	80.9
France	60.1	65.8	60.1	85.2	69.6
Germany	55.8	48.4	39.7	69.7	50.4
Italy	43.3	43.9	45.0	67.2	68.0
Sweden	80.0	89.4	85.8	—	81.0
United Kingdom	64.3	58.7	58.7	51.9	23.4
United States	68.5	65.0	52.5	65.3	45.1

a Women ages 60 to 64 are included in Canada and Sweden. Lower age limits are 16 for the United States and Sweden, 15 for Canada, and 14 for all other countries. For participation rates of women with children, no upper limit is applied for the United States or Canada. These differences do not distort the comparisons because very few women under 16 have children, while few women over 60 live with their minor children. Includes divorced, separated, never-married and widowed women
b Data for the United States are for March 1988; Canada and Sweden are annual averages for 1988; data for all other countries are for Spring 1986.
c Children under 16 years
Source: Sorrentino (1990), Kamerman (1995).

jobs for males, adjusted for population change, declined by about 25 per cent (Gregory et al., 1998). One can think of reduced employment prospects for men as decreasing the 'quality' of available marriage partners, and because marriage rates are related to the number of eligible and economically stable men (Lichter et al., 1991), marriage rates have declined. However, as McLanahan and Casper (1995) note, the 'marriageable males' hypothesis does not account for the decline in marriage among men with a college education who tend to be 'high-quality' marriage partners. It is, therefore, important not to minimise the significance of the changing social norms discussed above.

Differences in Social Welfare Programmes

Particularly in the United States, there has been much discussion about whether social welfare programmes have contributed to the increase in single-parent families. This issue has also been discussed in Great Britain, where the percentage of lone mothers dependent on public assistance increased from less than 20 per cent in 1960 to more than 50 per cent in the late 1980s (Land and Lewis, 1997). The latest research consensus for the U.S.A. is that income-tested welfare programmes do have small effects on family structure in the direction of encouraging single-parenthood (Moffitt, 1997). However, cross-national comparisons generate doubts about the welfare benefits hypothesis because welfare benefits to single mothers in the U.S.A. are so much lower than in other Western nations, whereas single-parenthood is higher.

Table 4.5 (column 1) illustrates the generosity of the social safety net for a single mother with two children in fourteen Western nations. Mean total government transfers to single mothers as a per cent of the median equivalent income in the United States (22 per cent) is lower than in any other country shown. This is followed by Canada (26 per cent) and Italy (29 per cent). Most others have transfer incomes ranging from 30 to 40 per cent of the median. This ratio is highest for the United Kingdom (46 per cent), Sweden (49 per cent), and the Netherlands (71 per cent).

Less variability is observed in the proportion of median income represented by government transfers to couples (Table 4.5, column 2). Italy (7 per cent) and the United States (8 per cent) provide the lowest amounts, followed by Germany (10 per cent), and Spain and Australia (both 11 per cent). Belgium, Denmark and Finland all provide transfers greater than 20 per cent of the median equivalent income, while Sweden is the highest at 32 per cent.

The data show significant variation in the extent of public support for single parents. Thus, in this context government spending is unlikely to be the major cause of the long-run rise in single-parenthood (McLanahan and Booth, 1989; Moffitt, 1997). McLanahan and Casper (1995) offer additional reasons why welfare is not primarily responsible for either the decline in marriage or the increased non-marital births as a percentage of all births in the United States. First, cash welfare benefits have become less generous in real terms since the early 1970s. Second, the decline in marriage and the increase in non-marital childbearing have occurred throughout the population, not just among welfare-eligible women.

4.3 Economic Status of Single Parents

In all industrial market economies, the economic status of single-mother families is lower than that of two-parent families. However, large cross-

Table 4.5: Mean Total Transfers as a Percentage of Median Equivalent Income

	Year	Single Mothers	Married Couples
Australia	1994	34.6	10.9
Belgium	1992	36.5	20.8
Canada	1994	26.1	13.0
Denmark	1992	40.2	23.3
France	1989	32.8	19.1
Finland	1991	31.9	22.8
Germany	1994	31.1	10.0
Italy	1995	29.4	6.6
Netherlands	1991	71.4	19.6
Norway	1995	39.5	17.8
Spain	1990	35.4	10.6
Sweden	1992	49.0	32.3
United Kingdom	1995	45.8	18.4
United States	1994	22.3	8.1

Source: Timothy Smeeding and Lee Rainwater, unpublished tabulations of data from the Luxembourg Income Study.

national differences are observed in their economic conditions. Wong et al. (1993) calculate the ratio of mean and median incomes of single-mother families and two-parent families in eight countries. Regardless of which income measure is utilized, single-mother families in the Scandinavian countries (Norway and Sweden) have net disposable incomes that are about 85 per cent of those of two-parent families. The ratios for other European countries (France, Germany and the U.K.) range from 65 to 76 per cent, and for countries outside Europe (Australia, Canada and the U.S.), the ratios are all less than 60 per cent.

These differences in economic status are largely due to variations in tax and transfer policies. The previous section highlighted the variation with respect to the latter. For example, based on market income only, the probability that a child with given parental characteristics (such as age, education and labour force status) will be poor is similar in both Sweden and the United States. But these countries have very different social policies, so the probability that a market-income poor child will be poor based on disposable income is much lower in Sweden (Jäntti and Danziger, 1994).

Differences in social welfare states are discussed in greater detail below. However, one underlying difference in social protection among Western countries is the extent to which government transfers are universal or means-tested. Single-mother families tend to fare worse in countries where a greater proportion of social support benefits are means-tested. According to Wong et al. (1993), the United States has the highest proportion of transfer income that is means-tested (89.4 per cent), followed by Australia (89.3 per cent) and Canada (61.2 per cent). France, Germany, Sweden and the United Kingdom range between 34.1 per cent to 54.9 per cent; Norway has by far the lowest proportion, at 6.0 per cent.[4]

Why means-testing should lead to worse welfare outcomes for single mothers is unclear, unless the targeting is poorly administered. However, it is probably the case that countries that choose to spend less on social welfare programmes use means-testing to better target the limited spending. It does not imply that, holding spending levels constant, shifting to universal programmes would lower poverty. However, some analysts (e.g. Skocpol, 1990), emphasize the political economy dimension and maintain that if universal programmes are first put in place, they will generate increased total spending over the long run because they will have a greater political constituency and will not stigmatize beneficiaries.

Overall spending levels on social protection (including spending on old age, health, childbearing and family, disability, and unemployment) as a proportion of each country's 1994 gross domestic product (GDP), are shown in Table 4.6. Greece spends the lowest fraction (15.6 per cent), followed by Ireland (20.4 per cent), the United States (21.2 per cent) and Portugal (21.7 per cent). Sweden spends the highest proportion of its GDP on social programs (37.7 per cent), followed by the two other Nordic countries shown in the Table – Finland (34.8 per cent) and Denmark (34.2 per cent) – and the Netherlands (32.8 per cent). Other European countries spend between 23 and 32 per cent of GDP on social protection.

Table 4.6: Expenditures on Social Protection as a Proportion of GDP[a] (percentages)

Country	1994
Austria	31.9
Belgium	27.0
Denmark	34.2
Germany	30.7
Greece	15.6
Finland	34.8
France	30.4
Ireland	20.4
Italy	25.8
Luxembourg	23.9
Netherlands	32.8
Portugal	21.7
Spain	23.6
Sweden	37.7
United Kingdom	28.1
United States[b]	21.2

a Includes expenditures related to old age, health, childbearing and family, disability and unemployment. Education is excluded.
b Figure is for 1995 and may not be directly comparable to others in table.
Source: European data from Eurostat (1997); U.S. figure from Committee on Ways and Means (1996).

Notable variations across industrialized countries are evident in both market income poverty rates (based on earnings and asset income only), and in poverty rates after social transfers, taxes and child support payments. Table 4.7 presents data from 16 countries in the Luxembourg Income Study (LIS), on poverty rates for children in single-mother families before and after government taxes and transfers. Poverty is defined as 50 per cent of a country's median adjusted income. Before government benefits are added (column 1), poverty rates range from a low of 31.7 per cent in Italy to a high of 79.7 per cent in the Netherlands. After government taxes and transfers, four countries have poverty rates less

Table 4.7: Poverty Rates for Children in Single-Mother Families[a] before and after Government Programmes[b]

Country	Year	(1) Pre-transfer poverty rate	(2) Post-transfer, post-tax poverty rate	(3) Ratio (2)/(1)
Australia	1990	73.2	56.2	.77
Belgium	1992	50.7	10.0	.20
Canada	1991	68.2	50.2	.74
Denmark	1992	45.0	7.3	.16
Finland	1991	36.3	7.5	.21
France	1984	56.4	22.6	.40
Germany	1989	43.9	4.2	.10
Ireland	1987	72.6	40.5	.56
Italy	1991	31.7	13.9	.44
Luxembourg	1985	55.7	10.0	.18
Netherlands	1991	79.7	39.5	.50
Norway	1991	57.4	18.4	.32
Sweden	1992	54.9	5.2	.09
Switzerland	1982	33.7	25.6	.76
United Kingdom	1986	76.2	18.7	.25
United States	1991	69.9	59.5	.85

a Single-mother families are families where one female adult resides in the household; cohabiting-parent families are not included here. Poverty is defined as 50 per cent of a country's median adjusted income.

b Government programmes include income and payroll taxes and all types of government cash and near-cash transfers.

Source: Rainwater and Smeeding (1995).

than 8 per cent (Denmark, Finland, Germany and Sweden); while most nations have rates between 10.0 and 25.6 per cent. At the upper end, the Netherlands, Ireland, Canada, Australia and the United States have rates ranging from 39.5 to 59.5 per cent.[5]

4.4 Social Protection and the Welfare State

How can public policies best meet the needs of single-parent families? This question is complicated by concerns related to ideological norms and perceptions of family roles and values. Some analysts and policy-makers view the increase in single-parent families as an indicator of the decline of the traditional family as a basic societal institution (Popenoe, 1988). They define the problem as the change in family structure itself – a departure from the traditional, nuclear family as the norm – and seek policies that would reverse the trend and encourage the formation and maintenance of two-parent families. Others view single-parenthood as a neutral, or even positive, development, particularly for women who may gain independence outside of marriage. They consider the low economic status of single parents as the key problem and propose policies to improve their income status, even if such policies were to increase the number of single-parent families. These different viewpoints lead to dis-agreement over the extent to which government should assume underly-ing responsibility for the economic (or perhaps social) circumstances of single-parent families (Duskin, 1990).

Family policies in some countries attempt to distinguish between the 'deserving' poor – those poor due to circumstances beyond their con-trol – and the 'undeserving' poor – those who are at least partly respon-sible for their problems (Wennemo, 1994). Public discourse about single motherhood is controversial because, except for widowhood, it is an 'achieved' rather than an 'ascribed' status (McLanahan and Sandefur, 1994). In this sense, divorced or never-married single parents who are poor may be viewed in the 'undeserving' category because they have 'chosen' that status. This distinction has historically affected the treat-ment of single mothers, especially in the United States. For example, widows with children have long been considered legitimate beneficiaries of public support in most countries. In contrast, until relatively recently, unmarried single mothers were deemed morally suspect and treated quite differently in the U.S.A. (Skocpol, 1992).

This tension is not confined to the United States, however. Policies intended to maintain societal notions of moral standards have often conflicted with those designed to improve the living conditions of poor single mothers. Historically, Western nations discouraged the formation of single-parent families (which implied not providing an incentive via generous government benefits for such families to form); yet, the poor economic status of such families required substantial assistance in order for them to remain economically viable and for their children not to be disadvantaged. In most countries, at least since the 1960s, a range of social support programs and policies have evolved that target benefits on single-parent families.

Many scholars have developed typologies of the welfare state to facilitate cross-national comparisons. Although countries have many distinctive features in their social welfare programs and policies, use of a typology can help to emphasise common features. One well-known typology is Esping-Andersen's *The Three Worlds of Welfare State Capitalism* (1990), in which the concepts of de-commodification (the ability of individuals to subsist by means other than the labour and capital markets) and stratification (differences between classes) are used to distinguish among Western countries. Although this model has been criticised, it is 'a well-established landmark' (Headey et al., 1997). In this typology, the three clusters of nations are *social democratic* (dominated by the Nordic countries), *conservative-corporatist* (mostly European continental countries), and *liberal* (primarily English-speaking countries).

Social welfare policies in the social democratic states developed as a way to further social ideals about equality, whereby all citizens are entitled to benefits and services commensurate with middle-class status. Work and welfare are intricately intertwined, however, and full employment is a both an objective and an expectation. Many benefits are nonetheless universal and government actively manages labour market policies. The Nordic countries represent this type of social welfare regime.

Conservative-corporatist nations are less focused on market efficiency and, instead, emphasize the preservation of status differentials.

Benefit levels are similar to those in social democratic states, and the provision of social insurance is linked to labour force participation and may differ by occupation. In most conservative-corporatist countries, the Church has had a major influence, and thus social policy typically upholds traditional values and expectations related to family (i.e. encouraging motherhood and traditional gender roles). Austria, France, Germany and Italy are representative conservative-corporatist regimes.

In the liberal welfare state, "means-tested assistance, modest universal transfers, or modest social-insurance plans predominate" (Esping-Andersen, 1990). Emphasis is on the market and individuals' labour force activity as the primary means for resource allocation. Benefit levels are typically modest when compared to average wage levels, and recipients are often stigmatized by non-recipients. Australia, Canada and the United States represent the archetypal 'liberal' welfare states.[6] Although, unlike the U.S.A., Canada and Australia offer non-means tested support for single mothers, all three nations have limited childcare or other social benefits to support the employment of mothers (Nichols-Casebolt and Krysik, 1998).

Other researchers have developed alternative typologies of the social welfare state. For example, Bonoli (1997) classifies welfare states by plotting social expenditures as a percentage of GDP against the percentage of social expenditures financed through employment-based contributions. Employment-based contributions are typically based on proportional taxes, as opposed to more progressive income-tax-based contributions. The net result would tend to be less re-distributive although the actual effect would depend on the details of various programmes. By this schema, the Scandinavian countries end up in the same cluster (high spending and low proportion through contributions), the United Kingdom and Ireland are in a second category (low spending and low proportion through contributions), and the remaining continental European countries all have a high proportion of social expenditures from employment-based contributions and are divided into two groups by high or low spending level (non-European countries were not included). Others have evaluated welfare state typologies from the perspective of gender and family and have based their categories on the generosity of policies toward women and children (Gornick et al., 1996; Sainsbury, 1996).

No typology uniquely captures the complex features of the social welfare states of disparate nations, as each has a particular culture, history, demography and national character that have shaped its choice of programmes and policies. Further, the social protection systems that exist today were implemented gradually through various reforms and more ad hoc adjustments over time. We adopt the three categories of Esping-Andersen as a heuristic device to facilitate understanding of cross-national similarities and differences and describe in greater detail the social support policies for single-parent families in a representative country of each type of welfare state. We then make some observations about the relevance of these models for the evolution of the Russian welfare state.

A Social Democratic Approach (Sweden)

Most European countries provide some universal cash benefits and target other programmes in an effort to raise the living standard of single-parent families. The Scandinavian countries have long provided the most generous supports in this respect. Single mothers have not been stigmatized because of their status; rather, policy debates have centred on how to improve the economic well-being of one-earner vs. two-earner families (Kiernan, Land and Lewis, 1998). Sweden has been very effective at reducing economic hardship among such families, as its welfare state emphasizes full employment, provides many part-time public jobs for mothers, and relies mostly on universal programmes, progressive tax rates and generous transfer policies. In the 1990s, however, unemployment rates have dramatically risen, raising the question as to whether the extent of public spending required to sustain such a welfare state model is feasible under different external economic conditions. Here we briefly review the evolution of the Swedish system.

In most Western countries during the twentieth century, the state increasingly intervened to support needy families, particularly those with children. Often policy initiatives first targeted the most needy groups, particularly single-parent families. Sweden was no exception—in 1937 four types of family support for mothers with children were introduced, including maternity insurance (for nearly all mothers) and advanced alimony (for single mothers) (Wennemo, 1994).

During and after the Second World War, emphasis shifted toward universal and away from targeted programmes. Sweden introduced a universal family benefit system in 1948, whereby all families with children received monthly cash benefits paid to the mother (Wennemo, 1994). The Swedish system today remains largely based on universal benefits and allowances, supplemented by specific programmes targeted to needy families. Unlike some other social welfare systems, Sweden's is largely based on the assumption that mothers work at least part-time (Björklund and Freeman, 1995).

Programmes providing benefits for Swedish single-parent families include a basic child allowance for each child under age 16 (under age 20 if still in school), child support and a housing allowance. If a child's parents live apart, the non-custodial parent pays a maintenance allowance. Parents can make their own child support agreement, but the social authorities ensure that it does not fall below an established minimum, which can be re-negotiated every six years. If the non-custodial parent fails to pay the required amount, or pays only a small amount, the custodial parent is assured a maintenance advance, paid for by the government until the child turns 18 (or age 20 if the child is still in school). The maintenance advance is indexed to a 'base amount', which is a sum of money determined annually and used in the social security system. The maintenance advance is not affected by the remarriage of the custodial parent.

Housing benefits are given to families with or without children, but the amounts differ by income and the presence of children. The housing allowance is paid as a per cent of housing costs up to a certain level. In 1992, approximately 28 per cent of families with children received housing allowances (Swedish Institute, 1994).

Childcare and parental leave are key components of Swedish family policy, enabling both men and women to combine parenthood and employment. As of January 1995, after the birth of a child, a parent is entitled to stay home with a child for 360 days at 80 per cent of his or her previous salary; for an additional 90 days, a small fixed sum benefit is available. One month of this total time can be used only by the father and is non-transferable. Once the mother decides to return to paid work, childcare facilities, at a high and relatively homogenous level of quality, are available for all children. Required parental payments cover only a small part of the cost of the care (about 11 per cent in 1992), with the remainder subsidised by government monies (Swedish Institute, 1994).

Because all persons have a right to a basic level of economic security, a family that cannot support itself on earned income and social insurance benefits is eligible for means-tested social assistance. Historically, a negative stigma has been attached to receiving such benefits, and, therefore, individuals use this programme as a last resort. Potential clients need only show that they have no other means of economic support. In 1996, 8.5 per cent of the population received social assistance, about one-third of whom were children (Statistiska Centralbyrån, 1998).

A Corporatist Approach (France)

France typifies the corporatist approach to social policy making. French social policy historically emphasized two objectives: (1) to encourage French parents to have many children, and (2) to provide families with sufficient support so that mothers could choose whether to stay home and care for their children or enter the paid labour force (Lefaucheur, 1995). The pro-natalist emphasis grew out of French defeats in wars in the late 1880s through 1940 as a way to overcome 'depopulation.' Women were provided with various supports for childbearing, including maternity homes which offered care during pregnancy. In France, where generous benefits are provided to mothers with children under age 3, single motherhood "is conceptualised as a risk rather than social deviance" (Kiernan, Land and Lewis, 1998).

The first government income assistance in France (established in the mid-1800s) was a means-tested monthly allowance to enable poor mothers to care for their babies. Today, this programme (now known as *Aide sociale à l'enfance*, or ASE) is managed at the local level, and in addition to monthly allowances, it provides educational support and emergency aid grants to low-income mothers with children. The amount of the allowance varies by locality, but on average it provides about 25 per cent of a standard minimum salary level (or SMIC), and approximately half of the grants given are to children in single-parent families (Lefaucheur, 1995).

After World War II, a national social security system was created to protect citizens against various social risks. Originally, access to the system was only offered to persons in families that had at least one worker, although after the unemployment crisis of the 1970s, this requirement was relaxed. Family allowances became integrated into the social security system by having them financed by payroll contributions. By 1955, the system offered six non-means-tested family benefits: (1) family allowances for families with at least one working parent and at least two children in the household; (2) single-income allowances for families with only one working parent; (3) prenatal allowances for all expectant mothers; (4) maternity allowances after the birth of their child[7]; (5) a supplemental benefit added to family allowances for children over age 10; and (6) a 'housewife allocation' for families of self-employed workers (ibid.).

The term 'lone-parent family' was not used in France until the 1970s; it was introduced by feminist academics who disparaged the traditional characterization of single-parent families as 'at risk' or 'broken' (ibid.). To address their special needs, in 1976 a means-tested 'lone-parent allowance' (*allocation de parent isolé,* or API) was introduced. This allowance provides about 71 per cent of the standard minimum salary amount (SMIC) for a single parent with one child. It is time-limited and is available for the first year after the separation of a couple (by death, divorce or legal separation) or until the youngest child reaches age three.

Consistent with pro-natalist aims, the French tax system encourages large families and provides special benefits to single parents. For a married couple, the first two children each count as half of an individual deduction, and the third and subsequent children as one deduction. For never-married, separated or divorced parents, the first child counts as one deduction, instead of half; for widowed parents, their own personal deduction counts as two, instead of one.

High-quality childcare for children under age three is available through local centres (*crèches*) where parents pay according to income (Lefaucheur, 1995). Although children of single mothers do not have legal priority on the waiting lists for such childcare, an informal practice of favouring children from single-parent families 'in difficulty' results in a greater likelihood that children of employed single mothers will be cared for in these centres than children of employed married mothers (ibid.). In addition, working single parents can deduct childcare expenses from their taxable income.

A network of mother and child centres across the country exists to provide medical care for expectant mothers and children under age six. Health insurance is provided to every person (and their spouse and minor children) who has worked 1,200 hours in the previous year or who has paid social security taxes for at least one year. Single parents who were previously eligible through a working spouse, but who become widowed or divorced, receive health insurance for one year after the loss of the spouse, or until their last child reaches age three. Single mothers who receive lone-parent allowances are also eligible for health insurance.

A 'Liberal' Welfare Approach (The United States)

The social welfare system in the United States has developed very differently from those in most other Western democracies. Though targeted support to some categories of needy families was introduced at the beginning of the 19th century and extended in the 1930s, a European-style universal family support system was never developed (Wennemo, 1994). Indeed, public social welfare programmes have never generated much political enthusiasm. Instead, the United States emphasizes personal reliance on the labour market and expects families to be primarily responsible for earning their own standard of living. Except for the elderly, targeted, typically means-tested, cash assistance and health insurance are available only to selected categories of needy families. As summarised by Ellwood (1990), "If there is a basic philosophy underlying the American system, it seems to be that people are expected to provide for themselves through their own work, unless there is a good reason why they cannot or need not assume responsibility for themselves".

Aid to Families with Dependent Children (AFDC), a means-tested programme, was historically the primary form of cash support for low-income families with children. Established in 1935, it provided cash assistance to single mothers (primarily widows) and their children, who were perceived as not responsible for their needy status and who were not expected to work. Since the programme's inception, the increased number of recipients who were single parents due to divorce, separation and out-of-wedlock childbearing changed the composition of and reduced public support for the programme. The AFDC program was run jointly by the Federal Government and the States. Each state defined 'need', set its own benefit level, established (within Federal limitations) income and resource limits, and administered the programme or supervised its administration. As a result, benefits varied widely across states. AFDC benefits were not indexed to inflation, and between 1970 and 1994, the median state benefit declined in real terms by 47 per cent (Committee on Ways and Means, 1996). In 1994, only about two-thirds of all poor children received AFDC, and 36 per cent of all female-headed families with children received either AFDC, Supplemental Security Income (for disabled children) or General Assistance (a state-based cash benefit) (ibid.). Thus, many poor children in single-parent families and most poor children in two-parent families received no monthly cash assistance.

In 1996, Federal welfare reform legislation dramatically changed the nature of social assistance for low-income families. The AFDC programme was eliminated and replaced by Temporary Assistance for Needy Families (TANF). Each state has increased authority to decide which families to assist, subject only to a requirement that applicants receive 'fair and equitable treatment'. Federal monies for families are essentially fixed at their 1994 levels by a block grant such that increased welfare expenditures due to demographic change or economic downturns are the responsibility of each state. If states are unwilling to spend more of their own funds, the poor have no entitlement to assistance. The centrepiece of the new reform is a time limit which stipulates that an individual cannot receive more than a cumulative lifetime total of 60 months of cash assistance. States have the option to grant exceptions to this time limit for one-fifth of all recipients at any time. Many fear that the consequences of this new system for low-income families will be deleterious, as families are no longer guaranteed support, even in a recessionary economy.

The Food Stamp programme is a means-tested, federal programme available to most low-income families. Designed to increase the food purchasing power of low-income households so that they can afford a nutritionally-adequate diet, it provides monthly vouchers for food. The maximum food stamp amount is about one-third of the official poverty line, or about 13 per cent of the median family income, and is adjusted annually for inflation. It treats poor two-parent families the same as poor single-parent families. In 1994, 41 per cent of all female-headed families with children received food stamps (Committee on Ways and Means, 1996).

Housing assistance in the United States has never been an entitlement. The federal government provides housing aid directly to selected lower-income households in the form of rental subsidies and mortgage-interest subsidies as far as the funds allow. Only 31 per cent of poor female-headed families with children received housing assistance in 1994, and 18 per cent of all female-headed families with children received such assistance (Committee on Ways and Means, 1996).

The Earned Income Tax Credit (EITC), enacted in 1975 to increase the incomes of low-income working families, is a refundable tax credit. If the amount of the credit exceeds the taxpayer's Federal income tax liability, the excess is payable to the taxpayer as a direct cash payment. The credit is equal to a specified percentage of wages up to a certain maximum amount that applies over a certain income range, and then diminishes to zero as wages further increase. Since its inception, the credit has been expanded significantly, with expenditures now exceeding the amount of cash assistance paid to poor families with children. Poor parents with children, in one-parent or two-parent families, working at the minimum wage are now eligible for tax credits equal to 34 to 40 per cent of their annual earnings. The EITC lifts more children out of poverty than any other government benefit programme (Porter et al., 1998).

Parents who live apart from their children are expected to provide child support. Historically, this private child support system was primarily a state government responsibility. Since the 1970s, the federal government has increasingly become involved in funding, monitoring and evaluating state programmes, providing assistance in locating absent parents and obtaining support from them. Traditionally, the amount of support ordered to be paid was determined by a court on an individualized basis, and the non-custodial parent was expected to make the support payment directly to the custodial parent. In recent years, states have increased child support enforcement by using routine procedures associated with taxation and social insurance programmes, such as wage-withholding of support orders from non-custodial parents.

Problems with the United States child support enforcement system are notable: first, in many cases, awards to custodial parents are never determined, often because paternity is never established. Second, awards are often set too low to cover the costs of raising a child, and are not consistent for similar cases in different states. Third, even when awards are ordered, many absent parents manage not to pay them. Unlike many industrialized countries, the United States has no guaranteed child support when private child support is not paid. Only about half of all custodial parents had orders to receive child support in 1992, and only about two-thirds of the total amount due to custodial parents was actually paid (Bureau of the Census, 1995). In 1994, only 39 per cent of all female-headed families with children received some child support or alimony (Committee on Ways and Means, 1996).

Unlike Sweden and other European countries, where childcare has for many years been universally provided and/or subsidised, governmental involvement in childcare in the United States has been minimal. Most such government assistance is targeted to lower-income families. The dramatic increase in the labour force participation of mothers in recent decades has focused attention on childcare needs. The largest Federal source of childcare assistance is a small non-refundable tax credit for working parents or those seeking work. Under current legislation, childcare is not universally available to welfare recipients, although States cannot reduce or terminate welfare assistance to mothers of children under age six who cannot accept employment because they have a demonstrated inability to locate adequate childcare.

4.5 Conclusions: Implications for Russian Social Policy toward Single Parents

As social policies in Russia evolve over the next decade, Russian policymakers are likely to evaluate their policy options with reference to these three major types of social protection systems that currently exist in Western nations. It is also likely that they will consider adopting some specific programmes and policies from each of the three approaches described above and, drawing also on their own Soviet experience, it is possible that a uniquely Russian hybrid model might emerge as a fourth, post-communist model. Just as social protection systems in Western countries were not wholly put into place at any one point, so too in Russia, social policy will evolve over time as the Russian government designs a system in the context of changing social, demographic and economic conditions.

Each of the major types of social systems described can shed light on the how Russian policy could develop most effectively. The anti-poverty effectiveness of the social democratic system is attractive to most policy makers concerned with poverty. However, the Scandinavian countries spend far more on social welfare than many European countries and all the English-speaking countries, and thus, the 'price' of the Swedish model is well beyond Russia's fiscal capacity. Further, the Swedish system is based on a complicated set of interacting programmes and incentives, and to implement such a welfare state requires an extensive system of taxation and significant and efficient national administrative capacity Given the many administrative and political problems with the current Russian tax system, it is highly unlikely that a Swedish-style social safety net would be fiscally or administratively feasible at least in the short-term.

Just as Sweden's early programmes aided only mothers, Russian programmes might begin with this group as well. This has, in fact, been the case, as will be shown in the next chapter by Klugman and McAuley. Because the Russian government has recently had trouble meeting its civilian and military payrolls, it will first be necessary to resolve the current fiscal crisis before considering extended social welfare programmes.

Similar to France, in the decades following World War II with concerns about 'depopulation', the Soviet Union also adopted goals to encourage childbearing and to provide sufficient support so that mothers could enter the paid labour force. However, during the transition towards a market economy, women have lost jobs at higher rates than men, state spending on day care and other children's services has declined, and the birth rate has fallen dramatically. Thus, it seems unlikely that these two goals remain attractive to Russian policymakers, an issue which is examined in the chapter which follows. In addition, France's extensive network of health centres for mothers and children has fiscal implications which are unrealistic for Russia at this time.

Because of Russia's current fiscal constraints, a programme for single parents similar to those found in the liberal cluster of nations might be most attractive and attainable in the Russian context. Such a programme could combine elements of a selective, less-centralized system as found in the U.S.A. with more re-distributive aspects of a model such as the one found in Australia.[8] Like the United States, Russia is a very large and diverse nation, with even greater regional variations in income levels and in the racial/ethnic composition of the population. In such an environment, with little national solidarity and little willingness to increase taxes to provide for the poor, an American-style means-tested, state-administered programme might be both appealing and feasible.[9] The United States programme is faulted by many analysts of the welfare state because the nation can surely afford a European-style welfare state. However, given Russia's budget constraint, targeting scarce benefits through selective programmes might be quite prudent.

To the extent that the United States has a model programme that might be attractive in both Russia and Western Europe, it is the Earned Income Tax Credit. The EITC raises the employee's take-home pay without increasing the employer's labour costs. It provides nothing to non-workers, so its major incentive is to increase work by low-skilled workers. The EITC has been shown to significantly increase work effort among single mothers, to remove a large number of families and children from poverty, and to moderate the widening gap between high-income and low-income families with children (Greenstein and Shapiro, 1998). In addition, because the family receives a payment only if it reports its income to the tax authority, such a programme could boost income reporting in Russia. However, the EITC does require sophisticated administrative capacity to avoid having taxpayers under-report their income in order to qualify for the credit.

In terms of support from non-custodial parents, the kinds of problems endemic to the child support system in the United States suggest that child support enforcement is also likely to remain a problem for Russian single parents. In the U.S.A., but not in Sweden, lack of centralization of information about absent parents and lack of federal authority has resulted in inadequate collections. Paternity is not routinely established in the United States for children born outside of marriage, making it difficult to locate and collect support from the non-custodial parent. Given the lack of administrative efficiency in Russia, its child support outcomes are more likely to look like those in the U.S.A. than those in Sweden.

In addition to pursuing a targeted approach and one that can function with only modest administrative capacity, Russia could also adopt some elements of programmes found in other liberal nations, such as Australia and the United Kingdom. In these nations, a strong labour movement uses collective bargaining to gain market-based social support through higher wages and pensions. For example, unlike the United Kingdom, the labour movement in Australia never fully accepted the universalistic social welfare state, but continued to advocate for means-tested family benefits which were viewed as more re-distributive (Esping-Andersen, 1990). Thus, Australia provides benefits to a wider range of low-income single-parent families than does the United States, but it does not approach the level of fiscal expenditure – nor the degree of universality – found in the Nordic countries.

With its heritage of socialist collectivism, a strong labour movement might develop in Russia which might then advocate greater public supports for working families and children. For example, minimal cash payments for families with children, or a parenting allowance for those not working, could supplement the incomes of poor single-parent families. Such programmes would not require extensive administrative capacity but would provide more generous assistance than the decentralized, means-tested system in the United States.

To summarise, we have provided an overview of the demographics, economic status and social welfare policies related to single-parent families in various Western nations. As Russian policy makers consider ways to improve living standards for single-parent families, lessons can be drawn from the experiences of other countries. We have suggested that budget constraints in Russia make it unlikely that Swedish-style universal cash benefits or French-style children's services are affordable. In fact, given the high poverty rates in Russia and problems of administration and fiscal capacity, the social policies of the liberal nations seem to provide the most appropriate models. However, as the next chapter shows, Russian policy will be influenced in the foreseeable future as much by its own past experience as by lessons from Western experience.

* We are grateful for the helpful comments of Markus Jäntti, Bruce Bradbury and the editors. This research was supported in part by a grant from the Ford Foundation to the Program on Poverty, the Underclass and Public Policy at the University of Michigan.

NOTES

1 It has proved particularly difficult to obtain comparable figures for the trend in single-parent families as a proportion of all families with children for the 1960s through the 1990s. McLanahan and Casper (1995) report the percentage of all family households that are single parent at two time points (1960-76 and 1985-88) for nine Western countries. Kamerman and Kahn (1988) show single-parent families with children as a percentage of all families with children for a single year from 1981 to 1985 for 11 countries. Kiernan (1996) provides figures for 10 countries in the 'late-1980s'. Eurostat (1998) shows data for 13 countries of the European Union in 1996. Appendix Table 1 provides alternative estimates, calculated by Markus Jäntti, for female-headed households as a percentage of all households with children for 15 countries in the 1970s, 1980s and 1990s using data from the Luxembourg Income Study. All of these estimates differ in their levels and trends for reasons that are not obvious. It is clear, however, that single-parenthood has been increasing in almost all countries for the past three decades.

2 In Scandinavia and most of Europe, cohabiting couples are counted as two-parent families; in the U.S., they are counted as single-parent families.

3 Wong et al. (1993) note that the proportions of transfer income that is means-tested in France, Sweden and Australia is overestimated because universal child-care subsidies are not included in the total accounting of transfers.

4 Similar differences in poverty for all persons are found across these countries. Using data from the LIS on 11 Western nations in the mid-1980s, Korpi and Palme (1998) find that both poverty and income inequality are significantly lower in the Scandinavian countries. Using a poverty line defined as 50 per cent of the adjusted median income, Finland, Norway and Sweden have the lowest poverty rates, from 3.5 to 4.9 per cent. Germany and the Netherlands (5.8 per cent), Switzerland (7.4 per cent) and France (8.5 per cent) have the next lowest poverty rates, while Australia (9.1 per cent), Canada (10.9 per cent), the U.K. (13.2 per cent) and the U.S. (17.9 per cent) have the highest poverty rates.

5 The liberal cluster could be subdivided into countries where liberalism has been combined with a relatively strong labour movement (as in Australia and England) or not (as in Canada and the U.S.) (Forssén, 1998). Because we simply use the typology to highlight overall differences among Western countries, we accept the general category of liberal nations.

6 Prenatal allowances and maternity allowances were eliminated in the mid-1980s and replaced with the young child allowance.

7 Australia's system is means-tested, but a greater percentage of the needy receive benefits than in the U.S.

8 Such programmes have been endorsed by international advisers: see World Bank, 1993.

Appendix. Table 4.8: Female-Headed Households as a Percentage of All
Households with Children

	Years	**1974-83**	**1984-89**	**1990-present**
Australia	1981,1985,1994	9.9	9.9	12.1
Belgium	1985,1992	—	5.6	9.9
Canada	1975,1987,1994	9.1	11.2	15.8
Denmark	1987,1992	—	13.8	16.9
Finland	1987,1991	—	11.0	12.3
France	1979,1989	5.4	9.8	—
Germany	1978,1984,1994	5.8	6.2	12.5
Italy	1986,1995	—	4.7	6.1
Luxembourg	1985,1994	—	7.5	7.6
Netherlands	1983,1987,1991	7.6	9.6	10.3
Norway	1979,1986,1991	12.2	12.5	19.4
Spain	1980,1990	4.3	—	5.3
Sweden	1975,1987,1992	13.0	14.9	17.4
United Kingdom	1979,1986,1995	10.1	14.2	21.6
United States	1974,1986,1994	15.4	19.0	23.5

—: Not available.
Source: Computations by Markus Jäntti, Åbo Akademi University, using data from the Luxembourg
Income Study.

Chapter 5: Social Policy for Single-Parent Families: Russia in Transition

Jeni Klugman and Alastair McAuley

The objective of this chapter is to analyse social policies with respect to single-parent families in Russia. Several of the chapters in this book touch upon various aspects of public policy and their impact on families, while the task of the present chapter is to present an analysis of key social policies in Russia over time. It provides a historical perspective because developments in the Soviet period help to determine the political and social context in which policies are currently being formulated. While Chapter 4 set out the implications of Western experience for Russian policy makers, we focus in this chapter on how policies to date have been influenced by and draw on Russia's own past and experience.

Social policy is viewed in the broad sense of policy about, as well as toward, families. The former includes state policies toward different types of marital and reproductive behaviour, whereas the latter focuses upon what is generally known as social protection. The former is reflected in the legislation regarding marriage, cohabitation and divorce, and the regulations which mandate private behaviour with respect to these events (such as rules about child support and alimony); whereas the latter is examined here in terms of the provision of income support for families with minor children (and especially single-parent families).

The primary interest of the chapter and this book is in the transition period, that is post-1991, although a longer-term perspective is provided in order to put the current system and recent changes into context. The ideology, institutions and approaches of the Soviet era still have an important bearing on family policy. The period under consideration thus extends from the October revolution of 1917 through to the reforms associated with the transition to a market economy in the mid-1990s.

On the whole, single-parent households in the USSR were worse off than conventional families (McAuley, 1981; Braithwaite 1997). The differences between single-parent and conventional family circumstances required the authorities both to adapt the overall framework of social support provided by the socialist system and to introduce a number of specific, targeted welfare programmes. At the same time, policy towards single-parent families was obviously conceived within the framework of a planned socialist economy. Hence it was based on a system in which enterprises were responsible for the delivery of a range of welfare services and in which economic security of the individual and family was achieved in large measure through full employment. That underlying approach is largely incompatible with the reality of a market economy. Transition has forced the governments of formerly planned socialist economies to reconstruct their approach to social policy – and to the provision of social safety nets (see, e.g. Barr, 1994). In this, Russia is no exception (World Bank, 1994). This has had important implications for the nature and type of support that is available to single-parent families.

In terms of the typology of welfare states set out in the previous chapter, we can observe that the Russian model has shifted from a model that was akin in many aspects to the social democratic approach of Sweden, to the other, U.S. style, end of the spectrum. The Soviet state, like the traditional Swedish model, emphasised full employment and mostly universal programmes. This was coupled with specific aspects peculiar to administrative command economies, including low controlled prices for basic goods and services. Many elements of this model have now disappeared in Russia – in particular, the commitment to full employment which has been eroded in the face of large output declines, so that open unemployment had reached 11 per cent of the labour force by 1998. General price liberalization and the rapid inflation which ensued in the first half of the decade also eroded previous guarantees for a minimal level of consumption. The pressures have most probably intensified following the financial crisis of August 1998.

This chapter is structured as follows. The next section examines the Soviet inheritance. Section 5.2 examines the key strands of Soviet family policy: Marx-Engels, pro-natalist tendencies and, especially in the later part of the period, concerns about poverty. The section continues by charting Soviet policy responses to the growth and needs of so-called incomplete families. This includes changing attitudes to marriage and the respective roles of parents and the state in the lives of children, and changes in family-related social protection and employment policies.

Section 5.3 analyses transition policies with respect to the family and social protection. The challenges and constraints created by the economic transition, then the changes in official policies with respect to marriage and in the social protection regime are reviewed. The chapter ends with some conclusions about the character of Soviet and post-Soviet social policy towards single-parent families.

5.1 The Soviet Inheritance

In this section, the evolution of Soviet policy towards single-parent families is described. In particular, we show how early socialist ideas about the family were modified by the nature of Russian reality and the evolution of the Soviet system. An understanding of the inheritance enables one to reflect on the degree of continuity that there has been between Soviet and post-Soviet policy towards the family in general and single-parent families in particular.

The background to this analysis is the evidence reviewed by Motivans in Chapter 2 about the number of single parents in Russia and changes therein over time. It was shown that there was very slow growth in the number of single-parent households during the 1970s and 1980s. However, between 1989-1994, the prevalence of children living with single-parents grew by one and a half million. Due to the lack of data, it is difficult to establish a definitive picture of changes over the longer term, however, and thus comparison with the Soviet past is problematic.

Family policy in Russia – and within that context, policy towards the single-parent family – has been influenced by socialist ideology, as well as by the actual development of the Soviet Union and by the political objectives of the different leaderships. The various strands of this heritage are briefly described here.

Ideological Influences

Early Bolshevik policy towards the family was motivated by two considerations: first, there was the Marxist tradition embodied primarily in the works of Engels but also put forward by activists and feminists like Alexandra Kollontai. Second, there was the practical political objective of wresting control over marriage and the family from the Orthodox Church. Engels had contrasted the loveless bourgeois family – designed to secure property relationships – with the proletarian family. This was supposedly a free union between a man and a woman based on affection. Such a union was to develop more fully under socialism in the context of the socialisation of housework and the liberation of women through wage labour. The kibbutz movement in Israel, or at least its socialist wing, gives some indication of what the early Bolsheviks hoped to create in Russia (Goldman, 1993).

The first Soviet Code on Marriage and the Family, which was enacted in 1918, was an attempt to legislate for such a family. Politically, it also challenged the church's control over marriage. As suggested below, however, this early idealism was undermined by the realities of post-revolutionary Russia and even more by the stresses imposed by Stalinist economic development. The collectivization of agriculture and the introduction of central economic planning, coming in the wake of the disruptions of revolution and civil war, resulted in a sharp fall in the rate at which the Soviet population was growing. This led to the suppression of the 1937 Census; it also resulted in the adoption of a pro-natalist stance by the Soviet government. Pro-natalism was accentuated in the wake of the Second World War with its massive population losses. In the face of a continuing decline in the birth rate, such attitudes continued to influence Soviet family policy at least until the Brezhnev period.

Under Stalin, the Soviet government was not particularly concerned with social policy; by the time Khrushchev took over in the early 1950s, Soviet society suffered from a range of social problems. Indeed, the USSR was characterised by significant income inequality and substantial poverty (McAuley, 1979). This in turn affected Soviet policy. For Khrushchev and for many of his successors, the objective of poverty reduction (that is, to ensure that most of the Soviet population enjoyed some of the fruits of economic growth and development) influenced the form of the social policies proposed – and, in particular, affected the evolution of policy towards the family. In the 1990s, a concern with poverty was still the overriding determinant of changes in family policy.

If socialist ideology, pro-natalism and a concern with poverty were significant influences on the content of Soviet family policy, its form was largely determined by the requirements of the planned economy (McAuley, 1996). The Soviet planned economy was characterized by full employment. The state owned the vast majority of enterprises and was responsible for price determination. Most social benefits were linked to employment and many social programmes were administered by state enterprises, providing inter alia an additional incentive for women's participation in the labour force. The authorities also assured minimal consumption levels through keeping the prices of basic consumer goods and services low, in particular foodstuffs, rent and utility items. Each of these elements became problematic during the transition to a market economy and, to different degrees, all have been amended.

5.2 The Evolution of Family Policy, 1917-1991

This section is in two parts. The first examines Soviet attitudes to marriage as reflected in the law and the respective roles of the family and the state therein. It reviews the 1918 Marriage Code and the subsequent revisions in 1944 and 1968, and rules about alimony and evidence as to its enforcement. The second part of the section sets out the policies of social protection that were established over the Soviet period, up until the social policy actions that accompanied the beginning of price liberalisation in 1991.

State Policies towards Marriage and the Role of Parents

The 1918 Marriage Code had three objectives: to establish equality between husbands and wives; to make marriage a union based on affection; and to establish the principle that parents were responsible for all their offspring (Goldman, 1993). To this end, the Code contained three important provisions. First, the only valid marriage was one registered with the civil authorities – the so-called ZAGS.[1] This was designed to undercut the position of the Orthodox Church and the various restrictions it had imposed upon marriage and the family in pre-revolutionary Russia. Second, the Code simplified the divorce procedure. Third, it tried to abolish the concept of illegitimacy and the distinction between children born to couples in and out of wedlock. Although various provisions in this code have been changed in the past eighty years, the principles underlying the 1918 Code provided the framework within which much of Soviet and Russian family policy was conceived.

In abolishing the distinction between legitimate and illegitimate offspring, the Code defined the family in terms of blood relationships – rather than via the legal concept of marriage. It asserted the responsibility of parents to support all their minor children. (Indeed, in 1918, the law went so far as to ban adoption but this provision was repealed in 1926 in the face of the so-called *bezprizornost'* crisis of the early 1920s (Goldman, 1993), that is, the massive rise in the number of homeless children in the wake of the civil war and the inability of state orphanages to cope.) The Code – and the courts – established the principle that after breakdown of a marriage, the non-custodial partner was liable to pay to support minor children. A similar liability arose in respect of children born out of wedlock. Nothing was to be paid, however, in respect of the spouse – she was expected to support herself out of her own earnings. Child support was set at a quarter of the non-custodial spouse's earnings for the first child, a third for two children and a half for three or more children. These proportions have continued to guide alimony settlements in the USSR, and now in Russia, as discussed below.

The 1918 Code also greatly simplified the procedure for establishing paternity. This was important because alimony payments from the non-custodial parent (usually the father) were typically the only source of support for single mothers. At that time, the state accepted no responsibility for the support of children unless they had been abandoned. Even then, it tried to place them with relatives rather than in an orphanage.

In practice, the Code did not achieve all of its objectives. There was conflict between Marriage Code and the Land Code, with the latter governing the division of property when peasant households broke up (Goldman, 1993). Women generally had difficulty in collecting the alimony settlements authorized by the courts. Also, there continued to be a certain stigma attached to out-of-wedlock births, particularly to younger women. Such stigma, which is not of course peculiar to Russia (see discussion in Chapter 4, and Lewis (1997) on Europe, for example), has persisted up to the present day (Yakovleva, 1979; Harwin, 1996).

There was a sharp fall in the rate of growth of population during the first decades of Soviet rule. The data show a sharp decline in the natural increase of the population (births over deaths).[2] At the same time, most of this drop took place in rural areas, suggesting that collectivisation and the famines of the period had a substantial demographic impact. Although this drop can be traced to the social and economic turmoil of the period 1928-35, the authorities attributed such trends to the failure of 'the Soviet family': that divorce was too easy, that abortion was too readily available and that families were failing in their obligations. In 1936, the Soviet authorities adopted a more pro-natalist approach to the family. In particular, abortion became illegal and divorce was made more difficult (Harwin, 1996). Also, the police were granted powers to pursue alimony-defaulters (Harwin, 1996). This innovation, together with the introduction of child benefits (see below), implied the acceptance by the State of a degree of responsibility for the support of children – at least in principle.

The Second World War resulted in further massive disruption to family life in the Soviet Union and the death of some 20 million or more persons – many of them civilians. In 1944, the authorities responded with further changes in policy towards the family – and single-parent families in particular. First, it was made more difficult to establish the paternity of children born out-of-wedlock. This was probably decided upon so as to avoid the problems of administering the alimony system in the face of the extensive population dislocation of the war years (Wimperis, 1960), but it also fitted in with the ideological norms of the period which led to a drive to strengthen 'traditional families'. At the same time, it was made more difficult for unmarried mothers to seek alimony. In compensation, however, the State made it easier for such women to place their children for adoption. The system of child allowances was extended and a separate allowance for single mothers, *odinokiye materi*, (in cases where paternity could not be established) was introduced. It is to these developments in the regime of social protection that we now turn.

Social Protection Policy

Benefits for children developed in an apparently ad hoc manner over several decades. The first step was taken in 1936, when the state introduced child allowances – though only for the seventh and subsequent children (Harwin, 1996). In 1944, alongside the family law reforms that were mentioned above, a series of changes to family-related social benefits were introduced. Child allowances were to be paid on the birth of the fourth and subsequent children, but only until the child's fifth birthday. (In 1948, the monthly benefit was extended to the third child.) Single parents received a more generous benefit. It was initially set at a level equal to the alimony a woman would have received if the father had been a skilled worker in rural areas or a semi-skilled one in town, and for those children payment was to continue until the child's twelfth birthday. However, the rates were halved in 1949 at the time of Stalin's currency reform (Wimperis, 1960).

The 1944 changes extended the principle that the State was responsible for the support of children even if in practice that support was rather limited. This is perhaps also reflected in the ambivalence shown during this period towards the fostering of children; and in a revival of adoption as a solution to the problems of long-term care where the natural family was not available. More generally, it has been argued that the thrust of policy at this time was directed toward supporting the child rather than the single-parent household (Harwin, 1996).

When Khrushchev assumed power in the mid-1950s, there was a widespread feeling that social questions had been neglected by the Party and that the country was suffering from an extensive malaise. While the new leader was not himself particularly interested in social policy as such, he did oversee a significant change in direction. In 1956, abortion was re-legalised. More importantly, Party policy became concerned with questions of poverty, inequality and living standards (McAuley, 1979). For example, an initial attempt was made to determine a poverty line and a minimum wage was established. Plans were made to extend state pensions for the elderly to the rural population who had worked on collective farms.[3] None of these innovations was addressed specifically to unmarried mothers – or to single-parent families – but those households that were among the least well-off did benefit disproportionately from the new directions in social policy (McAuley, 1987).

The leadership's concern with living standards of the population was maintained under Brezhnev. This resulted in increases in the minimum wage (by fifty per cent in 1968), and modifications to the social security system (as described below). The Party also revised the Marriage Code in 1968, liberalising the divorce procedure and making it easier for women to establish paternity again, thus reducing the stigma attached to out-of-wedlock births. It also made it easier for women to claim alimony. At about this time, the system of paid foster care was dropped (Harwin, 1996).

By the late 1980s, if not earlier, the vast majority of Soviet women were in paid employment. But they continued to earn significantly less than men (McAuley, 1981; Ofer and Vinokur, 1992). In part this was as a result of discrimination; in part it can be seen as a consequence of what is often referred to as the double burden borne by women in the Soviet Union. Because women were responsible for much of the work involved in running the home and bringing up children, they had less time than men for overtime, for second jobs – or even for raising their qualifications. The pre-eminent role of enterprises in the provision of many social services also tended to work to the disadvantage of women. Large enterprises tended to provide a wider range of higher quality services than small ones, whereas female employment was concentrated in sectors like trade and textiles, where enterprise size was smaller than average, and in social services (McAuley, 1981).

Despite the substantial increase in the minimum wage in 1968, poverty persisted in the USSR (McAuley, 1979; Braithwaite, 1997). It appears that the poor – and particularly women with children – were only weakly connected with the labour market and therefore they failed to benefit from wage increases. There was also a persistent gender gap in earnings (see Chapter 6 for further discussion). Women also continued to experience difficulty in collecting the alimony payments to which they were entitled – even though Soviet law allowed for automatic deductions from earnings (Harwin, 1996).

In the 1970s, the Party embarked on a rather more extended overhaul of the system of social protection. Measures which were adopted included liberalization of the system of maternity leave; injection of resources into pre-school childcare facilities; attempts to give young families a higher priority in housing queues; and finally, in 1974, a special income supplement was introduced for families with children under school age whose per-capita income was below the notional (unofficial) poverty line (McAuley, 1981).

Table 5.1 summarises the main state programmes aimed at dual- and single-parent families during the last two decades of the Soviet regime. It shows that the largest programme in terms of expenditures was maternity leave payments to women; these included both maternity benefits (social insurance payments to women on 112 days compulsory maternity leave) and payments to those women who chose not to return to work for up to twelve months after the birth of the child. This programme was also the fastest growing, and expenditures tripled over the period 1975-1989. This is consistent with the 'baby boom' that occurred in the USSR in the mid-1980s (see Chapter 2). Expenditures on the benefit for large families and lone mothers (a categorical programme which included both groups, traditionally considered to be disadvantaged) approximately doubled over the period. On the other hand, funding for the benefit paid to 'under-provisioned families', which was cash social assistance directed at families who were below the 'subsistence minimum', tended to decline.

As with the changes under Khrushchev, it is true to say that none of the changes under Brezhnev were addressed specifically to single-parent families (although the relaxation of the requirements for the establishment of paternity was intended to respond to a particular grievance). The motivation underlying the changes in benefits and increased spending is ambiguous. On the one hand, one can argue that the persistence of disadvantage among certain population groups was the motivating factor. The

Table 5.1: State Expenditures on Family Benefits in the USSR, 1975-1989
(million rubles)

	1975	1980	1985	1988	1989
Maternity leave	1257	1530	3565	3854	3700
Benefit for large families and lone mothers	389	311	592	703	732
Benefit for 'under-provisioned' families	866	783	781	763	710

Source: Goskomstat SSSR (1990).

social policy reforms could be seen to reflect a continuing, and possibly an increased, concern with the problem of poverty. The reforms were also a pro-natalist response to the continuing decline in the overall birth rate in the European parts of the USSR. On the other hand, an enlightened social policy could be argued to reflect more attempts to stimulate labour market participation, as the regime perceived labour shortages to be constraining output growth (Oxenstierna, 1990), in other words, average consumption and economic growth had priority, with social issues relegated to one of several secondary goals (Chinn, 1977). In this context one can observe that the Soviet regime of social protection was similar to continental approaches, where state benefits were largely insurance-based (see the discussion in Chapter 4), and those who did not formally participate in the labour market and therefore lacked a work history were forced to resort to second-class social assistance (see Lewis, 1997).

Whatever the underlying motivation for the policy change, the fact that women continued to earn less than men (McAuley, 1981), and a continuing rise in the divorce rate, meant that one-parent families were one of the major beneficiaries of the new social transfers and subsidies directed toward 'under-provisioned' families. This is not to say that these measures effectively eliminated poverty among single-parent families, not least because of the difficulties of reconciling the roles of mother and worker which are sharpened in the absence of a spouse.

The economic stagnation that ultimately led to the collapse of the communist system began under Brezhnev, in power from 1964 until 1982. But it intensified after 1985 under Gorbachev. Initially, the Gorbachev government expanded the social policies of its predecessor: maternity leave was extended and (partial) payment for those women who chose to stay at home with their children for the first year after birth was introduced. The State continued to invest (and to encourage enterprises to invest) in pre-school childcare facilities, so-called pioneer camps and other forms of collective consumption (Harwin, 1996). The government commissioned a new study of poverty and raised the notional poverty line in 1987 (Braithwaite, 1997). In 1990 (when inflation began to emerge) the government relaxed the limitation of child allowances to the third and subsequent children, making child allowances universal. In addition, the allowance for unmarried mothers was raised to half the minimum wage for each child (Harwin, 1996). Finally, in April 1991, the liberalization of a wide range of consumer prices was accompanied by the introduction of an extensive set of child allowances and other payments to offset some of the impact of the reduction in food and other subsidies on the family budget. In practice the compensations fell far below the price effects of the liberalization and the rapid inflation which ensued the following year. This is examined in the next section which explores changes during the transition period.

The Soviet Inheritance: A Summary

At the end of the Soviet era, family policy could be characterized in terms of some of the ideas embodied in the Marriage Code of 1918. The family was still conceived of as a consensual union and hence divorce was relatively easy. Husbands owed no general duty to support their wives – present or former. But parents were in principle responsible for the support of their children. Fathers were obliged to pay child support regardless of whether their children were born in marriage or out-of-wedlock, although in practice women continued to experience difficulty in collecting what was due to them.

Family policy was also influenced by a desire to raise the birth rate – or at least to avert further declines – and by a concern with poverty. As a result, the state had accepted a degree of financial responsibility for minor children: from 1990, at least, child allowances were paid to the parents of all children. Finally, family policy was conditioned by the general framework of the planned economy: the objective of expanding labour force participation to help offset perceived bottlenecks in production could be seen behind a number of measures, including the expansion of work-based childcare and a relatively generous system of maternity leave.

By 1990, the outcome in terms of social protection was an extensive range of benefits, many of which were linked to the minimum wage but not otherwise indexed for the level of prices. Social assistance was generally accorded on a categorical, as opposed to a needs-tested, basis. There was no general attempt to orient the system toward poverty alleviation through explicit means- or needs-testing. At the same time, however, family benefits were accorded on a per child basis, consistent with the general belief that large families were worse off. There was also a special allowance to single mothers – or, at least, to those who were not receiving alimony from the fathers of their children.

Since 1991, the transition to a market economy has wrought enormous changes to the economic well-being of families generally, and has had a major impact on the effectiveness of inherited approaches to social policy with respect to families. It is to these changes that we now turn.

5.3 Transition Policies for the Family and Social Protection

The task of this section is to provide an understanding of the fabric of family policy, especially toward single parents, during the period of economic transition which effectively began in 1991. We do not attempt to deal systematically with outcomes, which are the subject of the next two chapters of this volume. It is nonetheless important to note the major conclusions of those chapters: in particular, that poverty has risen rapidly during the transition, and especially among single-parent families; and that the outcomes for children in single-parent families on several measures of well-being beyond household expenditures are also relatively worse compared to those in dual-parent families.

Policies for the family and social protection affect the shape and impact of private, and especially public, transfers to single parents. Chapter 1 has already shown the scale of the economic changes that have occurred during the course of the transition, and to the severe fiscal constraints that have impeded government attempts to mitigate the social costs of the transition. A deep fiscal crisis has followed the state's inability to collect as much revenue as previously – and as it had budgeted for. As a result, the authorities have either failed to make the payments they were obliged to – to lower levels of the federal system, to suppliers, employees and those entitled to social security – or it has made them with considerable delay. Arrears in the payment of pensions, of child allowances and so on have increased inexorably – one estimate is that between 1994 and 1996, the share of eligible households not receiving child benefits increased from 33 to 62 per cent (Richter, 1998).[4]

The fiscal constraints have tended to worsen over time, and have resulted in sharp reductions in the levels of real public expenditure.

Public expenditure, at all levels of government and including extra-budgetary funds, has declined from about 63 per cent of GDP in 1992 to 44 per cent in 1997. It should be borne in mind that national income itself shrank considerably over the same period. This implies a very sharp reduction in the real value of spending on social benefits, even if the budget share was to be preserved. Figure 5.1 shows that while total spending on social protection as a share of public expenditures has increased by about one-fourth since 1992, pensions paid to the elderly account for the largest part of that rise.

Information on benefits for children is unfortunately not available for the whole period (in part because responsibility for financing has been transferred from the national government to local authorities). The data nonetheless indicates that child benefits, including payments paid specifically to children in single-parent households, accounted for a very small proportion (about 1.6 per cent) of expenditure and only 0.7 per cent of GDP in 1995.

We now turn to address the extent of change and continuity in

Figure 5.1: Trends in Social Protection Spending, 1992-1997
(share of Total Public Expenditure)

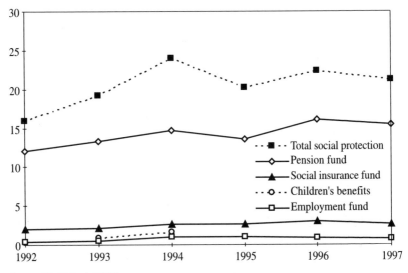

Source: World Bank (1999).

Russian social policy during the transition. The structure of the discussion mirrors that for the Soviet period, by addressing official attitudes toward and rules about marital dissolution, before turning to the regime of social protection.

Ideological Influences: Changes in Attitudes to Marriage
and the Role of Parents[5]

There have been some significant changes in marital behaviour, and in official policies about marriage, over the course of the transition.

The share of births out of wedlock has risen from 13.5 per cent in 1990 to 25.3 per cent in 1997. This figure is as high as 40 per cent in some regions (including Siberia, Komi and Tuva). The government remains committed to the principle that both parents should be responsible for the support of their children. Indeed, this responsibility has been strengthened by the reduction in the scale of direct financial aid from the State to all parents (not just those who are not married). These ideas underlie the 1996 Family Code (see below). If the child is born of unmarried parents, paternity can be established in court by an application of one of the parents or by the guardian (the trustee) of the child. The rules regarding acceptable proofs of paternity have been liberalized. Once paternity is established, "...children possess the same rights and obligations as those born to persons in a registered marriage" (Akademiya Problem Sotsial'noy Raboty, 1997).

There have been several important changes in the legislation governing family formation and dissolution. The Family Code was revised and adopted in December 1995 and has been in force since 1 March 1996. The most important changes allow nuptial agreements, the liberalization of divorce, and revision of rules about the size and procedure for enforcing the payment of alimony.[6]

The new Family Code has made it even easier to obtain a divorce. For example, the reconciliation term in the case of absence of spousal consent to dissolution was shortened from 6 to 3 months, and in the case of mutual consent to the dissolution of a marriage with underage children, the court dissolves the marriage without investigating the motives behind the divorce. The consensus among officials and legal experts is that the current laws governing divorce are very liberal and do not discriminate against women (Kuprianova, 1998).

The new Family Code established two regimes with respect to the division of property upon divorce. In addition to the 'legislative' regime whereby, as in the Soviet period, property acquired by the spouses during their marriage is joint property, there is a contractual regime governed by nuptial agreements. Under the former, women and mothers have equal, or in special cases, higher level of guarantees; under the latter, the division of property is governed by the nuptial agreement.

Recent legislation has changed the basis for calculating alimony from earnings to all sources of income.[7] This is an important shift, given the decline in the share of formal labour earnings in personal income, as entrepreneurship, private plots and informal sector activity generally has become more important. But, given the difficulty of establishing the size of non-wage income, it has added to uncertainty about the size of expected alimony payments.

There are two variants for the estimation of alimony amounts:
- formula (as in the Soviet period, one fourth of the parent's income for the first child, one third for two children, and a half for three and more children), which are automatically linked to changes in nominal income; or
- fixed monetary amount (which is indexed), set by the court.

Parents can conclude their own agreement on the maintenance of their underage children, but the agreed amount may not be less than that which would have been fixed by the court. About 16 per cent of cases in 1996 were effected by agreement of parents outside court. In such cases the size of the average paid alimony was twice as large, and more regularly paid (UNICEF, 1997).

The law does not set minimum or maximum amounts of alimony. It was estimated in June 1998 that in practice the minimum level of payments for one child was 20 rubles 87 kopecks (in the case of a father receiving only a minimum wage). This amounts to only 2 per cent of the average wage at that time.[8]

The 1996 Code contains some measures to enforce child support payments, including responsibility for late payment; alimony payments are indexed according to increases in the minimum wage; the absent parent is liable to a fine equal to one-tenth of one per cent of the sum overdue per day; finally, the Family Code allows property to be seized in lieu of payment (Semeyniy kodeks, 1996). Russian legislation also contains a criminal penalty for chronic non-payment of alimony.

There are, however, widespread problems with regard to the enforcement of alimony liabilities. Under market conditions, employers, especially in the private sector, do not tend to assume obligations to make transfers of alimony under writ of execution. The practice of under-declaring income for tax purposes also affects the calculation of alimony. Men also avoid paying alimony by living other than where they are registered, for example. The number of judicial cases of intentional non-payment of alimony rose from less than 10,000 in 1989 to almost 60,000 in 1995 (MONEE Project database, UNICEF). Survey results from two sites in 1995 – St. Petersburg and the small town of Vyazniki – revealed a desperate situation relating to the payment of alimony (Festi and Prokofieva, 1997). More than half of children remained without maintenance after divorce (St. Petersburg, 58 per cent; Vyazniki, 65 per cent). The period of non-payment of alimony averages 18 months (less than one year, 64 per cent; from one to three years, 23 per cent; more than three years, 13 per cent).

To summarize trends during the transition: divorce has been facilitated and the share of births taking place outside marriage has increased. Various legislative changes have sought to increase the financial support required from non-custodial parents – by changing the rules about paternity and alimony – but avoidance of these obligations remains widespread and is probably growing. In this context, the support provided by the state to single parents assumes even greater importance. It is to this subject that we now turn.

Social Protection Policy: The Regime of Public Transfers

Russia in the late 1990s lacks a coherent framework of social support for vulnerable groups. Rather, there is a hotchpotch of provisions – social insurance type benefits related to work history (in particular, labour pensions); maternity benefits and leave financed out of payroll taxation; and social assistance including child benefits.[9] These are administered by local government departments and, for those in formal paid employment, by the place of work. In addition, elements remain of the system of social services (like childcare) provided by enterprises – either because their managers have not yet transferred the relevant social assets to municipalities or because managers still feel a degree of paternalistic responsibility for their workforces.

Extensive and ongoing transfer of responsibility to local authorities from both high levels of government and from former state enterprises has had potentially disequalizing effects. The potential for widening disparities arises from variations in local fiscal capacity to finance benefits and services, and the absence of sufficient revenue transfers from the federal government (Klugman, 1997). This has further negative implications, since the revenue of local authorities is projected to decline a further 30 per cent in the wake of the financial crisis of August 1998 (World Bank, 1999). On the other hand, since local authorities substantially act as tax collectors for the federal centre, there is also evidence to suggest that they retain an increasing share of what they collect.

Changes in the Regime of Family Transfers

The Russian system of welfare has been marked by several themes during the transition: first, substantial declines in the real value of benefits; second, attempts to rationalize an array of benefits that had proliferated in the early stages of the transition; and finally, ongoing attempts to strengthen the targeting of benefits to poor groups. Each of these tendencies is examined in this section.

Before going on to discuss changes in social protection policies in the transition period however, it is worth summarizing the main features of the regime of public transfers to families which Russia inherited from the Soviet era. These comprise:

Maternity grant: a lump-sum birth grant (in 1990 equal to three times the minimum wage.)

Child allowances: these were originally paid to families with many children (four plus) until each child reached the age of six years. During the Soviet period they were extended to families with progressively fewer children and, from 1990, they were paid to all families with children. (After 1990, the size of child benefit was set equal to 50 per cent of the minimum wage for each child. This was subsequently raised to 70 per cent of the minimum wage.) Single parents received benefit originally until the child's twelfth birthday; after 1974 this was raised to the sixteenth birthday (or eighteenth if in full-time education). Single parents received twice the amount paid to married couples.

Family allowance for under-provisioned families: paid to families with a per capita income under the unofficial poverty line. This was not a measure aimed specifically at supporting single-parents, but they gained disproportionately from it, since they tended to be in the lower per capita income groups.

Post 1991 child / family allowances: replaced the above two benefits, and consisted of:

- universal benefits paid to (i) children under the age of eighteen months (after 1994), (ii) children from 1- 6 years, and (iii) children 6-16 years (18 if a student) at different rates and from different budgetary funds;
- a cost of living allowance paid to families with one or more children under the age of 16 years. Single parents no longer received special treatment.

Maternity benefits: employed women were entitled to a payment equal to 100 per cent of their average earnings during statutory maternity leave – 10 weeks before and 8 weeks after confinement (or longer for multiple births). Post-partum maternity leave was extended to 10 weeks (16 weeks for multiple births or births with complications) in 1993. Women who chose not to return to work at the end of their statutory maternity leave were entitled to a benefit equal to the minimum wage for a period of eighteen months. This was a universal benefit, and single parents did not have any special rights with regard to it. After 1991, unemployed mothers (and those with less than one year's covered employment) were entitled to a benefit equal to 50 per cent of the minimum wage until the child is eighteen months old. For single mothers, this benefit was set at 100 per cent of the minimum wage (DHHS, 1991).

Benefit Amounts

Publicly financed support provided to families with children has been seriously eroded during the transition. This is shown in Table 5.2. In December 1995 the child allowance was equivalent to less than 13 per cent of the child minimum subsistence level. The ratio of the child allowance to the average wage fell from 24 per cent in 1991 to about 5 per cent in 1994 and 1995, as shown in the table below (see also UNICEF, 1997). It should be borne in mind that the average wage also declined substantially in real terms over the same period, so that the fall in real benefit values is even sharper.

The special allowance for unmarried mothers was allowed to virtually vanish by September 1993, when it amounted to less than 2 per cent of the average wage. This was not done on 'moral' grounds; rather, it should be seen as resulting from fiscal pressures. In 1994, however, this situation was redressed somewhat, and the level was raised to about 8 per cent of the average wage.

Indeed, many of the benefits and allowances introduced in the final days of the communist period were allowed, through very high inflation and non-indexation, to decline into irrelevance. The fiscal crisis and the failure to increase benefits in line with changes in the cost of living threatened the actual existence of the whole system of child support. In the second quarter of 1996, the monthly amount paid to children aged under 6 years with a single parent was 36.1 thousand rubles (15 per cent of the minimum subsistence level at that time).[10] For children aged 6-16 years living with a single parent, the monthly amount was 31.0 thousand rubles. Moreover, as noted later in this section under the heading of financing and administration, and shown empirically in the next chapter, many of these children did not in fact receive the benefits to which they were entitled.

Table 5.2: Changes in the Value of Child Allowances in Russia, 1991-1996
(percentages of the average monthly wage)

Allowance for:	1991 Jan.	1992 Dec.	1993 June	1994 year	1995 year	1996 Jan.
Under-1½-year-olds	-	-	-	5.5	4.5	6.8
1½-6-year-olds						
- base benefit	10.7	2.5	4.0	5.5	4.5	6.8
- with compensation	13.0	6.2	6.0	-	-	-
6-to-16-year-olds						
- base benefit	5.9	2.8	1.4	5.5	4.5	6.8
- with compensation	8.8	3.7	4.0	-	-	-
Children of single parents	11.9	5.6	3.2	8.5	7.7	-

Sources: Fajth, 1994; UNICEF, 1997.

Benefit Eligibility and Administrative Responsibility

We now turn to look at administrative changes and attempts to rationalize the system of child benefits. As noted above, the system of child allowances proliferated in the early 1990s – being differentiated by the age of the child and the marital status of the mother (see also World Bank, 1994). There have been a series of major reforms, the success of which is difficult to gauge at this stage.

Table 5.3 sets out the major benefits for families with children, noting the major administrative and other changes that have been introduced during the transition. Note that, with one exception, none of these programs involve special arrangements for single parents. The exception relates to child allowance: for single parents the size of the benefit is doubled (to 140 per cent of the minimum wage).

There has been a shift from the old Soviet approach where enterprises were expected to fulfil an important role in the system of social protection. From 1998, employers have been freed from the obligation to administer monthly child benefits. Regional departments of social protection are now responsible for the payment and financing of these

Table 5.3: Changes in Benefits, Amounts and Administrative Responsibility

Benefit	Year	Amount	Financing Source	Delivery Agency
Child allowance	1991	70 per cent of minimum wage	Pension Fund	Enterprises
	1994		Local budgets	
	1998			Local social protection office
Maternity benefit[a]		Amount of wage, or if unemployed, minimum wage		Enterprise or local social protection office
Parental leave benefit[b]	1994	Minimum wage	Social insurance fund	Enterprise or local social protection office
	1996	2 x minimum wage		

a Duration increased to 140 days in 1992.
b This is paid from the expiration of maternity benefit (70 days after birth), until child is aged 18 months.

allowances. We have already noted that many local authorities are under severe and worsening financial pressure.

Widespread arrears in payment of benefits have persisted. According to the Ministry of Labour, in December 1998 the number of recipients of child benefits was 10 million less than the 34 million eligible to receive payment. Delays averaging six months were reported in 1998; regular and timely payment was limited, at best, to the largest cities of Moscow and St. Petersburg. The response of the Government to this growing problem was to set payment priorities: preference in payment of benefits was to be given to families with an income level which is lower than the minimum subsistence level.

Broadly speaking, there have been three major reforms of the eligibility criteria governing family allowances during the transition period. The initial step, in 1994, saw an extension of eligibility to all families with minor children, the second set of reforms in 1996 brought further simplification, before the most recent changes in 1998 re-introduced needs-based testing. Each of these initiatives is described briefly below.

The relevant changes in January 1994 can be highlighted as follows. The family allowance, which had been income tested during the Soviet period, became universal. The reform also extended family allowances to children under 18 months of age (formerly it was restricted to children of single parents). The compensatory payments that had been introduced in April 1991 with the removal of state child-related subsidies on food and clothing, which had been allowed to erode significantly in real terms, were terminated. Children under 16 years in single-parent families were eligible to receive both the universal child benefit and the incomplete family benefit, that is children of single parents were entitled to receive an allowance 50 per cent larger than those in dual-parent families. At the same time the maternity grant was raised to five times the minimum wage (DHHS, 1995).

In July 1995, the age-differentiation of child allowances was abolished and a single, somewhat larger, payment was introduced for all children under 16. The payment for children of single parents continued to be 50 per cent larger than that for children in complete families. From April 1996, children of single mothers were entitled to a monthly payment of approximately 80 thousand rubles. This amounted to approximately 22 per cent of the cost of subsistence. For other children, the payment was 53.1 thousand rubles. From 1 January 1997, the payment for children of single parents was raised to twice that for children in dual-parent homes. (Goskomstat, 1998). At the same time, however, the problems of non-payment continued to intensify (see Chapter 6).

The problems evident in the system of child allowances, together with growing fiscal pressures on the government, led to a decision to abandon the categorical child allowance – and the specific higher child allowance for unmarried mothers and replace it by a means-tested benefit for households in poverty. In July 1998, the federal legislation governing child benefits was amended so that the right to monthly benefit is limited to families with children, whose average per capita income does not exceed twice the minimum subsistence level. Effective implementation of this approach would be expected to benefit single-parent families – insofar as such families are more likely to be poor. Furthermore, if it increases regularity of payment, it will increase welfare of recipients. (Rossiyskaya Federatsiya, 1997).

Finally, it should be noted that in addition to the various cash benefits, various programmes support vulnerable families through the provision of support in kind. The measures for children in vulnerable families include the provision of free school meals, free school and sporting uniforms, free public transport, and free medicines until the age of six years.[11] Many such schemes are the responsibility of local or regional authorities. Hence the conditions experienced by single-parent families can vary substantially from town to town or *oblast'* to *oblast'*.

Impact of Family Allowances

Problems of exclusion of the poor and the relatively low level of benefits have tended to detract from the potential poverty alleviating effect of child benefits (Klugman and Braithwaite, 1998). This is confirmed by Russian academic studies, which have found that child allowances make very little difference to the standard of living of families with children (Khmelevskaya, 1997).

According to analysis of the RLMS for the period from 1992 to late 1995 public transfers accounted for almost 30 per cent of total household income (Foley and Klugman, 1997). As expected, the average contribution of transfers to the income of recipient households is higher: an estimated 42 per cent in late 1995. Coverage of family allowances has remained steady for the poor, but dropped for the non-poor (probably due to low take-up), and has also generally declined as a share of income, even of very poor households (defined as those at less than half the poverty line), given the erosion of their real value and payment arrears. The coverage of family allowances, and all transfers, for different groups – very poor, poor and non-poor – is shown in Table 5.4, as well as the contribution of the transfer(s) to household income of each group.

Table 5.4: Coverage and Significance of Public Transfers, 1994-1995 (percentages)

	Very poor		Poor		Non-poor	
	Receiving the benefit	Share of recipient household income	Receiving the benefit	Share of recipient household income	Receiving the benefit	Share of recipient household income
Family allowances						
1994	28.8	23.6	32.4	14.5	25.7	5.9
1995	29.3	16.3	32.3	13.1	17.2	7.1
All transfers						
1994	66.8	58.5	70.9	48.4	74.4	42.6
1995	61.6	43.3	67.7	40.3	70.0	43.3

Notes: All transfers include pensions, unemployment benefits, maternity and family allowances, and local social assistance.
Source: Foley and Klugman (1997), Kolev (1996).

In short, the stance of social protection policy helps to explain the observed trends in poverty among families, including single-parent families. While pension indexation has helped the elderly to cope during the transition, families with children appear to have been relatively neglected, with large numbers of poor and very poor families being practically excluded from state assistance. It remains to be seen whether the more recent attempts to strengthen needs-based targeting will successfully include the poor.

Employment and Childcare

Participation in the labour force is an important dimension of economic independence. For women, and especially for single mothers, the incentives to work outside the home are significantly affected by government policies with respect to parental leaves and childcare. These policies have been subject to change in Russia during the transition. In this section we briefly review state policies regarding female employment, as reflected in rules about maternity benefit and benefit levels, as well as access to childcare and labour market outcomes (as reflected in labour force participation and unemployment rates).

Maternity leave has been extended to three years, and the parents are now given the right to make a choice independently and decide which of them would take care of the child. However, the levels of parental benefit have declined significantly as a share of the average wage. By 1995 the parental leave benefit was less than one-tenth of the average wage (compared to, for example, one-third in Bulgaria, see Table 5.5). This is mainly because the benefit amount is linked to the minimum wage. The benefit level was raised to twice the minimum wage (19.3 per cent of the average wage) in January 1996.

Table 5.5: Parental Leave Benefit in Central and Eastern Europe
(percentages of the average wage)

	1989	1990	1991	1992	1993	1994	1995
Czech Republic	23.7	24.2	22.2	22.5	21.6		
Bulgaria	51.1	47.1	68.0	41.5	38.2	36.7	33.6
Lithuania	-	19.0	39.1	31.4	23.3	23.2	13.4[b]
Russia	-	-	25.6[d]	7.4	4.3	8.1	9.0[e]

—: Not available.
Notes: [a] Data are for benefits until the child reaches 1.5 years. Since 1991 the benefit level for children 1.5 to 3 years has been 50 per cent of the first benefit. [b] Estimate. [c] Until January 1994, the benefit for employed women with less than a one year work record (except those under 18 or on break from work for educational training) was about 20 per cent lower. [d] in April 1991. [e] The benefit level was raised to twice the minimum wage (19.3 per cent of the average wage) in January 1996.
Source: Fajth, 1996; UNICEF, 1998.

There have been significant changes in terms of access to and types of provision of childcare. The share of the relevant age cohorts enrolled at nursery and pre-schools has dropped substantially, as shown in Figure 5.2. This is especially evident for the younger children (aged up to three years) who are of nursery-school age, where the cohort share enrolled has almost halved between 1989 and 1997. Unfortunately, figures are not available by family type, but the general decline in participation has probably affected single parents without access to alternative childcare arrangements (see further the discussion in Chapter 7.4).

Figure 5.2: Kindergarten and Nursery Gross Enrolment Rate 1989-1997

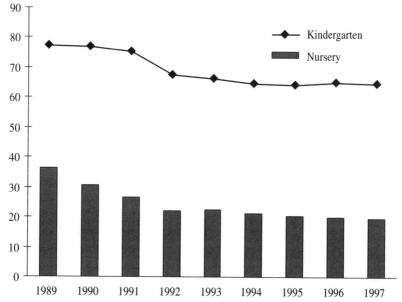

Source: MONEE Project database, UNICEF IRC.
Note: Nursery= 0-2 years, Kindergarten= 3-6 years.

Second, there has been a marked shift in the relative roles of enterprises and local municipalities in provision. During the Soviet period, provision was dominated by employers – who accounted for about three out of four places. Now, the employer share is less than one in five. Government provides the vast bulk of places, and the new private sector accounted for about 4 per cent of places in 1997.

Summary

There have been substantial shifts in the approach to family policy during the transition. Most recently, a concern for poverty relief has come to dominate social policy, at least with respect to the former array of categorical programmes (Harwin 1996). It makes little if any distinction between one- and two-parent families. It makes no distinction between unmarried and divorced or widowed mothers. It is questionable whether there is a specific *family* policy at the present time. Rather, there is a concern that children should be supported by their parents. Interestingly, our summary of the Soviet inheritance showed that both of these strands of family policy (i.e. the focus on poverty relief and the concern that children should be supported by their parents) have clear precedents in Russia's history of social policy.

The 'new poor', like the 'old poor' of the Soviet period, are frequently single-parent families (Braithwaite, 1997). This is not surprising in that women still earn significantly less than men on average, have fewer opportunities for overtime or second jobs (UNICEF, 1999). Women may also have been at greater risk of unemployment. They therefore stand to benefit disproportionately from whatever financial assistance is provided on a needs-tested basis. But there are still substantial problems involved in identifying those who are needy and delivering support to them in a timely way (World Bank, 1999).

5.4 Conclusions: Is There a Social Policy for Single Parents?

This chapter has provided a brief overview of the evolution of Soviet policy towards the single-parent family and shown how far the contemporary Russian picture resembles its historical origins. We have also shown how far the Russian government's policies to support the needs of single parents have been influenced and constrained by the circumstances of transition from a command economy. The main conclusions can be highlighted as follows.

First, in 1917 the Bolsheviks were ideologically committed to a policy which reduced the sanctity of marriage as a 'bourgeois institution'. These ideas continued to influence Party policy, although they were tempered after the end of the heroic attempt to build socialism and the onset of Stalinist industrialization. The incidence of incomplete families was affected by war, civil war and repression. As a result, the Soviet Union witnessed a significant increase in the number of single-parent households both during the inter-war period and, more particularly, after the Second World War. On the whole, the evidence suggested that they were less well off than traditional families.

The USSR government responded after 1944 by providing special allowances for single mothers; they were also given certain privileges in the workplace. It did not, however, make it easy for women to establish the paternity of their children and hence to force fathers to support their children. Single-parent households were also protected and supported by the collectivist welfare system that characterized the planned economy, insofar as prices for basic goods and services were kept low and employment opportunities were relatively abundant. State support was based primarily on the fact that the family contained children – and that the household was poor – rather than on the absence of a second parent, as the problem of poverty gained official recognition during the late Soviet period. There was little support for single-parent households as such.

The transition to a market economy has undermined the rationale of the collectivist welfare system. The nature and extent of support provided for single-parent households has been altered, not least because of the economic crisis and the collapse of state revenues that has characterized the transition period.

The transition to a market economy has intensified the economic disadvantage traditionally faced by single-parent families, a topic which is addressed in depth in Chapters 6 and 7. Increased emphasis on targeting of public transfers would be expected to benefit single parents, who are disproportionately represented among the poor. At the same time it is desirable that women, and single parents in particular, have access to employment; special efforts should be made to ensure that they receive the necessary training and are not discriminated against in hiring or promotion decisions. Equally important, the state needs to establish a clear policy on childcare for young children. How far should this be provided as a social service or should it be available largely on a commercial basis? The cost and availability of such services can have a significant influence on women's employment and thus on the living standards of single-parent households.

We have drawn attention to some of the policy alternatives facing the Russian government. The changing patterns of child allowances were reviewed, and factors such as the payment rate, the introduction of targeting, and the supplements for the children of single parents were described. The present situation is far from optimal, even taking the existing budget constraints as given. Very little public support is provided to single mothers, and fathers are often evading their responsibilities with impunity. In view of the high and rising rates of poverty among single parents, together with a number of indicators of worse welfare outcomes for their children, which are examined in depth in the next part of this volume, there is a strong argument for providing the children of sole parents with a higher supplement. For a neutral budget impact, this would have to be offset by reduced benefit levels for two-parent children or better targeting to exclude the non-poor from social assistance. The next chapter reveals that the current system of social protection is characterized by extensive leakage to the non-poor. The policy options to improve targeting include an expansion of the proxy means testing which has been piloted in several *oblasts* already, although care is needed to avoid wrongful exclusion of the poor under this approach (see World Bank, 1999).

Finally, in relation to the economic interests of single-parent households, it is appropriate that fathers (or, more properly, non-custodial spouses) continue to support their children. The state needs to re-examine the alimony system and how it operates in the market economy. It should make it as simple as possible for the parent with responsibility for care to collect the financial support to which she (or sometimes he) is entitled. At the same time, however, it should try to ensure that awards are seen to be fair as this will make collection easier.

In sum, the Russian authorities have retained their traditional conception of marriage as a consensual union and their belief that parents should be responsible for the maintenance of their children, whether born in or out of wedlock. But they have modified the state's commitment to the support of children. First, they have substantially abandoned any commitment to the provision of earmarked assistance for children of single mothers; second, it has been decided to concentrate available resources upon the needy – where need is defined in almost exclusively material terms. This change in policy has largely been dictated by increasingly severe fiscal constraints as the so-called transition recession has continued and deepened. But it is also consistent with the changing social values noted in Chapters 2 and 3, and with the priority past Soviet social policies gave to poverty relief. Chapter 4 has suggested that Russia could be best advised to draw on the liberal less-extensive welfare state model, and there are also signs within the country of a growing belief that individuals should assume greater responsibility for their own lives. It is not certain, therefore, that these recent policy changes will be reversed when economic recovery begins. Finally, also as a result of the fiscal crisis, responsibility for many areas of social policy has been devolved to *oblast'* or city governments. As a result there are now considerable regional differences in the level of support available to single-parent households.

NOTES

1 Civil Registration Offices of Vital Statistics that keep records of marriages, births, deaths and divorces. ZAGS stands for 'Zapis aktov grazhdanskogo sostoyaniya', which translates roughly as 'Register of acts of civil condition'. But the registration of marriages with the accompanying ceremony gives them their image as a marriage bureau.

2 For example, the rate of natural increase per thousand for the USSR as a whole was 23.7 in 1926 and 13.2 in 1940; in the RSFSR, the rate of natural increase in 1940 was 12.4 per thousand. The fall was due mostly to a decline in births, as death rates were stable, albeit at very high rates (Goskomstat SSSR, 1987).

3 These changes were in fact introduced by Khrushchev's successors in 1965.

4 In December 1998, the Moscow Times reported that wage arrears amounted to about 85 billion rubles; arrears in pension payments were 30 billion and overdue payments to families stood at 24 billion rubles.

5 The description and evaluation of recent changes in family law and alimony in particular draws heavily on Kuprianova (1998).

6 Men and women who cohabit as husbands and wives without being registered as such enjoy the same rights. But if an unregistered marriage breaks up, the woman, in contrast with a divorced woman, has no right to receive maintenance from the former partner. Nor does she receive a pension in case of the loss of the bread-winner.

7 Even in the Soviet period, a woman was entitled to a share of the value of produce produced on the private plot for the support of the children of a union.

8 This is primarily because the minimum wage was set at less than 10 per cent of average earnings. But few if any workers were paid the minimum wage. In 1997, only 2.4 per cent of employees received less than 100 rubles a month. The minimum wage was 84.5 rubles (Goskomstat, 1998).

9 Lack of an overall coherent framework for social protection is not, of course, peculiar to the Russian case. The U.S. system can be similarly characterized (see Burtless et al., 1997).

10 The minimum subsistence level, or poverty line, is based on an austere level of living comprising about 70 per cent food expenditures (see Chapter 6).

11 For the children of other families, medicines are available free, at least in principle, until the age of three.

PART III

POVERTY, WELFARE
AND SINGLE PARENTS
IN THE TRANSITION

Chapter 6: The Welfare Repercussions of Single-Parenthood in Russia in Transition

Jeni Klugman and Alexandre Kolev*

The past several years of economic transition in the Russian Federation have been associated with enormous social and demographic changes. A number of studies have documented rises in the overall incidence and depth of poverty and changes in the composition of the poor (see e.g. Klugman, 1997; Klugman and Braithwaite, 1998). One group that is frequently mentioned among those at risk of poverty are single parents. Earlier econometric analysis (e.g. Foley, 1997), as well as anecdotal and sociological evidence has suggested that women on their own with young children are especially vulnerable. Tchernina (1996), for example, adopts a case study approach to social exclusion in rural areas to highlight the plights of, for example, a single mother with a toddler who receives little and often delayed social assistance, and a divorced mother with three small children without regular employment.

In Chapter 4, Danziger and Carlson showed that there has been a surge in the incidence of single-parenthood in a number of Western countries since the 1970s. There are concerns about the welfare repercussions of single-parenthood. For example, in 1989 the United States poverty rate among families with a mother only was over 50 per cent, compared to a national average of 19 per cent (reported in Lerman, 1996). Thus recent economic and demographic trends in Russia naturally pose questions about the impact on household and child welfare. This chapter represents the first detailed economic investigation of single-parent families in Russia in the mid-1990s based on nationally representative micro-data.

The first task is to document the extent of poverty among single-parent families, relative to other family types, and to explain the greater vulnerability of single-parent families in terms of family composition and individual characteristics of family members. The second is to investigate the impact of family structure on income and earnings inequality in order to establish the effect of domestic responsibilities and other potential constraints. The final aims are more directly policy-related: to assess what has been the poverty impact of public transfers for single parents, and the impact of support received from private sources outside the household. The analysis is undertaken in the context of a rich and growing literature about single-parenthood in Western industrial countries though, as we have seen in Chapters 4 and 5, the policy issues and implications differ significantly. The Russian situation is in many senses distinct, not least in the dramatic falls in average household income and rising poverty and inequality experienced in recent years, and the significant fiscal and institutional constraints that characterize and hamper policy responses (see Chapter 1).

The analysis is structured as follows. The next section covers a range of definitional issues related to classification of family type and the measurement of poverty, and describes our data source, the Russian Longitudinal Monitoring Survey (RLMS). The following section presents a range of poverty measures and tries to isolate the observed characteristics associated with single-parenthood that are responsible for the high poverty risk observed for single-parent families. The third section investigates the impact of family structure on the distribution of income. Part four explores the extent and incidence of public and private transfers, highlighting errors of exclusion. The final section concludes by highlighting the most disturbing trends revealed by the analysis.

6.1 Data and Definitions

The data source exploited for this analysis is rounds V-VII of the Russian Longitudinal Monitoring Survey (RLMS) as described in Chapter 1. We utilize both information collected on households as well as extensive information at the individual level. For example, expenditures and sources of income refer to those reported at the household level, while additional information on labour force status comes from the individual questionnaire. The analysis was limited to those families headed by an adult and reporting positive expenditures on food. After data cleaning, we were left with a sample size of 3,693 observations for round V, 3,509 for round VI, and 3,419 for round VII.

According to common Western usage, a single-parent family consists of a parent with her (his) dependent children, either living as a separate household or in the household of others, for example the grandparents of the children (Ermisch, 1990). Variations in definition can surround the specification of the dependent child, and whether single-parent families living in the households of others should be included. In the present analysis, as set out in Chapter 1, single-parent families include households in which children under 18 years of age live with less than two parents (father and mother), whether or not with anyone else.

As noted in Chapter 1, in Russia a distinction is commonly drawn between 'incomplete' and 'complex' families. The former comprises single parents living alone with their children while the latter extends to single parents living in the households of others. According to census data, between 1989 and 1994, the number of children living in incomplete and complex families rose by 11 and 27 per cent respectively, to 15 and 6 per cent of all children (see Chapter 2). In a number of places we distinguish between incomplete and complex single-parent families. In general, our reference point for purposes of comparison is dual-parent families with children. We also make comparisons to the overall category of 'all households'.

Patterns of Family Structure

Chapter 3 has already investigated patterns of household structure based on the RLMS.[1] To summarize, single parents represented about one in five households with children, and about 9 per cent of all households in 1996 (see Figure 6.1). The group of single parents divides fairly evenly between incomplete and complex families: about 49 per cent fall into the incomplete family category, and 51 per cent are complex, i.e. living in a family headed by someone else.

Between 1994 and 1996, the proportion of children living in single-parent families remained around 16 per cent (Appendix 6.2).

Figure 6.1: Distribution of Households by Type, RLMS 1996

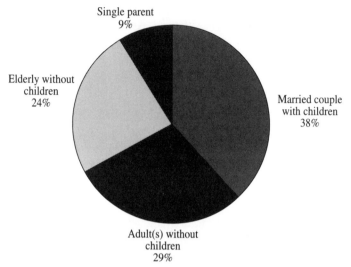

Figure 6.2 shows the distribution of those children by type of single parent – we can see that for almost two-thirds their mother is either divorced or separated; only about 14 per cent had never married, confirming the point made in Chapter 2 that divorce remains the main route to single-parenthood in the transition period.

Figure 6.2: Distribution of Children in Single-Parent Families by Type, RLMS 1996

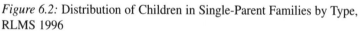

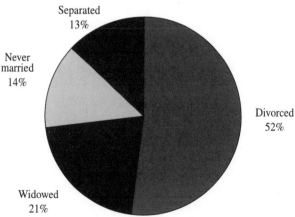

Defining Poverty, Incomes and Expenditure

This analysis employs several widely used measures of poverty. The different measures – the poverty headcount, the poverty welfare ratio and poverty depth and severity – are defined in Appendix 6.1. These indicators are derived from consumption data.[2] We aggregate the total consumption (expenditure) of the household in the month preceding the survey, plus the monthly imputed expenditures represented by the consumption of home-produced goods (such as food), less expenditures on consumer durables. This definition of consumption does not impute expenditures for subsidised social services nor for owner-occupied housing. The latter omission should not have a dramatic impact, since rental expenditures remain low in mid-1990s.[3] The treatment of social services (health care and education) is possibly more problematic. However, since access to subsidised services is fairly universal, comparisons between households should not be greatly affected.

Reliance on expenditure rather than income data has a number of advantages in Russia, given the widespread incidence of wage arrears and unpaid leave, residual stigma, and the desire to avoid tax by understating income often derived from the informal sector. Moreover, income is subject to larger variation than consumption, which households may try to smooth over time.[4] There are nonetheless some disadvantages. First, people may choose to consume less, despite stable or growing income, and total expenditures (and thus our picture of household welfare) will thereby influenced. Second, consumption patterns may be influenced by the purchase of durable goods (e.g. car, house, etc) and therefore we exclude them. Third, it may be more difficult for respondents to recall past expenditures than income. On balance, however, we consider household expenditure to be preferable to reported income as a measure of well-being in Russia during the transition.

This analysis focuses on absolute poverty. In fact, in Russia there is an official national poverty line (referred to as the Minimum Subsistence Income or MSI) that has been in use since 1992. In the present analysis, we use regional MSIs, which are based on a methodology similar to that used to derive the national threshold with several important adjustments. The national minimum subsistence level is based on a basket of food products, adjusted upwards by a certain percentage of the cost of this basket to account for non-food expenditure. We construct a household-specific threshold for each household. First, variation in the level of regional prices is taken into account. Second, the actual composition of the underlying food basket varies according to observed regional consumption patterns. Third, the different needs of families of varying composition and size are taken into account through the inclusion of both equivalence scales and economies of scale.[5]

High rates of inflation have characterised much of the transition. During the years under investigation the annual national consumer price index ranged from 195 in 1994, to 875 in 1996 (UNICEF, 1998). These national averages conceal significant variation in regional rates of inflation (Stewart, 1998). To adjust our poverty estimates for inflation, nominal monthly expenditures were compared with the corresponding monthly subsistence minimum income. Since the latter is indexed for inflation, this normalization also adjusts for price changes over time.

6.2 Single-Parent Families and Poverty: 1994-1996

In this section we investigate poverty status by family type. The results reveal a dramatic rise in the incidence of poverty across all family types over the period 1994-1996.[6] We then look at several characteristics that could explain the high rates of poverty among single-parent families, relative to other family types.

Family Structure and Poverty Status

There have been steep rises in overall poverty rates during the transition that can be broadly traced to falls in the level and widening distribution of labour income and social transfers.[7] It is natural to expect that family dissolution would tend to be associated with increased poverty and inequality simply because families become divided into groups with one earner and groups with two earners. Even during the Soviet period, households could generally only be assured of a decent standard of living where there were at least two earners (Braithwaite, 1997). Studies of the industrial town of Taganrog found a much higher incidence of poverty among single parents relative to average families in 1989 (Mozhina and Prokofieva, 1997). This tendency has become more pronounced during the transition, as illustrated by the much higher incidence of poverty among families affected by unemployment, (see Foley, 1997). In the West also, there tends to be a strong correlation between single-parent status and poverty, as was shown in Chapter 4 above (see also Lerman, 1996).

Figure 6.3 presents trends in poverty head counts based on regional poverty thresholds.[8] The increase in aggregate poverty incidence has been dramatic. Between 1994 and 1996, the proportion of families that fell below their regional poverty line nearly doubled, rising from about 12 to 21 per cent.[9] Even more striking is the surge in poverty among single-parent families, whose poverty rate more than doubled from about 12 per cent to about 28 per cent. By way of contrast, poverty incidence among elderly households rose by only 2 per cent over the same period.

There has been widening dispersion in poverty rates among family types. Whereas in late 1994, poverty incidence for each of the different family types was similar, by late 1996 the highest poverty rate (of 28 per

Figure 6.3: Poverty Status and Family Structure, RLMS 1994-1996 (percentages)

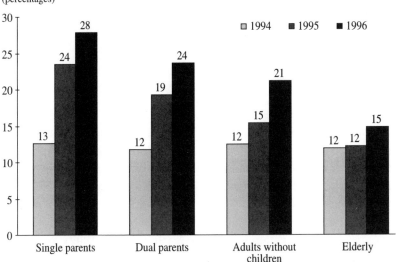

cent among single parents) was almost twice the lowest (found for the elderly). This dramatic shift presents important questions for empirical investigation, which we address below.

Not only are poverty rates highest among single parents, but their real per capita expenditures are the lowest among all family types. In 1996 their per capita expenditure was only about 80 per cent of the average reported for all families.

Indicators representing poverty depth and severity are also markedly worse among single-parent families. These indicators suggest that single parents are not close to the threshold but more frequently report very low expenditures (Table 6.1). Moreover the trend in recent years has been toward deepening and more severe poverty among single parents, a trend that can be seen for dual-parent families as well.

Table 6.1: Severe Poverty and Family Types, RLMS 1994-1996
(percentages)

	Very poor			**Depth**			**Severity**		
	1994	**1995**	**1996**	**1994**	**1995**	**1996**	**1994**	**1995**	**1996**
All households	3.0	4.3	6.1	4.0	5.6	7.5	2.0	2.8	4.0
With children									
Single-parent	3.3	6.9	8.3	4.0	8.1	10.2	2.1	4.0	5.4
Dual-parent	2.3	4.4	7.4	3.6	6.2	8.4	1.7	3.0	4.7
Without children									
Adult	3.4	3.6	5.5	4.2	5.0	7.4	2.2	2.5	4.0
Elderly	3.8	3.9	4.0	4.4	4.5	5.1	2.5	2.4	2.6

Notes: See definitions of poverty measures in Appendix 1. For depth (100*P1); for severity (100*P2).

Moving from the household to the individual, Table 6.2 presents the poverty head count indices for different age groups. In each year, the incidence of poverty is the highest for children, especially for young children. In late 1996, more than 26 per cent of all children were living in poor households, compared to 22 per cent of working-age adults and 19 per cent of pensioners.

The trend of worsening poverty has also been sharper for children, especially younger children, in single-parent families. Nearly 30 per cent of children in single-parent families in late 1996 were poor, and 36 per

Table 6.2: Individual Poverty Incidence by Demographic Group and Family Type, RLMS 1994-1996
(percentages)

	All families			Single-parent families		
	1994	**1995**	**1996**	**1994**	**1995**	**1996**
All children	13.4	21.6	26.5	13.2	25.7	30.2
Children aged 0-5 years	17.1	25.1	26.3	16.2	33.3	35.6
Children aged 6-17 years	11.6	20.1	26.6	12.0	23.1	28.4
Working-age adults	11.5	18.0	22.4	13.2	23.4	27.6
Pensioners	11.3	13.7	19.4	11.4	22.0	27.5

cent of under six year-olds. Although the elderly have experienced lower than average poverty risk generally, the poverty incidence among the elderly living in single-parent families is similar to that for working-age adults.

Observed Family and Individual Characteristics

We have seen that single-parent families had higher poverty rates. It is now interesting to investigate and compare the characteristics of single-parent families, relative to dual-parent families. Do the characteristics of single-parent families diverge significantly from overall patterns? Broadly speaking, we can distinguish between family and individual characteristics, both of which may have a significant bearing on the risk of poverty.

Single-parent families are generally, but not necessarily, headed by the single parent: almost 78 per cent of single-parent families were headed by the single parent.[10] In the overwhelming majority of cases (97 per cent), the single parent is the mother (or a female adult). This is not surprising since in Russia, like elsewhere, children generally stay with their mother in the event of birth out-of-wedlock or marital breakdown.

Single parents often live in an extended family context, an arrangement which may be partly explained in terms of the severe housing shortages that still characterize Russia, and which were noted in Chapter 1. Census data suggests that there has been a substantial rise in the number of extended families in the 1990s, which may reflect a type of coping strategy in response to economic stress (see Chapters 2 and 3). About half of single-parent families had other adults in the household (Appendix 6.2). This is significantly higher than the figure reported for the United States in 1994, for example, where only 15 per cent of single parents comprised a 'sub-family'.

Given what we know from previous studies about the positive association between the presence of children and poverty risk (Foley, 1997), we would expect both single-parent and dual-parent families with children to face higher than average risk of poverty. At the same time however, single parents tend to have fewer children than dual-parent households, 48 per cent of which have two or more children. Again we know from earlier analysis that the presence of young children in the household is a significant risk factor for poverty (ibid.). Only one third of single-parent families have one or more children under six years of age compared to 42 per cent for dual-parent families.

A striking, but not unexpected, finding is that about 70 per cent of single-parent families have only one working-age adult. By way of contrast, among dual-parent families with children, 97 per cent have two or more working-age members. This in turn would be expected to affect the relative earning capacities of different household types, especially in the presence of young children (a hypothesis that we investigate below). Nonetheless, highlighting the importance of complex households, about 27 per cent of single-parent households have at least two working-age adults. However there are more elderly people in single-parent households than in dual-parent families, presumably because the divorced spouse returns to his/her parents after the split: about 34 per cent of single-parent households have at least one pension-age adult, compared to 20 per cent for dual-parent households.

Individual Attributes of Family Members

Along with the composition of the family, the attributes of the individuals living in single-parent families is likely to affect family welfare. Since the single parent is often at the same time the head of the family and the mother of the children, it is interesting to compare the characteristics of single mothers with both married mothers and heads of dual-parent households. In particular, we investigate how far the divergences between single-parent families and dual-parent families can be related to gender differences, as opposed to characteristics specific to single-parenthood. The evidence suggests that gender differences cannot explain all the change in poverty rates.

The overall age pattern for single-parent heads is roughly similar to that observed for dual-parent heads, though the share of very young and older heads in single-parent families – respectively under 25 years and above 46 years – is significantly higher than in dual-parent families. On average, single mothers are older than married mothers. This is consistent with the finding that half of single mothers were divorced. In most OECD countries, the vast majority of single parents are divorced or separated mothers, followed by widows, and on average they are older than married mothers (Ermisch, 1990).

Education level is an individual characteristic that would be expected to impact upon household welfare status. It is perhaps contrary to expectations to find that heads of single-parent families are on average more educated. In late 1995, about three-quarters had completed more than 9 years of school compared to 59 per cent for household heads on average (Table 6.3), though this partly reflects age cohort effects. In fact, comparison with dual-parent household heads suggests no real educational differences relative to heads of single-parent families. Similarly, we could not find any evidence of an educational gap between married

Table 6.3: Education Characteristics by Family Type, RLMS 1995 (percentages)

	Heads in:			Mothers in:	
	Single-parent	Dual-parent	All households	Single-parent	Dual-parent
Years of school					
≤ 5 years of school	4.0	1.0	10.4	2.4	0.3
6-8 years of school	20.2	25.5	30.6	20.1	20.1
9-12 years of school	75.8	73.4	59.0	77.5	79.6
Highest level of school completed					
Secondary or less	29.5	30.5	39.8	24.2	22.1
Vocational education	46.0	46.2	38.8	50.8	54.1
University education	24.5	23.3	21.4	25.0	23.8

and single mothers. However, the achievements of the latter tend to be more disparate: the share of heads of single-parent families with less than 5 years of school and more than 9 years is higher than that observed for heads of dual-parent families.

Labour Market Status

A vast majority (72 per cent) of single-parent heads in the 1995 sample were working (Table 6.4). Nonetheless, this rate is still some 12 percentage points below that reported for dual-parent heads. This may reflect female rather than single-parent disadvantage, given that dual-parent heads in Table 6.4 are mostly men, whereas heads in single-parent families are virtually all women. Comparison with married mothers suggests that single mothers tend to have higher labour force participation rates and, for those employed, longer hours of work. Recall that about half of single parents live in an extended family context, so that other family members may contribute to childcare. This picture is consistent with other evidence for Russia: a survey of urban families in 1993 found that 90 per cent of single-parent women had labour market earnings compared to 77 per cent for women in dual-parent households (Mozhina and Prokofieva, 1997).

Access to informal sector employment is lower among single-parent heads than for dual-parent heads of household, which is a cause for concern since empirical evidence shows that participation in the second economy is an important way to escape poverty (Kolev, 1996). Again however, this may reflect a gender difference rather than a single-parent disadvantage. Single mothers are in fact more numerous in the informal labour market than married mothers. Of course, access to the informal labour market tends to vary by region, with higher rates in metropolitan areas. Mozhina and Prokofieva (1997) report from a survey of urban families that almost one in four single mothers had secondary earnings, compared to 11 per cent of women in dual-parent families.

The rate of unemployment is 30 per cent higher among heads in single-parent families than in dual-parent family heads. This does not seem to be a question of female disadvantage: in general, unemployment affects more males than females. Rather, single mothers are more affected by unemployment than married mothers.[11] We would expect higher unemployment to be associated with worse living conditions (Commander and Yemtsov, 1997).

The share of heads on leave to take care of children is also higher in single-parent families, which is not surprising given the gender distribution of heads.[12] Hence, overall, a higher share of heads in single-parent families (about one in eight) are not working either because they are on leave or because they are unemployed, and this would increase the risk of poverty among single-parent families. On the other hand, fewer single than married mothers are on official leave, presumably because

Table 6.4: Labour Market Characteristics by Family Type, RLMS 1995 (percentages)

Status of Heads / Mothers	Household heads		Mothers	
	Single-parent	Dual-parent	Single-parent	Dual-parent
Employment Status:				
Employed	72.2	84.3	71.3	65.8
Disabled	4.3	2.0	4.1	0.6
Pensioner	5.0	2.4	4.1	0.8
Unemployed	11.6	8.9	10.9	8.1
Out of labour force [a]	4.0	1.3	5.5	13.3
Official leave [b]	1.0	0.1	4.8	10.7
Student	1.7	0.5	1.0	0.6
Occupation (for employed)				
Senior manager	3.2	5.3	2.7	2.1
Professional	15.1	9.6	13.3	14.8
Technician	20.6	6.3	19.4	17.7
Clerk	10.1	1.5	7.8	8.9
Service and market worker	11.5	5.3	10.6	8.6
Skilled agricultural worker	0.0	0.9	0.0	0.0
Craft and related trade	7.8	27.7	3.4	4.9
Plant and machine operator	15.6	34.0	6.8	5.8
Unskilled	14.2	7.5	11.6	13.9
Army	0.9	1.9	0.7	0.2
Engaged in the informal economy	11.9	16.6	12.6	9.0
Average monthly hours of work in main job	159	184	157	154

Notes: a 'Out of labour force' includes housewives, those caring for other family members or raising children, and others that are not seeking employment.
b 'Official leave' refers to individuals on maternity leave or official leave for looking after children.

they have fewer young children, but also because the extremely low benefit levels act as a disincentive for sole wage earners in a household.

The occupational breakdown by family type largely reflects gender segregation in the workforce at large. The persistence of the gender segregation during the transition has been shown (UNICEF, 1999). Just as women tend to be concentrated in low status white-collar and other low paid jobs, we see also that heads in single-parent families are disproportionately working as technicians, clerks, in the service sector and in unskilled occupations. Very few are engaged in crafts or related trades or working as machine operators, whereas these occupations account for more than half of married heads. Gender segregation is also found in the lower share of single-parent heads in managerial positions.

6.3 Family Structure and the Distribution of Income

So far, we have seen that poverty rates are substantially higher among single-parent families, and have worsened disproportionately compared to those among dual-parent families over time. In this section we introduce another dimension of welfare – the distribution of income – and explore the impact of family composition on levels of income inequality over the period 1994-1996.

Differences in Levels of Income and in Sources of Income

Levels of real family income per capita have decreased sharply. In 1996, average family income per capita was only 76 per cent of its 1994 level for all households, and 83 per cent for single-parent families. Income differences between family types have been large and fairly stable during the period and so has been the ranking of family types from highest to lowest income (Figure 6.4). Family income per capita for single-parent families has been consistently lower.

In terms of the relative importance of different income sources, labour market earnings represent the largest share across all family types, including single parents (Appendix 6.3). For the latter, labour market earnings represented 37 per cent of income in 1996. Differences in income sources across family types are found in the relative impor-

Figure 6.4: Real Household Income Per Capita by Household Type, RLMS
1994-1996 (June 1992 rubles)

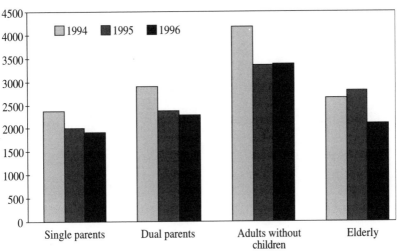

tance of social transfers and home production. This is discussed in
greater detail in section 6.4. The contribution of home production –
which is an important way for families to protect their level of real consumption – is lower for single parents, which is consistent with their
greater time constraints.

Differences in Labour Market Earnings

Income-earning opportunities have a critical impact on family welfare
status, especially in Russia, where the scope and generosity of public
transfers will be limited for at least the foreseeable future. Here we
investigate the earnings component of incomes, to measure the extent to
which single-parent families differ from other population groups in
terms of labour supply and rates of pay.

Looking at families with positive labour market earnings shows
that average salaries per employed member for single-parent families
represent only 84 per cent of those for married families with children.
This reflects both the lower rate of pay and the lower average hours of
work among single-parent family members, relative to dual-parent fam-

ilies (Appendix 6.4). There are several possible explanations, that we attempt to verify empirically below.

In Russia, possibly even more so than in the West, the general organization of work does not facilitate participation of single mothers in employment. In particular, part-time work is much less common. According to official statistics only 1.2 per cent of Russian women worked part-time in 1990 (Katz, 1994). More recent nationally representative surveys suggest that in 1994 only 8 per cent of women worked part-time outside the home when their children were of pre-school age. Family-related tasks such as childcare and household maintenance usually cannot be performed by the worker during working hours (Sussman and Steinmetz, 1987). This would be a particular burden for poor single parents who may not be able to afford to pay for such services to be carried out by others.

One factor that we might expect to influence the labour market participation of single mothers is the availability of childcare. The decline in the provision of this formerly widely accessible service during the transition was noted in earlier chapters: overall enrolments of children aged 3-6 years have fallen by about 15 percentage points between 1989 and 1996, to 55 per cent (Cusan and Motivans, 1997). Studies elsewhere have suggested that the availability and cost of childcare can severely constrain single mothers' participation in the work force. A national survey of single mothers carried out in the UK found that more than one-third felt that the cost of childcare prevented them from working more than 16 hours a week (Ford, 1996). The same study found that among working single parents, about two-thirds used childcare and the remainder either worked at home, left their children alone or took their children to work with them. Among those using childcare services, fees represent on average 20 per cent of their net income. In sum then, we would expect that family-related constraints would reduce the average number of hours that single mothers spend working, relative to adults in two parent families.

However, as noted in Section 6.2, for Russia in late 1995, the employment rate of single mothers is lower than for male heads but higher than for mothers in dual-parent families. Moreover, we found that on a monthly basis, single mothers work three hours more than married mothers in primary employment. The higher average employment rate and hours of work can be partly explained, at least in one out of two cases, by the presence of other adults that can take care of the children. Also, in Russia, the cost of childcare does not yet represent the same burden as in Western Europe: in 1996, according to the RLMS, the cost for single parents purchasing childcare represented about only 7 per cent of their household expenditure.

More so than the number of hours spent in employment, differences in total earnings among family types reflect the differences in the rate of pay: in late 1996 the hourly rate of pay in single-parent families was only 82 per cent of that in dual-parent families. Since virtually all single parents are women, it is not surprising to find lower hourly earnings for household members in single-parent families. Earlier studies have documented the persistence of a gender wage gap of the order of 30 per cent during the transition, which is only partially explicable in terms of women's labour market experience and other 'objective' factors (Katz, 1996; Newell and Reilly, 1996).

Quantifying the Effects of Family Structure on Income and Earnings Inequalities

Single parents, as a group, have experienced significant relative deterioration in welfare status since 1994. Another important dimension of family welfare is the extent of income and labour market earnings inequalities, both within the group of single-parent families, and between family types. In terms of household welfare, are single-parent families closer to each other than to other parts of the population? Or are differences among single parents more important? In other words, what is the extent of heterogeneity among single-parent families?[13]

Following the approach used by Jenkins (1995) to assess inequality trends in the United Kingdom, we distinguish the effects of family structure from the effects of within-group income level on the distribution of income, as described in Appendix 6.5. After dividing the population into mutually exclusive sub-groups based on family type, total inequality is decomposed into two parts: within-group inequalities (the weighted sum of the inequalities within each family type), and between-group inequalities (inequalities remaining where each family's income is equal to the family type's mean income).

Table 6.5: Within-Group and Between-Group Inequality, RLMS 1994-1996

	Income per capita			Salaries in cash		
	1994	**1995**	**1996**	**1994**	**1995**	**1996**
Mean logarithmic deviation index	35.1	44.9	51.7	44.5	46.0	50.1
Within-group inequality	33.7	43.4	49.5	41.6	43.5	48.0
Between-group inequality	1.4	1.5	2.2	2.9	2.5	2.1
Gini coefficient	45.6	49.0	50.4	46.6	48.8	51.4

Note: Technical details are set out in Appendix 5. "Income per capita" refers to real family income, and "Salaries in cash" to real family earnings from main and second jobs, (June 1992 rubles). Mean logarithmic deviation index and Gini coefficients are multiplied by 100.

We apply this methodology to Russian household incomes. The trends in aggregate income and earnings inequality between 1994 and 1996, as well as its within- and between-family structure components, are summarized in Table 6.5. The Gini coefficient and mean log deviation suggest substantial increases in overall income inequality over the period. This is consistent with the findings of other recent work (e.g. Commander et al, 1997; Flemming and Micklewright, 1999). Our concern here, however, is not to investigate trends in inequality generally, which have clearly worsened over the period, but rather the contribution of household composition to these outcomes. Interestingly, the decomposition of aggregate inequality suggests that the within-family-type inequality term dominates the between-family one. Between-group inequality accounts for only 13 per cent of total inequality.

This finding lends further support to the evident heterogeneity within the different family types. Mozhina and Prokofieva (1997) cite a 1993 survey of urban families where the decile ratio for the incomes of the single-parent group was 8.6 and about 6 per cent of single parents were classified in the high income group (three or more times the subsistence minimum). It is also consistent with recent Western studies. For the United States, for example, Tilly and Albeda (1994) found that within-family-type inequality is larger than inequality between family types, which was attributed to the many different factors affecting earnings that vary within family types. The same conclusions are drawn for the United Kingdom by Jenkins (1995).

Inequality in labour earnings has also increased significantly over the period 1994-1996. At the same time, trends in within- and between-group inequality in earnings appear to have diverged – within-group inequality has worsened sharply while between-group inequality has narrowed slightly (this is explored further below, see Table 6.6).

At the same time, the extent of inequality within the group of single parents is still evidently less than that found for dual-parent families and families headed by a working-age adult without children. This is illustrated by the positions of the respective Lorenz curves in Figure 6.5. That is, in terms of income, single parents are less heterogeneous than other family types.

The Determinants of Earnings Inequality

Labour market opportunities for single parents appear to be constrained in various respects, but we need to examine the sources of differences in earnings. In particular, do inter-family inequalities in salaries depend more on differences in the rate of pay across family types, on the number of wage earners in the family, or on the average hours worked by employed members in the family?

To answer to these questions, we modify an approach used by Tilly and Albeda (1994). We decompose family salaries in cash into three

Figure 6.5: Lorenz Curves for Real Family Income Per Capita, RLMS 1996

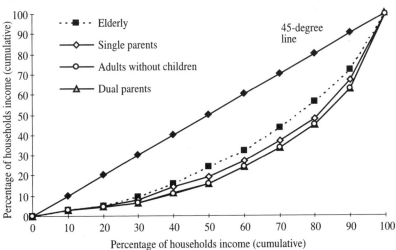

components, for those families with positive labour earnings, as follows:

$$E = P * H * N$$

where E is total labour earnings received by the family as a whole; P is the hourly rate of pay, that is, E divided by total hours worked by those employed in the family; H is the average hours spent working by the employed members of the family; and N is the number of employed individuals in the family. The reference period is the month preceding the interview.[14]

To look at the impact of these three variables on inter-family earnings differences, we performed a simulation, by setting each of these variables in turn equal to the mean value for all families as a benchmark. We then recomputed salaries for each family type, using the aggregate mean values. Between-group inequality measures based on the mean logarithmic are then used to assess the impact of the three components on labour income inequality between family types.

The results are summarized in Table 6.6. Inequalities in labour earnings between family types are generated mainly by the differences in the number of wage earners, and in the variations in the rate of pay between families. But the average hours spent working by the employed members of the family do not seem to be a source of between-family-group inequalities in earnings. This confirms the finding above that the diminution of childcare access associated with the closure of facilities has not affected labour force participation, possibly because about half of single parents live in extended family contexts where other adults may assist in childcare tasks.

Table 6.6: Between-Group Inequalities in Per Capita Family Labour Earnings, RLMS 1994-1996

	1994	1995	1996
Between group inequality:	3.0	2.5	2.1
- Holding rate of pay constant (P)	1.0	1.0	0.8
- Holding number of employed members constant (N)	1.3	0.9	0.7
- Holding average hours worked constant (H)	2.2	1.9	2.4

Note: Mean logarithmic deviation is multiplied by 100.

The foregoing provides a better understanding of differences in earnings across family groups, but these account for only a small part of aggregate inequality, indicating a large degree of heterogeneity within family type. We now turn to the task of examining the impact of public and private transfers on family welfare.

6.4 Support for Single-Parent Families

We might expect government, as well as friends and family, to provide assistance to single parents that would improve their welfare status. This is indeed the case in Russia, as described in the previous chapter. At the same time, our detailed empirical analysis of the incidence of public transfers confirms that errors of exclusion are a serious cause for concern for single-parent families, and generally.

Russia inherited an extensive range of public transfers from the Soviet period, even if the system of social assistance targeted to the poor was limited in scope and generosity (see Chapter 5). In the mid-1990s the range of benefits included pensions, unemployment benefits, child benefits, student stipends, and subsidies for housing and fuel. However, the real value of transfers generally has been very low. For example, the level of unemployment benefits, which we approximate by referring to the minimum wage,[15] stood in 1995 and 1996 at less than one-fifth of its late 1991 level.

Table 6.7 reports the crude impact of all transfers on the poverty head count, by family type. Over time, there was a clear weakening in the poverty alleviation impact of transfers: for all households the reduction in the poverty head count after receipt of transfers dropped from 29 to 24 percentage points between 1994 and 1996. The weakening has been even sharper for single-parent families, of the order of ten percentage points. This is not surprising against the background of declining value and increasing incidence of arrears in payment.

Public and private transfers nonetheless remain an important safety net against poverty. This is especially true for single-parent families (and even more so for pensioners), for whom these transfers have played a larger role than for other groups. The reduction in poverty incidence among single parents brought about by transfers is double the average for families with children. At the same time, this highlights the dependence of single parents on outside support to prevent further welfare deterioration during the transition.

Table 6.7: Impact of Transfers on the Poverty Head Count, RLMS 1994-1996
(percentage points)

	1994	**1995**	**1996**
All households	-28.7	-26.4	-24.3
Single-parent	-32.3	-23.8	-22.7
Dual-parent	-10.4	-11.1	-11.2

Note: Includes both public and private transfers.

How many poor single parents receive public transfers, and what contribution do they make to household income? Appendix 6.6 shows the share of poor and non-poor households receiving each of the major transfers, and the contribution to their income. Poverty here is defined on the basis of pre-transfer household income. Figure 6.6 shows that the share of poor households receiving public transfers has decreased significantly among single parents and for dual-parent family types. For

Figure 6.6: Poor Households Receiving Public Transfers by Family Type, 1994 and 1996 (percentages)

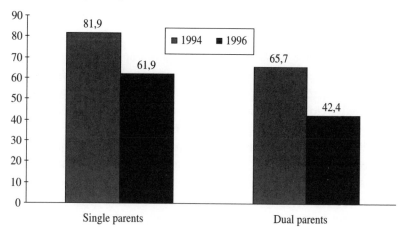

recipients, however, public transfers accounted for practically the same share of total household income over the period (Appendix 6.6).

In late 1996, the share of families with children receiving public transfers was generally higher among non-poor households than poor households. The share of single-parent families receiving public transfers and the contribution of transfers to their income has been larger than that of married families. About 62 per cent of poor single parents receive public support compared to only 42 per cent of poor dual parents.

There has been a sharp decline in the share of poor single parents receiving support since 1994 – from 82 to 62 per cent – a trend that has also affected other family types. Interestingly, however, the share of transfers in household income for single-parent recipients of transfers has remained around 50 per cent. Hence those poor single parents remain vulnerable to reductions in the size of public support.

Pensions and child benefits were the most widely received transfers in the sample overall. For poor single parents in late 1996, child benefits were the most frequently received transfer and, despite their small nominal size and the extensive errors of exclusion detailed below, made an important contribution to household income for recipients, of around 23 per cent. As noted in Chapter 5, child benefits were dramatically eroded in real terms in the early years of the transition (UNICEF, 1997). However, since 1993/94 the real values of child benefits including the allowance for children of single parents, have increased.

The share of poor single parents who receive unemployment benefits is low, and has actually fallen further over time. We know that over 11 per cent of single parents are unemployed, yet only one per cent of poor single parents were receiving unemployment benefits in late 1996. Among the poor who do receive such support, the contribution to household income is nonetheless significant, around 24 per cent (Appendix 6.6).

The foregoing patterns suggest not only that many poor single parents are not receiving public transfers, but also that many of the non-poor do. If we accept the proposition that public transfers ought to be directed to those who need them the most, errors in coverage are a cause for concern. Without revisiting the appropriateness of targeting objectives and implementation problems (see van de Walle 1998 for a recent review), we examine errors of leakage and exclusion, corresponding respectively to cases where ineligible individuals receive assistance, and cases where eligible individuals do not. The weight given to the different types of error is a value judgement: do we care more about minimizing leakage to the non-poor, or about ensuring that all the poor receive assistance? While most Russian households receive some government transfer, a significant proportion of the very poor (almost three out of ten) and of the poor (one out of five) do not receive any such benefits, and almost four out of five households that are not poor do receive public transfers (Foley and Klugman, 1997). Here we estimate the extent of errors of exclusion in the context of single-parenthood.

We compare the extent of errors of exclusion among all households and among single-parent families by looking at whether households who apparently qualify for the various categorical transfers in fact reported receipt. It is clear from Figure 6.7 that errors of exclusion are large and have increased for pensions, child benefits and unemployment benefits. Our definition of exclusion encompasses those families affected by delayed payment, so that the large increase in the proportion of eligible families not receiving any pensions is likely to reflect the phenomenon of pension arrears. The same may be the case for child benefits financed by fiscally-constrained local authorities. Overall however, the data does not suggest that exclusion is more serious for poor single-parent families (Appendix 6.7). They are less likely than all families to be excluded from child benefits and pensions, though slightly more likely not to receive unemployment benefits.

Very high rates of exclusion are observed for child benefits. In late 1996, about 69 per cent of all eligible poor and 61 per cent of poor single-parent families who were eligible were not receiving such allowances. Among non-poor single parents, about 63 per cent are excluded.

We found that the vast bulk of families affected by unemployment do not receive unemployment benefits, which is presumably either due to non-registration or expiry of benefit (Appendix 6.7). More than nine out of ten single-parent families affected by unemployment did not report receipt of the benefit. Apart from unemployment benefits, student stipends are the least well-administered benefit in terms of errors of exclusion. In late 1996, over 81 per cent of eligible poor families were not receiving any student stipends, significantly above the 54 per cent found for 1994.

Figure 6.7: Errors of Exclusion of Poor Single Parents, RLMS 1994 and 1996
(percentages)

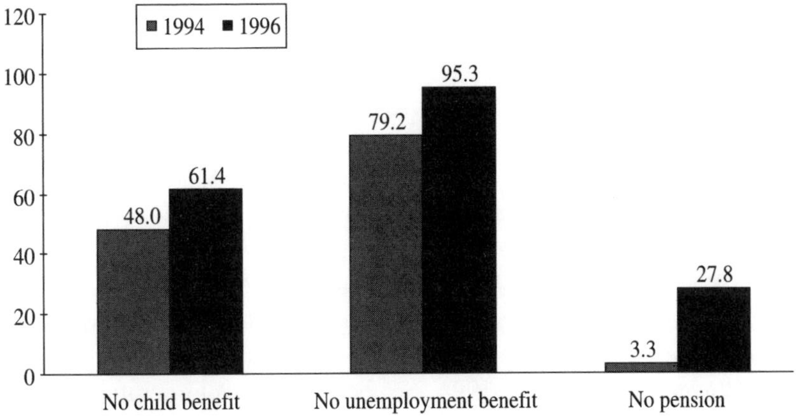

Note: Figures refer to the percentage of eligible group excluded; e.g. of families with children not receiving child benefits or households with an unemployed person not receiving unemployment benefit. The figures are reported in Appendix 6.7.

Private Transfers

Earlier studies have found that private transfers in Russia are large, widespread and responsive to households' socio-economic characteristics (Cox, Eser and Jimenez, 1997). While assistance from the extended family has always been important in Russia, by 1993 surveys found that this was considered by one third of single-parent respondents to be "the most significant" source of household income (Mozhina and Prokofieva, 1997). In this section we investigate the quantitative impact of such transfers for single-parent families.

Our analysis confirms that private transfers in Russia are quite large: they represented 8 per cent of total household income in 1994, 6 per cent in 1995, and 8 per cent again in 1996. The contribution to household income for single-parent families is virtually double this average in each of the years. Among recipient single-parent households (that is, those receiving such transfers), the contribution of private transfers is even higher, rising from 35 to 38 per cent over the same period.

Not surprisingly, the share of single-parent families receiving some kind of private support was higher among incomplete families than among complex families: 46 and 33 per cent respectively. The contribution of private transfers to total household income is also higher for incomplete than for complex families. Among the former, private transfers represent 20 per cent of family income – which is similar to the average for all households – while for the latter, they represent more than 9 per cent. Single parents that cannot benefit from other household members' income are therefore compensated partially by private transfers from outside the household from relatives, friends, or non-governmental organisations. In turn, this may be one reason why we did not find any differences in the poverty rate between incomplete and complex families.

Private transfers do benefit poor single-parents (Appendix 6.8). A slightly higher percentage of poor households (defined in terms of pre-transfer income) benefit from family networks. This pattern was particularly pronounced in late 1994 for poor single-parent families, among whom more than 50 per cent were receiving some private assistance, compared with 37 per cent for non-poor single-parent families.

The contribution of private transfers is especially important for poor households. In late 1996, for the one in two poor single parents receiving such assistance, the average contribution to their household income exceeded 47 per cent. The contribution was sizeable even for the non-poor, about 21 per cent. This support has tended to rise over the period under review.

In most cases, private transfers flow from parents to children. In late 1996, more than 22 per cent of poor single-parent households with children reported assistance from their parents, which in turn represented about 41 per cent of their income. This pattern is evident for families in general, in fact single parents do not appear to be especially advantaged either in terms of the frequency nor the size of support received from their parents. Children and grandparents are a much less frequent source of support in general, also for single parents. Relative to other family types, the proportion of poor single parents receiving assistance from friends is higher: almost 6 per cent in late 1996. For recipient families, these transfers represented more than 23 per cent of total income.

Alimony naturally is a much more frequently received and more important source of income for single parents relative to other types of families. At the same time, problems associated with the size and regularity of alimony payments have been documented (see Chapter 5). One survey of 1200 women in six towns in European Russia found that alimony amounted on average to only half the cost of children's basic food needs (Mozhina and Prokofieva 1997). It has been argued that the adoption of tighter legislation to govern alimony liabilities does not yet seemed to have improved the regularity of payment (ibid).

In 1994 more than one-fifth of poor single parents reported receipt of alimony, but by 1996 the share had dropped to 13 per cent. For non-poor single parents the share hovered around 13 per cent over the period. This is consistent with the rise in cases of officially reported non-payment of alimony in Russia, which has almost tripled over the period 1990-1995 (UNICEF, MONEE Project database).

The data nonetheless suggest that the real value of alimony for recipients rose significantly over the twelve months to late 1996, and as a share of income for poor recipients from 30 to 35 per cent. This could be a sign that the new Family Code adopted at the end of 1995 has effectively increased compliance in terms of amounts paid.

Finally, it is evident that the voluntary non-governmental sector is not, at least yet, providing much material support to poor single parents. Few households reported receiving such assistance, and among single parents the proportion was about the same for poor and non-poor families (3.5 per cent).

6.5 Conclusions

There have been several striking changes in the welfare status of single-parent families in Russia during the transition. Our analysis of nationally representative survey data over the period 1994-1996 has shown that, in the context of increasing aggregate poverty incidence, there has been widening dispersion in poverty rates among family types. Most dramatic has been the surge in poverty among single-parent families, whose poverty rate has almost tripled over a three-year period.

The family and individual characteristics of single-parent families suggest that their higher poverty incidence largely reflects gender disadvantage in the labour market, both in terms of lower employment rate and lower rate of pay in formal and informal jobs. However, there are clearly several characteristics that affect the welfare status of single-parent families and that cannot be attributed to a gender disadvantage. The absence of a spouse alters a Russian family's welfare status through three main effects: absence of a potential additional wage earner in the family; reduced capacity to engage in home production; in the case of marital split, the disruption of family income is only partly compensated by the receipt of alimony. A further factor characterizing single parents is the higher incidence of unemployment: single mothers had higher unemployment rates than both mothers and male heads in dual-parent families, even though Russian women generally experience lower unemployment rates than men.

The second task of the paper was to look at the impact of family composition, in particular single-parenthood, on income inequality. Our results suggested that in certain basic respects single parents do not comprise a homogeneous group distinct from the rest of the population. The analysis drew attention to the heterogeneity among single parents in terms of income levels. Within-group income inequality is far more important than inequality between different family types, even if the extent of inequality is less among single parents than among dual parents

International evidence suggests that the specific labour market characteristics and constraints facing single parents differ significantly from those faced by household heads in general, a possibility that was investigated using the RLMS. For Russia, we found that single-parent family earnings differ from dual-parent families not only in terms of the number of wage earners, but also in terms of the rate of pay and the number of hours worked by employed members. This confirms the general pattern of gender disadvantage in the labour market noted above. At the same time, inequalities in labour earnings between family types are generated mainly by the differences in the number of wage earners and in the variations in the rate of pay between families, more than the hours spent in the work force.

We saw that the value of public transfers, an important component in the income of single-parent families, contracted sharply. Yet errors of exclusion of the poor remain extensive. Single parents remain vulnerable to further diminution of the system of public transfers. Private transfers have helped to alleviate the poverty status of single parents, despite evident problems with respect to non-payment of alimony. They were also higher among incomplete than complex single-parent families, boosting the welfare status of the former relative to the latter.

In sum, we have identified a range of disturbing trends that have characterized single parents in Russia during the transition. Given that the number of single-parent families is expected to increase in conjunction with the wider social and economic changes that are taking place, these findings point to major social issues to be addressed by policy makers. Policy responses to date, as reviewed in this and the previous chapter, have been severely fiscally constrained and generally inadequate. The next chapter identified how children have been affected.

Appendix 6.1 Measures of Poverty

The **head count index** of poverty is given by the proportion of the population for whom total household expenditures (income) y is less than the poverty line z. It is the most frequently cited figure in this analysis, and has the advantage of simplicity. If q is the proportion of poor people in the sample population of size n, then the head count, H, is given by:

(1) $H = \dfrac{q}{n}$.

We present 'head counts' in terms of the share of individuals in the population, but also in terms of the share of households. We also use a simple head count measure of severe poverty. A household is considered as very poor if total expenditures are 50 per cent or less than its specific (regional) poverty line.

The poverty headcount measure is insensitive to differences in the depth of poverty. A way to look at the poverty deficit of the poor relative to the poverty line is to used the **poverty gap index**. Let Q be the subgroup of poor, the poverty gap is then given by:

(2) $P1 = \dfrac{1}{n} \displaystyle\sum_{i \in Q} \dfrac{(z_i - y_i)}{z_i}$

The poverty gap sheds light on the potential fiscal cost for eliminating poverty in a society. Summing all the poverty gaps in the sample population and taking the average provides an estimate of what would be the minimum cost of eliminating poverty, assuming perfect targeting.

The poverty gap measure may not adequately capture differences in the severity of poverty. The *Foster-Greer-Thorbecke* measure of the **severity of poverty**, sometimes referred to as 'P2', is a way to tackle this problem. It gives more weight to the consumption (income) gap of those households located furthest below the poverty line and is defined as:

(3) $P2 = \dfrac{1}{n} \displaystyle\sum_{i \in Q} \left(\dfrac{z_i - y_i}{z_i} \right)^2$

The severity index facilitates comparison of policies which are aiming to reach the poorest, but it is less intuitive and more difficult to interpret than the other two poverty measures.

Rather than estimating a binary model of the probability of being poor, a increasingly common practice is to estimate the ***expenditure-to-need ratio***, which is the ratio (or its logarithm) of total expenditure over the poverty threshold

$$(4)\ \frac{y_i}{z_i}$$

where y_i is total family expenditure, and z_i is the poverty threshold specific to family i (Ravallion, 1996). Lower values of this welfare ratio mean that a typical member of the household is absolutely poorer. In particular, the proportion of the population for whom the (log) ratio is lower than (zero) one gives the poverty headcount index.

Appendix 6.2 Family Characteristics, RLMS 1996
(percentages)

Characteristics	All households	Dual-parent households	Single-parent families
Number of adults (18 years or older)			
1	23.1	0.0	50.6
2	52.9	69.9	29.5
3	17.1	20.0	13.9
4 or more	6.9	10.1	6.0
Number of children			
0	52.6	-	-
1	25.7	51.5	73.8
2	17.9	40.5	23.5
3 or more	3.8	8.0	2.7
Number of children under six years			
0	81.0	57.8	68.2
1	15.8	34.2	30.8
2 or more	3.2	8.0	1.0
Number of working-age adults			
0	25.3	1.3	3.8
1	18.5	1.6	69.2
2	42.3	79.8	17.5
3 or more	13.9	17.3	9.5
Number of above working-age adults			
0	54.0	80.7	65.6
1	30.4	14.6	26.8
2+	15.6	5.7	7.6
Rural household	25.5	25.7	18.5
Average number of family numbers	2.8	4.0	3.0
Average number of employed in primary job	1.1	1.6	1.0
Average number of unemployed	0.1	0.2	0.2

Note: Elderly is defined according to Russian pension eligibility norms, that is, aged over 54 for women and 59 for men.

Appendix 6.3　Income Sources for Families with Children, RLMS 1994-1996

	Share of total family income		
	1994	**1995**	**1996**
Labour income	**38.1**	**36.5**	**36.7**
Single-parent	37.3	38.2	38.8
Dual-parent	53.0	50.7	51.2
Public transfers	**30.2**	**29.5**	**24.5**
Single-parent	28.0	25.6	23.4
Dual-parent	11.4	11.1	9.9
Private transfers	**7.1**	**7.0**	**9.1**
Single-parent	15.8	14.7	15.6
Dual-parent	8.0	7.7	9.7
Home production	**18.4**	**18.2**	**18.8**
Single-parent	13.0	11.9	13.1
Dual-parent	19.6	19.0	16.5
Other income	**6.2**	**8.8**	**10.9**
Single-parent	5.9	9.6	9.1
Dual-parent	8.0	11.5	12.7
Total	**100.0**	**100.0**	**100.0**

Source: RLMS rounds V, VI and VII.
Note: total income refers to real family income adjusted to June 1992 prices. Labour income includes salaries in cash and non cash. Public transfers include pensions, unemployment benefits, child benefits, student stipends, fuel benefits and apartment benefits (except for 1994). Private transfers include interfamily transfers, including alimonies, and charity transfers. Home production refers to the imputed value of home-produced goods. Other income includes capital income and sale of personal belongings.

Appendix 6.4 Components of Real Family Earnings, RLMS 1996

	Family earnings per employed members (rubles)	Hourly rate of pay (rubles)	Avg. monthly hours of work per employed members	Avg. number of wage earners
Single parents	3107	21.4	161.8	1.3
Dual parents	3710	26.1	168.7	1.8
Adults without children	3404	21.7	167.3	1.7
Elderly without children	2093	14.7	155.3	1.1

Note: Refers to family income and family earnings from main and second jobs.

Appendix 6.5 Inequality Decomposition Methodology

Following the approach used by Jenkins (1993), the mean logarithmic deviation (MLD) is the preferred inequality index because of its decomposability properties. If N is the population group of size n with mean income m, the MLD is given by:

$$(4) \quad I = \frac{1}{n} \sum_{i \in N} \log \left(\frac{m}{y_i} \right)$$

The population group can then be partitioned into K mutually exclusive sub-groups, according, for instance, to family structure. Considering that the kth groups have n_k members and group mean income m_k, the population share of group k is then $s_k = n_k/n$, and group k's mean income relative to the population mean income is given by $l_k = m_k/m$. The additive decomposability of I allows (4) to be rewritten as:

$$(5) \quad I = \sum_{i \in K} s_k I_k + \sum_{i \in K} s_k \log \left(\frac{1}{l_k} \right)$$

The mean logarithmic deviation index is decomposed into two components: the first term measures within-group inequalities – the weighted sum of the inequalities within each family type – and the second shows the contribution of between-group inequalities – inequalities remaining where each family's income is equal to the family type's mean income.

Appendix 6.6 Significance of Public Transfers in Household Income for Recipient Families with Children, RLMS 1994 and 1996

Public Transfers	Non-Poor (pre-transfer)				Poor (pre-transfer)			
	Per cent receiving the benefit		Income share for recipients		Per cent receiving the benefit		Income share for recipients	
	1994	1996	1994	1996	1994	1996	1994	1996
Pensions								
Single-parent	45.0	39.5	24.1	22.1	55.9	36.0	54.4	57.2
Dual-parent	20.5	17.4	19.7	17.9	28.6	15.7	52.7	46.0
Unemployment benefits								
Single-parent	2.7	1.6	6.9	5.8	4.7	1.1	44.4	23.5
Dual-parent	0.9	1.0	10.1	9.5	2.9	1.8	27.1	38.2
Child benefits								
Single-parent	56.8	37.1	5.8	7.3	52.0	38.6	12.1	22.8
Dual-parent	57.9	35.0	3.9	6.0	49.3	29.3	12.8	20.5
Student stipends								
Single-parent	8.1	5.5	3.8	5.2	11.2	5.3	9.4	12.2
Dual-parent	10.0	4.9	3.9	4.3	7.9	2.3	12.7	17.5
All public transfers[a]								
Single-parent	75.7	64.5	19.4	18.6	81.9	61.9	48.8	49.8
Dual-parent	70.8	50.4	9.7	11.4	65.7	42.4	36.3	34.6

Source: RLMS rounds 5 and 7.
[a]Includes fuel benefits for 1994 and both fuel and housing benefits for 1996.

Appendix 6.7 Errors of Exclusion for Specific Public Transfers

Household type	Per cent among non-poor		Per cent among poor	
	1994	1996	1994	1996
Not receiving any child benefits	42.3	64.7	49.9	68.4
All families with children	43.2	62.9	48.0	61.4
Single-parent				
Not receiving any unemployment benefits				
All families with unemployed members	90.4	94.4	91.3	92.9
Single-parent with unemployed members	70.0	85.7	79.2	95.3
Not receiving any pensions				
All families with pensioners				
or disabled members	5.8	28.9	1.6	31.3
Single-parent with pensioners				
or disabled members	5.8	15.6	3.3	27.8
Not receiving any scholarships				
All families with students	56.8	80.0	53.4	81.4
Single-parent with students	62.5	79.4	65.8	81.8

Source: RLMS rounds V and VII.

Appendix 6.8 Significance of Private Transfers in Household Income for Recipients

Type of private transfers	Non-poor (pre-transfer)				Poor (pre-transfer)			
	Per cent receiving the benefit		Income share for recipients		Per cent receiving the benefit		Income share for recipients	
	1994	1996	1994	1996	1994	1996	1994	1996
All private transfers								
Single-parent	36.9	37.9	26.3	20.7	50.4	40.2	45.9	47.3
Dual-parent	28.9	26.1	19.2	17.2	34.3	31.7	45.7	44.8
From parents								
Single-parent	13.5	11.3	29.1	18.7	18.9	22.2	47.5	40.5
Dual-parent	22.5	19.3	18.2	16.5	26.1	24.7	44.8	44.6
From children								
Single-parent	2.7	2.4	13.6	8.4	5.5	1.1	26.2	23.5
Dual-parent	0.3	0.1	5.2	11.5	1.1	1.8	21.5	31.9
From grandparents								
Single-parent	1.8	1.6	7.4	22.7	1.6	1.6	12.8	29.8
Dual-parent	1.9	2.2	9.9	4.5	1.8	1.5	22.3	27.6
From grandchildren								
Single-parent	0	0	0	0	0	0	0	0
Dual-parent	0.3	0	2.1	0	0	0.1	0	4
From other relatives								
Single-parent	6.3	5.6	21.3	23.1	11	10	27.6	27.8
Dual-parent	3.8	5.4	15	12.1	5.4	4.1	15.1	24.1
From friends								
Single-parent	4.5	8.1	18.1	14.7	10.2	5.8	25.8	23.4
Dual-parent	3.3	4.1	8.2	7.7	3.2	2.6	18.4	22.7
From other non-state organization								
Single-parent	4.5	0.8	5.5	19.8	3.9	3.7	15.5	22.2
Dual-parent	2	0.9	6.6	9.3	2.5	0.8	26.7	27.3
Alimony								
Single parent	22.5	20.2	12.8	12.4	20.5	13.2	30.3	34.9
Dual-parent	2.6	1	10	13	3.6	2.1	36.3	17.7

* We would like to thank Aline Coudouel, John Micklewright, Michel Sollogoub and Kitty Stewart for constructive comments and suggestions.

NOTES:

1 It is important to note that in some sections of this chapter we cover similar ground to Chapter 3, but from a completely different perspective. This chapter uses households as the unit of analysis, while Chapter 3 uses children. The categorization of households used in Chapter 3 is also different from the one used here, due to the former's specific objective of using panel data to look at changes in the living arrangements of children. This required a more detailed categorization of households and a different unit of analysis. The purposes of this chapter are, however, better served by using households as the unit of analysis and referring to the standard official categories of households.

2 As pointed out by Atkinson (1989), poverty may be analysed either in terms of a 'standard of living' or 'minimum rights to resources'. We adopt the former approach, and this leads to poverty being defined in terms of consumption (expenditures), as opposed to income. This also has further practical advantages that we discuss in the text below.

3 In late 1995, average expenditures on rents and utilities amounted to less than 4.5 per cent of total expenditures.

4 However, this is more the case in countries where capital markets are well developed, so that families are able to dissave or to borrow to finance current consumption.

5 See Popkin et al. (1996) for an elaboration of the approach used. Note that the consumption patterns were those of the second lowest income decile, collected by the official Family Budget Survey.

6 All the results reported here are derived from the RLMS for this period, unless otherwise stated.

7 See Klugman and Braithwaite (1998) for an overview.

8 The higher rates of poverty among single-parent families are also observed using the national poverty line adjusted for equivalence scales and economies of scale.

9 Poverty incidence by type of single parent – using the conventional Russian distinction of complex and incomplete families – was basically similar in 1994 and 1996.

10 This figure is based on the assumption that a single mother is not the head if there is a working-age male (e.g. her brother or father) in the household.

11 In late 1996, the share of (self-reported) unemployment was respectively 14 per cent among working-age males and 11 per cent among working-age females.

12 Background on the benefits paid in respect to childbirth and maternity is given in Chapter 5.

13 This heterogeneity is analyzed here in terms of income inequality. More recent Western sociological literature also stresses that families with one parent are probably as diverse as dual-parent households along psychological and interactional dimensions (see Sussman and Steinmetz, 1987).

14 We use actual hours worked, and wages received (rather than contract wages owed) in the preceding month. Given the prevalence of wage arrears, the latter figure would be misleading. We also include labour earnings from all sources, including primary and secondary employment. Similarly the hours worked include those worked in secondary as well as primary employment.

15 Due to benefit calculation rules, high inflation meant that the vast majority of beneficiaries received only the minimum unemployment benefit.

Chapter 7: Family Structure and Child Welfare Outcomes

Aline Coudouel and Mark Foley[*]

The trends in poverty that were examined in the previous chapter suggest increased hardship for large sections of the population. Increasing poverty incidence and increasing income and wage inequality are being compounded by decreasing allocation of government resources to social sectors. One would expect the decrease in income levels to be paralleled by a general deterioration in other aspects of well-being, such as health, security, and education (see UNICEF, 1998a).

In order to go beyond the household level monetary-based assessments of welfare, this chapter analyses the welfare outcomes for children and looks at the differences in outcomes by family structure in 1996. Looking at these differences without controlling for other determinants of child welfare outcome (such as income) does not permit us to estimate the overall impact of family structure on welfare. However, it provides a picture that is relevant for policy formulation. Knowing the dimensions of the disadvantages faced by children living in single-parent households is important per se, irrespective of the reasons for such differences. It is needed to motivate action from policy-makers and to inform on the appropriateness of targeting additional support to such children.

The next section reviews available evidence on the non-monetary dimensions of child welfare in transition. Section 7.2 looks at various frameworks for examining the impact of family structure on child welfare outcomes and provides a brief review of the evidence available, mainly for North America and Western Europe. Section 7.3 presents the data set used for the analysis and elaborates a framework for the analysis by defining both the different types of household and the various welfare measures under consideration. Section 7.4 presents the empirical results of the analysis for children in three different age groups. Section 7.5 concludes.

7.1 Deterioration in Child Welfare during the Transition

The transition has seen a general deterioration in child welfare indicators (see UNICEF 1999 for the most recent review). This reflects the increasing risks being faced by children in Russia. The fulfilment of basic needs, including survival, good health, and adequate nutrition in addition to the ability of children to avert risks, through inclusion and participation, have been jeopardised in the past few years.

The deterioration can be illustrated, for young children, along several dimensions relating to both health status and access to services. First, by the increase in the mortality rate of young children: from 21.9 deaths of under-five year-olds per thousand live births in 1989 to 25.0 in

Figure 7.1: Trends in Child Welfare Indicators: Education Enrolment Rates, 1989-1996

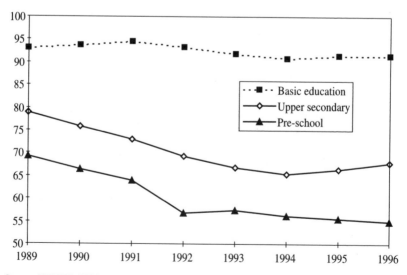

Source: UNICEF (1998a).

1996 (UNICEF 1998a); second by the deterioration of preventive basic health care; and third by the decline in enrolment in pre-school facilities and in participation in developmental activities (Figure 7.1).

The teenage and young adult age group has also experienced falling enrolment in post-compulsory education (Figure 7.1). Unemployment for young persons (15-24 years-old) was estimated to be 19.1 per cent in 1996 (OECD-CCET labour market database), much higher than for the older age cohorts within the working age population.

Some health indicators also indicate changes in behaviour among young people. For example, the number of cases of syphilis has soared (Figure 7.2), and an increasing proportion of teenage mortality rates is caused by accidents, poisonings and violence (from 45.4 deaths per 100,000 children aged 5-19 years in 1989, to 54.9 in 1996) or by suicide, especially among boys. Overall crime rates have gone up, and the increased participation of children in criminal activities is also a sign of the troubles facing Russian youth (Figure 7.2).

Figure 7.2: Trends in Child Welfare Outcomes: Criminal Sentencing and Sexually-Transmitted Disease, 1989-1996

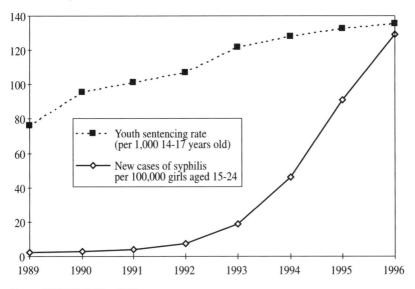

Source: UNICEF (1998a, 1999).

The above indicators cover only a limited number of dimensions but point to a general deterioration. Given the findings of the preceding chapters about poverty in single-parent households and the increase in the number of children who live in single-parent households, we might well expect particularly adverse welfare outcomes for this group of children. Indeed, income can be expected to play an important role in shaping child welfare outcomes.

Similarly, the situation of children living in reconstructed households is of concern, since they are likely to have experienced changes in resources and spells in a single-parent household, and there is some reason to assume that the household resources might be less readily allocated to stepchildren. Many single parents eventually remarry and therefore numerous children who once lived in single-parent households now live with a step-parent (about 10 per cent of 15-22 year-olds and 9 per cent of 11-14 year-olds in the RLMS 1996).

Basing the analysis of children's welfare on the current level of household consumption can be restrictive for different reasons. First, the measures of income or consumption available in most household surveys can only be used as a proxy and remain imprecise (for a review, see Ravallion 1994). In addition, monetary measures suffer from well-documented limitations since the valuation of in-kind incomes or benefits is approximate at best.

Second, household-based measures assume pooling of resources and their fair distribution among household members. While household consumption is important for the living standards of women and children, it is not inevitable that all members of the household will share the same living standards (Haddad and Kanbur, 1990). There are many social and cultural factors that might influence the allocation of resources within households. These include the prevailing social norms of gender and kinship relationships, the manner in which income enters into the household and the relative economic power of household members. It might be the case, for instance, that single parents invest in their children despite low incomes, that stepchildren are neglected by step-parents, or that natural children receive preferential treatment over stepchildren. There is a need to go beyond household-level data and to focus on child-specific characteristics in order to avoid the assumption of equality within the household.

Last but not least, child welfare outcomes can be expected to be influenced and determined by a broad range of factors and not merely by the household income or consumption level. In particular, changes in family structure can be expected to have long-term cumulative effects on child welfare. Income as a measure of well-being does not capture elements contributing to the quality of life, such as access to clean water, living conditions, health status, access to education, etc. In May 1995, opinion polls suggested that Russians regarded low income as their most serious problem, but other elements, such as poor health and medical care, a sense of hopelessness about the future, and job insecurity, were also major concerns for large parts of the population (Zubova and Kovalyova, 1997). Thus, focusing on current household income and expenditures may mean that other important factors influencing child welfare are neglected.

7.2 Family Structure and Child Welfare Outcomes: Theory and Evidence

Analytical frameworks for the study of the impact of family structure on child welfare outcomes distinguish between direct and indirect mechanisms.[1] The direct mechanisms by which family structure may affect child outcomes are related to economic resources, socialization and family stress. We examine each of these in turn, although they are not mutually exclusive.

The first emphasizes economic resources as a determinant of child welfare outcomes. The formal economic model which underpins this approach is the human capital framework developed by Becker (1981) and applied to children by Becker and Tomes (1986). According to this theory, parents decide to allocate the family's available economic resources for consumption, with the aim of improving their own well-being and investing in their children. The argument is that, in single-parent households, fewer resources in terms of time and income can be expected to result in lower investment in children. Similarly, fewer resources are expected to be available for children in reconstructed families because income from step-parents may not be as readily available to the child as that from biological parents, and because the non-custodial parent might be less likely to invest in the child if there is a step-parent in the household. This approach is based on the hypothesis that economic resources influence achievement, net of other background elements such as the education levels of parents.

Second, factors which can be expected to have a direct influence are sometimes summarized as the 'socialization' mechanism (Seltzer, 1994). This acts through the influence of role models and socialization during childhood, and more generally through the child-rearing environment. This in turn suggests the need for adequate support, supervision and control of children. It is possible that single parents or step-parents have less time or inclination to perform these functions, although it is also possible that single parents develop a particularly close relationship with their children precisely because of the absence of a spouse.

Finally, the stress perspective focuses on the disruptions experienced by children rather than on situations themselves and suggests that changes in living arrangements have a negative impact on child welfare. Conversely, living in dual-parent households where conflicts arise can also generate important stress. Changes in economic status, residential move, loss of family, school friends and social networks can all be stressful events, which have implications for child welfare. This mechanism suggests that it is important to distinguish the route by which the child enters into a period of time in a single-parent household (death of a parent, divorce, or non-marital birth).

While a large number of single-parent households have low income, changes in income levels are more likely to be experienced by those who enter single-parenthood through divorce rather than via non-marital births. The dynamics of poverty have been shown to be different for divorce-related single-parent households (Garfinkel and McLanahan, 1986; Duncan et al., 1984). These enter poverty following the loss of a bread-winner (structural change), while in other types of households poverty usually results from a decrease in income (due to unemployment for instance) but without loss of earning capacity (the unemployed can engage into home production or return to the labour market).

In addition to the direct influence of family structure on child outcomes, there are indirect mechanisms of influence. Parents choose the community in which their children grow up and such choices might be constrained by family structure (although it is more likely to be constrained by economic resources). The local community or neighbourhood can be expected to affect attainments through the influence of role models, peer behaviour and collective monitoring, and through the importance of the relative situation of a child compared to that of other children in the community (Jencks and Mayer, 1990).

The impact of these mechanisms, however, will also depend on the environment in which they take place. Society and governments (as agents of society) set the basic environment within which families and children make their choices. Some government policies will have a direct effect on children, others have indirect effect, as the comparative analysis of government family policy toward single parents in Chapter 4 suggests. State social investments in education, childcare, nutrition, health, and public health can, for instance, weaken the link between some child welfare outcomes and parental economic and human resources. The Russian Federation inherited a strong and universal system of basic social services, including childcare, health and education provision, which can be expected to limit the adverse influence of low parental income on child welfare outcomes. In addition, income inequality was until recently relatively limited in the Russian Federation and the guarantee of low pay employment, together with the extensive system of social benefits, tended to limit income differences between various types of households.

In the transition, however, some of these equalizing tendencies have been weakened, and this may exacerbate differences between types of households. For example, access to childcare and primary health care services has been eroded and social benefits have lost most of their value. This can be expected to lead to an increased polarization of Russian society with regard to socio-economic indicators, and implies that the impact on different types of households will vary.

The relative significance of the different mechanisms described above can be expected to vary according to the age of the child, since both the effect of reduced economic resources and the emotional impact of shock or disruption on the child's well-being will be different for the various age groups. For instance, parental divorce is often found to be more detrimental for children of pre-school age, even if harmful consequences are also reported in late adolescence (Longfellow, 1979; Wallerstein and Blakeslee, 1989). Furthermore, the impact of changes in family structure on family resources also depends on the timing of the changes in the life-cycle of the parents. The impact of divorce for young parents who have limited economic resources can be expected to be greater than the impact among older parents with greater earning capacity and a greater number of assets. In addition, the length of the spell in a single-parent household could be expected to be an important influence on child welfare outcomes. The gender of the child is also important because boys and girls are likely to react differently to family changes (for example, Ermisch and Francesconi, 1997, find different results in terms of educational attainment).

Empirical investigation of the link between family structure and child welfare outcomes is largely limited to the West and in particular to the United States. A useful review of the literature is provided by Haveman and Wolfe (1995). In terms of educational outcomes, children and adolescents from single-parent households have been found to have lower educational achievement and higher drop-out rates from school (Entwisle and Alexander, 1995). Some studies distinguish between adolescent girls and boys, and find that having had spells in a single-parent household (even if the child later lives in a reconstructed family) has an impact on boys' educational attainment but has only a minor effect on girls (Ermisch and Francesconi, 1997; Ni Broclchain et al., 1994). The evidence is not conclusive as to the magnitude of the effect of family structure, which varies largely across studies, from modest to rather large. The survey reports that the probability of high school graduation by children who have lived in single-parent households is 5-16 per cent lower than that of children in intact families (Haveman, Wolfe and Spaulding, 1991; Sandefur, McLanahan, and Wojtkiewicz, 1992).

When looking at labour market achievements, it appears that having lived in a single-parent household results in lower earnings, even after controlling for educational levels. Studies also suggest that adolescent girls living in single-parent households, and especially those experiencing family disruption, are more likely to have a non-marital birth or experience a broken marriage themselves (Plotnick, 1992; Bumpass and McLanahan, 1989).

Children living in intact families are also less likely to suffer from health problems than those who have experienced divorce or separation (Mauldon, 1990). This study also shows that the relationship between health problems and a history of family disruption persists even if the mother remarries. It also argues that the impact on health depends on the age and gender of the child, with younger children being particularly vulnerable. Other studies point to the importance of distinguishing between single parents who are divorced, separated, widowed and never-married, and between those who live alone and those who share with other family members (Aquilino, 1996).

There is mixed evidence with regard to the relative importance of the various mechanisms through which family structure can influence child welfare outcomes. Most surveys however point to the key role of economic resources as the main determinant of outcomes (Enstwisle and Alexander, 1995; Mauldon 1990; Ermisch and Francesconi, 1997). Economic differences account for many of the adverse effects of having lived in a single-parent household, and much of the single-parent effect is in fact an income effect. Thus, while the previous section showed that a narrow focus on monetary indicators when evaluating the effect of family structure on child welfare is likely to lead to an incomplete picture of the welfare outcomes, the available evidence on the actual mechanisms through which family structure influences child welfare suggests that income accounts for a large part of the negative welfare outcomes for children in single-parent households.

7.3 Data and Variables

In this Chapter the analysis of family structure and the welfare of Russian children is carried out using the Russian Longitudinal Monitoring Survey (RLMS). This section describes briefly the data set and the different household types which were defined. We then turn to the definition of the different measures of child welfare outcomes which can be computed using the RLMS.

The Data Set

The RLMS was described in Chapter 1. This chapter draws on a special questionnaire which covered topics related to children, including child-care arrangements, children's physical activities, utilisation of medical services, health evaluation, anthropometric measurement, time-use, and food consumption. The questions for children under 16 years-old are usually answered by their mother, or by the adult in the family who looks after the child. Children aged 16 years and older answered the question-naire for adults which covers education, labour market situation, income and health evaluation.

In the present chapter, we focus on child welfare outcomes and therefore chose the child as the unit of analysis. All children, including sib-lings or children living in the same households, are taken as separate units.

Rounds V - VII of the survey (conducted in 1994, 1995 and 1996) comprise a panel, with households and individuals being followed for the three points in time. The limited attrition rates and the relatively low mobility of young individuals means that the number of children observed over the period is stable. However, the data set does not include information for the intervening periods; i.e. retrospective infor-mation on changes in family structure is not collected, nor on past changes in income and parental activities. Thus the 'snapshot' nature of the information prevents us from using the panel structure of the data to build a model explaining causality; we therefore limit ourselves to analysing the relationships between variables.

A typology appropriate for the present purposes was defined for the last three rounds (V to VII). Since these cover only two years and many of the outcomes measured react to changes with a lag, we limit our analysis to the last available observation (Round VII). The situation in previous rounds is referred to only when this is directly relevant to the discussion of the results.

Household Types

In line with the discussion of the mechanisms in section 7.2, the analysis should ideally distinguish between the following different types of house-holds: (1) number of parents; (2) type of parents (natural versus step); (3) presence of other adult members; (4) type of entry into single-parent households; and (5) duration of the child's spell in a single-parent house-hold. The analysis therefore classifies the households using three criteria.

First, a distinction is made between households with a single parent and those with two parents. The hypothesis is that the former are likely to provide lower stimulus to educational achievement, as well as less involvement in and less supervision of the child's education activities. In addition, the economic resources of single-parent households are likely to be lower than those of dual-parent households with negative effects for child welfare. Throughout the analysis, the living arrangements of parents are taken into consideration rather than their marital status. Therefore, no distinction is made between married or cohabiting couples, when referring to either natural-parent households or step-parent households.

Second, within dual-parent households a distinction is made between biological parents and step-parents. The hypothesis is that children are likely to receive less stimulus to educational achievement, and less commitment and involvement from step-parents than from natural parents. While the economic conditions of reconstituted households are usually similar to that of natural parents families, the children may receive less of the income from the step-parent or less income from the non-custodial parent. The presence of step-parents might offset part but not all of the losses, since the formation of such reconstituted families can generate tensions and require residential mobility, all of which will affect child welfare.

Lastly, within single-parent households a distinction is made between those with no other adults present, and those with other adults (non-parent) in the household. The presence of additional adults could be expected to increase family resources (especially in terms of income and childcare), which in turn would influence child welfare outcomes.

Ideally, the analysis should also distinguish between the routes of entry into single-parent households,[2] the child's age when beginning a period in a single-parent household, and the duration of the spells in various types of household structures. However, these dimensions cannot be captured by the available data.

The categories used throughout the chapter are based on the typology developed in Chapter 3 (see Table 3.2). We collapse the more detailed categories into the following five categories: dual-parent households, subdivided into households with two natural parents and households with one natural parent and one step-parent; single-parent households, subdivided into households with only one adult parent and households with one parent and other adults; and households with no parents.

The number of children in each category for 1996 (Round VII) is presented in Table 7.1. The Table shows that the main category is that of dual-parent families: almost 80 per cent of the children in the sample are covered by this category. Within this category, most children live in natural-parent families, although the proportion living with step-parents increases with age, with up to around 10 per cent of children aged 15-22 years living with step-parents. The share of children in single-parent households varies between 15 per cent for children under seven years and 22 per cent for those aged 19-22. Within this category, it is interesting to note that younger children are more likely to live in households with other adults (11 per cent of children under 7 years) than older children.

Table 7.1: Distribution of Children by Family Type and Age Group, RLMS 1996

	Number of children by age group [% of column]					
Family type	0-6	7-10	11-14	15-18	19-22	Total 0-22
Dual parents	**688**	**553**	**553**	**425**	**216**	**2435**
of which:	**[82.1]**	**[82.3]**	**[79.2]**	**[75.8]**	**[63.5]**	**[78.3]**
2 natural parents	663	518	492	374	179	2226
	[79.1]	[77.1]	[70.5]	[66.7]	[52.7]	[71.6]
1 natural and 1 step-parent	25	35	61	51	37	209
	[3.0]	[5.2]	[8.7]	[9.1]	[10.9]	[6.7]
Single parent	**129**	**107**	**121**	**105**	**73**	**535**
of which:	**[15.4]**	**[15.9]**	**[17.3]**	**[18.7]**	**[21.5]**	**[17.2]**
1 parent alone	40	50	67	53	44	254
	[4.8]	[7.4]	[9.6]	[9.5]	[12.9]	[8.2]
1 parent and other adults	89	57	54	52	29	281
	[10.6]	[8.5]	[7.7]	[9.3]	[8.3]	[9.0]
No parents	21	12	24	31	51	139
	[2.5]	[1.8]	[3.4]	[5.5]	[15.0]	[4.5]
TOTAL	**838**	**672**	**698**	**561**	**340**	**3109**
	[100.0]	**[100.0]**	**[100.0]**	**[100.0]**	**[100.0]**	**[100.0]**

Most results in this chapter are presented in a way that allows comparison of children in dual-parent households with those in single-parent households. However, reference will also be made to the two types of dual-parent households and to the two types of single-parent households. Note that details on the outcomes for all the categories are given in Tables 7.3, 7.4 and 7.5 in the appendix. When referring to 'all children', we also include children living without parents (either on their own or with other adults). This last category is small and heterogeneous. For example, it includes a 3 year-old girl living with her aunt and uncle and also a 17 year-old teenager who lives with older siblings. The situation of the children in this category can therefore be expected to vary greatly, with some living in almost typical dual-parent households and others in potentially insecure environments.

Outcome Measures

Having defined a typology of family types, we turn to the definition of the different measures of child welfare outcomes used in the analysis. The selection and definition of such measures is motivated by the theoretical frameworks reviewed in Section 7.2, as well as specific features of the Russian context and by the types of information which can be derived from the RLMS. The groups of indicators used focus on children's health status, their education and employment, and health and risk-taking behaviour.

In this chapter, the focus is on child-specific outcomes. As argued in section 7.1 above, income is very important to the well-being of children, but there are also other determinants. The choice of indicators in this analysis is motivated by the basic needs approach and the capability approach developed by Streeten and Burki (1978) and Sen (1985, 1992) respectively. The first approach considers the fulfilment of a set of basic needs as a measure of well-being. Basic needs include survival, good health, adequate nutrition and clothing. The second approach widens the range of welfare components by defining well-being in terms of capability to perform a wide range of human functions. 'Functioning', in addition to the fulfilment of basic needs, covers elements such as inclusion and participation in community and measures of satisfaction, happiness, or self-respect. These approaches have become accepted in the development economic literature, as well as by such international organisations as UNDP and the World Bank.

The domains considered in this analysis reflect the 'functioning' which children should be capable of achieving, whether as children or when they become adults. They include health, education, economic independence, and healthy lifestyles. While direct measurement of such functioning is not possible, the analysis concentrates on indicators which capture elements of these domains. Some of the measures selected are immediate outcomes, while others are also important for the child's future since they turn into enabling or risk factors for other child outcomes.

The selection of these dimensions is also motivated by the current Russian context. It has been emphasized in this and the previous chapters that there has been a decline in basic indicators of well-being since the early 1990s. Access to education and primary health care have deteriorated during the transition and indicators of negative health behaviour have increased.

The choice of indicators of child well-being, however, also represents a compromise between what should be measured and what can be measured. The present data set, although extensive, does not cover some aspects of child well-being which would be relevant for the current analysis. In particular, information on mortality, sexually-transmitted diseases, subjective well-being, integration in social networks, educational achievement, time use, quality of life, and criminal activities are not included in the survey.

The indicators selected vary according to age group (and sometimes gender) in order to reflect the different problems associated with different stages of life. In the present analysis, three different age groups of children are analysed separately for different reasons. First, the framework presented above suggests that family structure and family-related changes are likely to affect children in different age groups and gender in varying ways. In addition, children at different ages have different needs. For instance, teenagers are usually healthy and have passed the most critical age in terms of health risks. On the other hand, they are exposed to new types of risks (such as teenage pregnancy) largely irrelevant for younger age groups. Another example comes from the fact that, because school is compulsory for a certain age group (and almost universally provided in practice), enrolment in education might have greater consequences for younger pre-school children in terms of development, and for older children (post compulsory school age), in terms of opportunities for their future. Consequently, children have been classified in three groups: children under 7 years, children aged 7-14 years (compulsory school age), and children aged 15 years and older.

Child health is in itself an important welfare outcome but is also an important determinant of, and condition for, other outcomes, some of which we cannot examine here. The data set provides a number of variables that can be analysed in order to assess different aspects of health status, including:

- Anthropometric measurement (measurement of body size). This reflects the past and present nutritional status of young children, and is a particularly important indicator of child welfare, as it can capture indicators of the child's physical and intellectual development (reflecting also future capabilities) and can also be linked to child morbidity and mortality. (UNICEF 1998b; Behrman, 1992).
- Immunisation prevalence. This is an important preventive measure against child morbidity and mortality.
- Health problems incidence. This subjective measure attempts to capture general health status.

Another group of variables is used to measure the child's participation in education and employment. Participation and attainment in education partly depend on other welfare outcomes (such as the child's health status) and in turn influence other welfare outcomes (such as the future ability to achieve economic independence). The following measures are used here:

- Attendance and enrolment in the educational system are analysed by age group. For young children, this is relevant due to the developmental and socializing role of pre-school. For children in the age groups for which education is compulsory, non-enrolment strongly inhibits the development of capabilities. For children beyond this age (15 years), participation in education can be taken as an indicator of the choices available to the individual and of future well-being.

- The number of grades completed compared to age of the child is used to assess education performance (as evidence of repeating grades etc.).
- The number of grades completed, for older children, is taken to measure their educational attainments, which in turn will affect their future well-being.
- The occupation (work versus economic inactivity) of children who have finished their education is used as a measure of economic achievement and future opportunities.

Finally, indicators of behaviour are selected, which will partly depend on past health and education status, and which will in turn influence the capacity of a child to invest in human capital and obtain economic security in the future. Two main variables provided in the data set are used:[3]

- The prevalence of drinking and smoking. This is taken to reflect negative health behaviour and to be an indicator of future well-being.
- The prevalence of pregnancy and abortions among girls. This can be interpreted as acting as a constraint on girls' education and their economic and social participation.

These variables do not cover all the dimensions which should ideally be covered. However, the data set does provide a valuable set of indicators which can be used to build up a picture of child welfare outcomes.

7.4 Child Welfare Outcomes and Family Structure in Russia in 1996

Following the analytical framework developed above, the analysis of child welfare outcomes distinguishes between children of different ages: children of pre-school age (0-6 years), children of compulsory school age (7-14 years) and young adults or adolescents in the post-compulsory school age group (15-22 years).

Children of Pre-School Age (0-6 years)

Here we look at the health and educational status (for those in the kindergarten age group) of the pre-school children.

The health status of a child in the first years of life is both an important welfare outcome in itself and an extremely important factor which will in turn influence the child's future development. In the Russian Federation, the health status of the population has been worsening in many dimensions since the onset of transition, with the lowest point being reached during 1993-1994, after which some of the trends are more favourable (UNICEF, 1997). Children are now born with less favourable conditions than at the beginning of transition (a higher share of children with low-birth weight, congenital malformation and complications at birth, UNICEF, 1999). Both morbidity and mortality of young children has shown negative trends. The child mortality rate increased over 1989-1996 (from 22 to 25 per 1,000 for those under 5 years) and the incidence of some infectious diseases has increased dramatically since 1989 for both children and adults (UNICEF, 1998a). Some of these trends might be linked to drops in living standards, but they are also connected to the reduced supply of health services – state expenditure on health has remained constant in relative terms, at 2.2 per cent of GDP in 1989 and 1995, but GDP has dropped by over 40 per cent in the same period (WHO, 1998; EBRD, 1997).

In order to test whether household structure is an important correlate of the child's health status, we focus on three aspects of child health: (1) nutritional status; (2) immunization status, which indicates the degree of preventive health care; and (3) health problems which reflect the rate of occurrence of illness. Figure 7.3 presents some of the main differences observed between single- and dual-parent households, while Table 7.3 in the appendix provides more information on all categories of households used in this analysis.

Anthropometric information can be used to measure the prevalence of 'wasting' and 'stunting'. Wasting (low weight for height) is usually interpreted as an indicator of recent severe malnutrition, while stunting (low height for age) is an indicator of persistent malnutrition over a longer period of time. RLMS data suggests that the prevalence of stunting increased dramatically in Russia in the period 1992-1994, rising from 9 to 15 per cent for children aged 0-24 months.[4] There was a subsequent decline to around 8 per cent in 1996. Information for older children (aged 2-6 years) shows less variation over time, while the preva-

Figure 7.3: Welfare Outcomes by Family Type, RLMS 1996
(percentages)

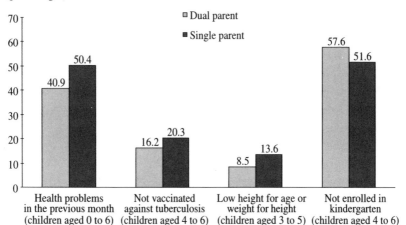

lence of wasting does not indicate any major acute nutritional problems among young children. The improvement between 1994 and 1996 is particularly surprising given the overall increase in poverty discussed in the previous chapter, as well as the general decrease of food consumption over the period.[5] It should, however, be kept in mind that stunting develops slowly and reflects past nutritional intake.

The anthropometric status of children aged 6 to 36 months shows a greater impact of malnutrition. The difference in the incidence of stunting or wasting across household types was negligible in 1994, but relatively large in 1996, with 13.6 per cent of the children living in single-parent households being affected and only 8.5 per cent of those living with two parents. This suggests that dual-parent households have been better able than single parents to benefit from the general improvement.

Immunization is an important preventive measure which can help combat child morbidity and mortality. It has become particularly important in the Russian Federation where the incidence of some infectious diseases has been increasing during the transition. The number of new cases of diphtheria in the population increased sevenfold from 1989 to 1997 (and reached a peak in 1994/1995), while the number of cases of tuberculosis doubled (UNICEF, 1999). Although official statistics report an increase in vaccination coverage (up to 95 per cent of the relevant population in 1996), the RLMS shows both a lower level of, and a decrease in, coverage in most vaccines over 1992-1996[6] (see Zohoori et al., 1997).

Differences in immunization coverage across household types are relatively small. However, the general pattern points to lower coverage for children in single-parent households (for children in the 4-6 years age group, who should have received all the vaccinations under consideration). One exception is tuberculosis, with over 20 per cent of children from single-parent households not vaccinated compared to 16 per cent for those in two-parent households. Since tuberculosis tends to be associated with poverty (UNICEF, 1997) and single-parent households have a higher – and more rapidly increasing – poverty incidence, the risk of contracting tuberculosis is even larger for children in single-parent households.

The foregoing evidence on differences in nutritional status and preventive care suggest that children from single-parent households might be more likely to suffer from health problems than those from dual-parent households. The self-reported occurrence of problems is indeed higher among the former category (over 50 per cent of children under 7 years in single-parent households) than among the latter (41 per cent). This pattern is particularly strong for children under three years, with a higher than average incidence for single-parent households. Interestingly, within two-parent families, the frequency of illness is higher among children in stepfamilies, at levels similar to those in single-parent households (see Table 7.3 in the appendix).

When looking at the prevalence of specific symptoms, the pattern is the same as above (although the differences are not always statistically significant). Children in dual natural parent households show the least number, followed by those in single-parent households and finally those in reconstructed households.

It should, however, be noted that, in the case of sickness, the probability that a child visits a doctor, is prescribed medicine, or takes medicine is very similar across the different family structure categories. This suggests that health services remain accessible to all, although the quality of the services might vary widely.[7]

To summarise: the health situation of children in single-parent households appears to be worse than that of children living with two parents, although the differences are not always statistically significant. The presence of other adults in single-parent households does not appear to make a difference to the health status of the child. Among dual-parent households, there are signs of relatively large differences between children from natural and reconstructed households, which would place the latter in a similar or worse situation than children in single-parent households. This is in accordance with studies in the USA which concluded that children who have experienced a parental separation are significantly more likely to experience health problems than those in intact families, irrespective of the presence of a step-parent (Mauldon, 1990).

The motivation for looking at kindergarten enrolments lies in the developmental and socializing roles which such institutions can play. The decline in aggregate enrolment rates to 55 per cent in 1996 (UNICEF, 1998a) has been noted in chapters 5 and 6. Part of the reduction has taken place on the supply side, with numerous kindergartens attached to enterprises or co-operatives being closed or handed over to local government authorities. Some have been replaced by modern private kindergartens, but these tend to charge high fees. As a result of a deterioration in the quality of care, increases in fees, decreasing income levels and lower female labour force participation, the demand for childcare has also decreased, and parents have been looking for alternative childcare arrangements (Klugman et al., 1997; and UNICEF, 1998a). The problems posed by the reduction in the supply of kindergartens can be expected to be particularly important for single-parent families. This is especially true for those without other adult members, who thus have fewer alternatives with respect to childcare.

The educational system in Russia has traditionally played a significant role in the provision of health services and nutritional programmes. Children who attend kindergartens not only receive instruction in cognitive and social skills, but they are also given vaccinations, regular medical check-ups and nutritious meals. Our data shows the correlation between enrolment in kindergarten and immunization to be relatively strong in 1994, with 82 per cent of those enrolled fully immunized, against 60 per cent of those not enrolled. In 1996, the correlation is still positive but no longer statistically significant.

In terms of household structure, it appears that children from single-parent households are more likely to be enrolled in kindergartens (children aged four to six years) than those from dual-parent households (enrolment rates of 48 and 42 per cent respectively). However, enrolment in kindergarten appears to be conditioned more by access to alternative childcare arrangements than by the type of household structure. Both the labour force participation of the mother and the presence of other non-working adults in the household are the main factors determining enrolment. There appears to be a strong link between labour force participation of the mother and attendance, with only 21 per cent of children with non-working mothers enrolled, versus 45 per cent of those with working mothers in 1996 (14 and 43 per cent respectively in 1994). Within single-parent households, the presence of other adults in the household is also correlated with enrolment in kindergarten. In 1994, children aged three to six years living with one parent and other adults were less likely to be enrolled (27 per cent enrolled) than those living only with one parent (36 per cent). By 1996, the overall enrolment rate had increased from 30 to 46 per cent, and the difference between the two categories of single-parent households had declined.

In summary, the RLMS data suggests that the health status of preschool children living in single-parent households is worse than that of children living with their two natural parents. In terms of educational advantage in early childhood development, the evidence presented here on kindergarten enrolment suggests that the probability of enrolment depends more on the presence of alternative childcare possibilities (which in turn depends on the labour force participation of mothers or on the presence of other adults in the household) than on the type of family structure.

Children of Compulsory School Age (7-14 years)

This group should be looked at separately from the younger and older age cohorts for several reasons. First, as noted above, education is compulsory for these children, and they can be expected to be relatively healthy, having survived the critical first years of life, and not yet being subject to the health problems linked to adolescence. It should also be noted that, unlike younger children, children in this group were born before the beginning of transition. They can therefore be expected to have benefited from previously higher coverage levels – both in health care and in kindergarten facilities – during their early years. Finally, children in this age group are usually not confronted with the choices and opportunities their older siblings face during adolescence. For all these reasons, variation by household structure can be expected to be small – at least smaller than for other age groups.

The general picture of health status provided by the data is that of children healthier than their younger siblings, especially those in the 10-14 years age group. However, despite better average health status, some (small) differences between children in dual- and single-parent households persist. The health status of those living in a stepfamily, as was the case for younger children, is lower than that of children with two natural parents, with levels similar to those living with only one parent (see Table 7.4).

For instance, the proportion of children having health problems is very similar among the different groups but, as shown in Figure 7.4, the proportion of children with a cough over the week preceding the survey is less than 1 in 5 in dual-parent families and more than 1 in 4 in single-parent families (significant difference). When looking at other health

Figure 7.4: Welfare Outcomes by Family Type: Children Aged 7-14, RLMS 1996 (percentages)

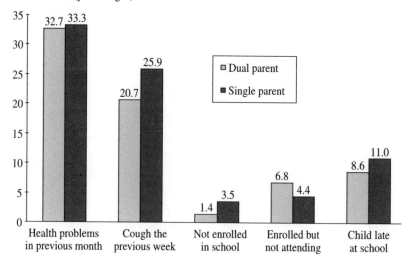

problems, this general pattern is maintained, with children from natural dual-parent households scoring best and children from single-parent households and with two non-natural parents alternating for second and third position.

Access to medicine and to health services does not appear to depend on family structure. Children from single-parent households see health workers and take medicine slightly more frequently than those from complete families, which is consistent with their higher reported morbidity.[8]

The most commonly used indicator of child educational outcomes is school enrolment. Being enrolled is a necessary condition for efficient learning of appropriate subject matter, but it is not a sufficient one. Learning also depends on attendance, progress through the system, success in assimilating the material, quality of teaching, and relevance of the curriculum. We have direct and secondary information on these additional dimensions.

Overall enrolment rates for compulsory education in the Russian Federation have decreased only marginally since the beginning of transition, from around 93.0 per cent in 1989 to 91.4 per cent in 1996 (UNICEF, 1998a), showing that the drop has been mainly in attendance rates for pre- and post-compulsory education. Previous analysis using the RLMS has shown that enrolment rates do not differ significantly between urban and rural areas and across income groups. The RLMS confirms very high rates of enrolment, with less than 2 per cent of children in the 7-14 years old group not being enrolled. Despite high enrolment rates, children from single-parent households are less likely to be enrolled than those with two natural parents, and children from households with stepparents rank between the two other categories, as shown in Figure 7.4 and Table 7.4 in the appendix. The difference is larger at the lower secondary level (children aged 10-14 years), with four per cent of the children from single-parent households, 2 per cent of those from stepfamilies and only 1 per cent of those with two natural parents not enrolled.

The non-attendance rate – absence from school the week preceding the survey – for children in compulsory education is 6.3 per cent. This means that a total of around 8 per cent are either not enrolled in school, or are enrolled but not attending – a relatively low rate by Western standards. Children in primary school (age 7-10 years) are found to miss school more frequently if they live in dual-parent households (whether natural or reconstructed) than if they live in single-parent households, possibly reflecting the availability of alternative care arrangements in the case of sickness in dual-parent households.

In order to assess the development of the child at school, we analyse the extent to which children are 'late' in their studies. Lateness is defined as being more than one grade below the standard grade for the age of the child. This might indicate late entry in school or repetition of a class and is a sign of disadvantage. Children from single-parent households are found to be at a disadvantage, with 11.0 per cent of them being 'late', versus 8.6 per cent for children of dual-parent households, as shown in Figure 7.4. Once again, within dual-parent households, children living in a reconstructed household have a situation similar to those living with a single parent. The difference across household types is more important for children in lower secondary than for those at primary levels (see Table 7.4 in the Appendix).

Finally, we use a survey of the determinants of achievements in science and mathematics for 13 year-olds to complement our analysis.[9] The results of this survey showed that achievement is strongly influenced by parental education (also taken to reflect income, which is not dealt with by the survey) and by school characteristics. Interestingly, family structure (number of parents present) did not have any significant relationship with achievement once the other dimensions were taken into account. This would support the hypothesis that the influence of household structure on child welfare is mediated by household resources, as argued in section 7.2 above.

Overall, the disparities among children of compulsory school age in different household types are small. Children aged 7-14 years appear to be relatively healthy and their educational process does not appear to be much affected by their household environment. Some small differences emerge between children from different types of households, pointing again to lower child welfare outcomes in single-parent households and in reconstructed families with respect to health and education status.

Children of Post-Compulsory School Age (15-22 years)

Individuals aged 15-22 years face a different situation from those in the younger age cohorts.[10] First, they are past the age of compulsory school-ing. Their participation in education therefore results from a choice, likely to depend on – and be constrained by – a combination of elements, including the characteristics of the household in which they live. In addi-tion, adolescents are also at the age where the opportunities and options they have are greater. In particular, adolescence is the period when risk-taking and problem behaviour are most likely to develop. In this section we examine first the main occupation of adolescents (education, employment, etc.) before turning to their health behaviour.

The situation of adolescents in Russia has changed in many respects since the beginning of transition. Participation in education has undergone dramatic changes. The network of vocational schools has collapsed, so that more students now pursue academic-based education. Overall, how-ever, there has been a large decline in enrolments among 15-18 years old in any type of education, from 79 per cent in 1989 to 68 per cent in 1996 (with a rate as low as 65 per cent in 1994; see UNICEF 1998a). Enrolment in tertiary education, for young adults aged 18-22 years, has been rela-tively stable over transition, from 17 per cent in 1989 up to 18 per cent in 1996 (after having reached 16 per cent in 1994, UNICEF 1998a).

The alternatives to further education for young people have also deteriorated, with rising unemployment rates especially among youth and new entrants. In the first quarter of 1996, the overall unemployment rate was 9.5 per cent while the youth unemployment rate (age 15-24) was twice as high, at 19.1 per cent (OECD-CCET).

Basically, adolescents and young adults can be divided into those who study, those who work, and the others (unemployed or out of the labour force and not studying). Children from single-parent households can be expected to face a different set of constraints when making their choice. Indeed, the lack of economic support in single-parent households might force those children to work, or at least to look for work, rather than continuing their education.

The percentage of children enrolled in education facilities varies significantly by type of household. Figure 7.5 (and Table 7.5 in the Appendix) presents the distribution of children in the three different types of occupation. Those living in a dual-parent household have higher enrolment rates, in all age groups and for both genders. The difference is more pronounced among the older group, with, for instance, 41 per cent of girls aged 19-22 years from dual-parent households enrolled compared to 31 per cent for those living with a single parent. When separating those living with two natural parents from those living in reconstructed households, it appears once again that the latter are in a situation similar to those from single-parent households.

Further analysis of the determinants of enrolment in education for children aged 15-18 years, suggests that the main factor influencing enrolment for children beyond the compulsory school age is the educa-

Figure 7.5: Activities of Young Adults by Age, Gender and Family Type (dual or single parent), RLMS 1996 (percentages)

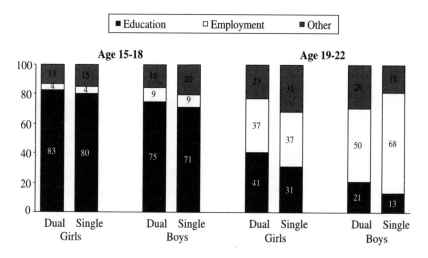

tional level of the parent(s). Household income appears to play a more limited – but not insignificant – role in the decision, while family structure does not seem to play any significant role.[11] Lower enrolment rates for children living with single parents seem to be related to their parents' lower educational achievements and lower income levels rather than to be directly caused by household structure.

Another measure of the differences in terms of human capital between different groups is provided by the percentage of those who have attained a certain educational level (whether they still study or not).

Table 7.2 shows that those who live with two parents, both boys and girls, have attained higher levels of education. The situation is particularly of concern for girls in single-parent households, with 20 per cent of them having less than 10 years of education.

As for those who are not enrolled in the educational system, the patterns vary according to age and gender. For the younger age group, employment rates are similar across the different household types and

Table 7.2: Educational Attainment by Family Type and Gender, RLMS 1996
(percentages of 19-22 year-olds)

	Boys		**Girls**	
	2 parents	**1 parent**	**2 parents**	**1 parent**
Less than 10 years of schooling	12.5	13.2	5.2	20.0
10-11 years of schooling	27.5	42.1	19.8	20.0
12 or more years of schooling	60.0	44.7	75.0	60.0

the difference in enrolment is only compensated by the 'other' category (see Figure 7.5). The situation of girls from the older age group is similar, with much higher rates of non-participation for those from single-parent households (31 per cent versus 23 per cent for those from dual-parent households). Girls seem more likely to simply drop out of education rather than to leave education for employment.

Older boys present a different picture. The participation rate is much higher among children from single-parent households (68 per cent) than among their peers (50 per cent). The 'other' category is also smaller for those boys from single-parent households. This suggests that they are more active in seeking employment – or ready to accept a wider range of employment – than those living with both parents. Older boys from reconstructed families appear to be very similar to those with single parents (14 per cent study and 62 per cent work) while older girls from reconstructed families appear to leave education in order to work (19 per cent study and 63 per cent work).

In terms of changes in behaviour, recent years have witnessed a decrease in social cohesion generally, with the crime rate increasing by over 60 per cent in the period from 1989 to 1996. Crimes committed by young persons have also soared, with the youth sentencing rate increasing by 80 per cent over the same period (see Figure 7.2). Risk-taking behaviour has also become more frequent, with drug use and substance abuse becoming major public health issues (UNICEF, 1999). The number of new cases of sexually transmitted diseases, and in particular of syphilis, has also increased dramatically among adolescents and young adults. For instance, the number of new cases of syphilis among girls aged 18-19 years skyrocketed from around 2 per 10,000 in 1989 to 130 per 10,000 in 1996 (UNICEF 1999).

Negative health behaviour is assessed using indicators of smoking and drinking, and for girls, pregnancy and abortion. The overall finding with respect to these outcomes is that dual-parent households are correlated with lower incidence. As shown in Figure 7.6, children from single-parent households are more likely to smoke and drink than others, except for the drinking pattern of girls. Boys are particularly likely to smoke and drink.

As far as pregnancy and abortion are concerned, girls living in single-parent households are almost twice as likely to become pregnant as those living in dual-parent households, with 10 per cent and 5 per cent of them respectively having experienced a pregnancy (Figure 7.6). The incidence of pregnancy appears to have decreased since 1994. When

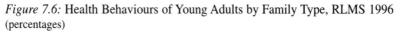

Figure 7.6: Health Behaviours of Young Adults by Family Type, RLMS 1996 (percentages)

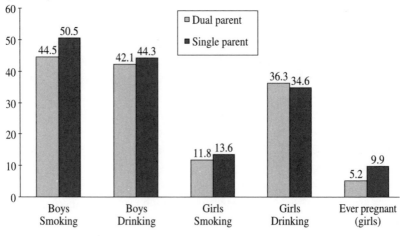

concentrating on younger girls, in the 15-18 years age group, for whom pregnancy would represent a greater barrier to education, the prevalence is very low and similar across family types (the samples are, however, too small for such findings to be robust).

The probability of having an abortion following pregnancy is similar among the different groups (although, in 1994, girls from single-parent households were more likely to continue their pregnancy than those from dual-parent households). While teenage pregnancy is not necessarily the result of risk-taking behaviour but might reflect deliberate decision, it still represents a constraint for the young women concerned. In particular, the capacity to pursue further education will be greatly affected.

Overall, the differences between adolescents living in households of different types appear to be larger than for their younger siblings of compulsory school age. Adolescents living in single-parent households are less likely to be enrolled in education, especially in tertiary education. The situation for children from single-parent households differs by gender, with girls seemingly dropping out of education into non-activity, while boys appear to leave education for employment. Important differences between household types are also noted in terms of behaviour, with a higher proportion of those living in single-parent households engaging in smoking or drinking and a higher proportion of girls experiencing pregnancy.

7.5 Summary and Implications

This chapter started out with a series of hypotheses about the potentially adverse impact of family structure on child welfare outcomes. Children living in single-parent households or in reconstructed households were expected to be negatively affected by lower economic resources, greater time constraints on custodial parents and by the stress generated by disruptions in family life.

The results of the analysis presented above have pointed to differences in welfare outcomes between children in various types of households. The differences were usually found to be small but systematically underlines a range of disadvantages for children living in single-parent households and reconstructed households. Furthermore, the differences in the various child welfare outcomes, even if small, are bound to have a cumulative impact on children, and their combined effect can be expected to be substantial.

It appears that the differences in welfare outcomes for children in different family structures are greater for those in pre-school age and those past the age of compulsory schooling. This can be taken partly to reflect the fact that children aged 7-14 years (the middle age group) face fewer health and behavioural problems than their younger or older siblings. It also, however, points to the important role played by the educational system, which is compulsory for that age group. Close to full enrolment does contribute to a reduction in differences with respect to several indicators.

The situation of younger children, especially with regard to health, is worrying. One might expect health deficiencies in childhood to have a long-term impact. As for older children, the rapid deterioration of the economic situation and the development of negative health behaviour represent threats, in particular for those living in atypical families.

Various trends raise concerns for children from atypical families for the future. First, child welfare outcomes generally can be expected to further deteriorate as the economic situation worsens after the crisis of August 1998. Second, the particularly vulnerable – and worsening in relative terms – situation of single parents in terms of poverty (reviewed in Chapter 6) can be expected to deteriorate further. Third, any further increase in the prevalence of single-parent households and reconstructed households would tend to increase the number of children potentially 'at-risk'. Finally, the reduction of state involvement and contribution to social welfare, in particular in terms of public financing and provision of health and education, will contribute to the deterioration of child welfare outcomes, especially for those children whose parents lack private resources. The combination of these various elements is likely to increase the differences among children from various household types. The polarization of the Russian population, already observed in terms of income and poverty, could be further accentuated in terms of child welfare outcomes.

Table 7.3: Welfare Outcomes among Young Children, RLMS 1996 (percentages of relevant age group)

	Both parents	of which: Natural	Step	Single parents	of which: Alone	Other adults	Total	(N)
Health outcome								
With health problems in previous month (0-6 year-olds)	40.9	40.5	52.0	50.4	60.0	46.1	42.3	837
Without vaccination against tuberculosis (4-6 year-olds)	16.2	16.7	...	20.3	20.0	20.5	16.8	406
With low height for age or weight for height (6 month- to 3 year-olds)	8.5	8.6	...	13.6	...	...	9.7	258
Education outcome								
Not enrolled in school or kindergarten (4-6 year-olds)	57.6	57.1	...	51.6	48.0	53.9	43.1	406
Not enrolled in school or kindergarten (3-6 year-olds)	59.0	58.3	72.7	54.3	50.0	56.9	58.9	533

Note: ... small sample size.

Table 7.4: Health and Education Outcomes among Children, RLMS 1996 (percentages of relevant age group)

	Both parents	of which:		Single parents	of which:		Total	(N)
		Natural	Step		Alone	Other adults		
Health problems in previous month								
7-14 year-olds	32.7	32.2	37.9	33.3	34.2	32.4	32.9	1366
7-10 year-olds	35.3	35.2	37.1	35.5	40.0	31.6	35.2	671
11-14 year-olds	30.0	29.0	38.3	31.4	29.9	33.3	30.8	695
With a cough the previous week								
7-14 year-olds	20.7	20.4	23.9	25.9	24.3	27.6	21.7	1275
Not enrolled in school								
7-14 year-olds	1.4	1.3	2.1	3.5	3.4	3.6	1.7	1370
7-10 year-olds	1.8	1.7	2.9	2.8	4.0	1.8	1.9	672
11-14 year-olds	0.9	0.8	1.6	4.1	3.0	5.6	1.4	698
Enrolled but not attending								
7-14 year-olds	6.8	6.7	8.3	4.4	6.0	2.7	6.3	1370
7-10 year-olds	7.6	7.2	14.2	2.8	4.0	1.7	6.7	672
11-14 year-olds	6.2	6.3	5.0	5.8	7.5	3.7	6.1	698
Not attending/not enrolled in school								
7-14 year-olds	8.2	8.0	10.4	7.9	9.4	6.3	8.0	1370
7-10 year-olds	9.4	8.9	17.1	5.6	8.0	3.5	8.6	672
11-14 year-olds	7.1	7.1	6.6	9.9	10.5	9.3	7.5	698
Child late at school								
7-14 year-olds	8.6	8.4	10.4	11.0	10.3	11.7	8.9	1370
7-10 year-olds	9.9	10.2	5.7	12.2	12.0	12.3	10.4	672
11-14 year-olds	7.2	6.5	13.1	9.9	9.0	11.1	7.5	698

Table 7.5: Welfare Outcomes of Adolescents and Young Adults by Family Type, RLMS 1996 (percentages of relevant age group)

	Both parents	of which: Natural	of which: Step	Single parents	of which: Alone	of which: Other adults	Total	(N)
Behaviours								
Smoking among 15-22 year-olds								
Boys	44.5	41.1	67.4	50.5	50.0	51.2	47.0	475
Girls	11.8	9.6	24.4	13.6	14.6	12.5	13.4	426
Drinking among 15-22 year-olds								
Boys	42.1	41.8	44.2	44.3	39.3	51.2	44.0	475
Girls	36.3	34.5	46.7	34.6	46.3	22.5	37.8	426
Girls aged 15-22 ever pregnant:	5.2	4.6	8.9	9.9	9.8	10.0	6.8	426
of these, ever had abortion	37.5	...	...	37.5	...	...	41.4	29
Occupation								
Boys aged 15-18 in:								
Education	74.9	74.6	77.3	71.2	73.3	70.0	73.1	294
Employment	9.3	9.3	9.1	8.5	10.0	6.9	9.5	
Other	15.8	16.1	13.6	20.4	16.7	24.1	17.4	
Girls aged 15-18 in:								
Education	82.9	84.5	72.4	80.4	78.3	82.6	81.7	267
Employment	3.8	3.3	6.9	4.4	0.0	8.7	4.5	
Other	13.3	12.2	20.7	15.2	21.7	8.7	13.9	
Boys aged 19-22 in:								
Education	20.8	22.2	14.3	13.2	15.4	8.3	21.0	181
Employment	50.0	47.5	61.9	68.4	65.4	75.0	53.6	
Other	29.2	30.3	23.8	18.4	19.2	16.7	25.4	
Girls aged 19-22 in:								
Education	40.6	45.0	18.8	31.4	38.9	23.5	37.7	159
Employment	36.5	31.3	62.5	37.1	38.9	35.3	39.0	
Other	22.9	23.8	18.8	31.4	22.2	41.2	23.3	
Educational attainment								
Boys aged 19-22 with:								
Less than 10 years	12.5	11.1	19.1	13.2	...	...	11.6	181
10-11 years	27.5	27.3	28.6	42.1	...	...	30.4	
12+ years	60.0	61.6	52.4	44.7	...	...	58.0	
Girls aged 19-22 with:								
Less than 10 years	5.2	5.0	6.3	20.0	...	...	8.2	159
10-11 years	19.8	16.3	37.5	20.0	...	...	18.9	
12+ years	75.0	78.8	56.3	60.0	...	...	75.0	

Note: ... small sample size.

* We are very grateful to Michael Swafford for the provision of the household structure variables and for his assistance in defining the typology.

NOTES

1 See, for example, the framework presented and developed in Haveman and Wolfe (1995) and the literature reviewed therein.

2 As noted above, instability and abrupt changes in income are important factors, over and above the actual absolute level of income.

3 Ideally this could be extended to include, for instance, analysis of prevalence of contraception or sexually transmitted diseases.

4 A child is considered stunted if height for age or wasted if weight for height is below two standard deviations of the median of a reference population.

5 For example, the average per capita consumption of dairy products decreased by 23 per cent between 1994 and 1996 (UNICEF 1999).

6 In addition, the RLMS is likely to overestimate the actual coverage since the data indicates whether the child has received any vaccination, and does not differentiate between children who have received all the necessary injections on schedule, and those who have not.

7 The percentage of children taken to hospital over the 3 months preceding the survey varies from 6 per cent in dual-parent families to 9 per cent in single-parent households (children under 4 years). It is possible that part or all of the difference reflects the need for childcare for working single parents, since the presence of other potential caretakers in single-parent households reduces the probability of being taken to hospital to levels similar to that in dual-parent households.

8 As was the case with younger children, children from incomplete families visit hospitals more frequently than their peers (6 per cent versus 2 per cent for those with two parents for the 7 to 10 years group). The hypothesis that this reflects the lack of alternative child-care arrangements for single parents living without other adults could however not be tested due to the small sample size.

9 The Third International Mathematics and Science Study carried out by the International Association for the Evaluation of Educational Achievement. See Beaton et al. (1996a and 1996b); Vari (1997).

10 This analysis considers only children who are not married (within the 15-22 age group, 266 individuals were married, and these are excluded from our analysis). It is interesting to note the very low prevalence of single-parenthood among individuals aged 15-22 years. In 1996, less than one per cent of them were single parents.

11 Preliminary multivariate analysis of enrolment shows the strong impact of parental education and child gender on enrolment for those aged 15-18 years and the smaller importance of parental income. Household structure variables do not have significant coefficients.

Bibliography

Agence France Presse (AFP) (1998), Newswire, 12 December 1998.

Akademiya Problem Sotsial'noy Raboty (1997), *Rossiyskaya entsiklopediya sotsial'noy raboty [Russian Encyclopedia of Social Work]*. 2 vols., Moscow.

Alwin, Duane F., Michael Braun and Jacqueline Scott (1992), 'The Separation of Work and the Family: Attitudes Towards Women's Labour-Force Participation in Germany, Great Britain, and the United States'. *European Sociological Review*, 8(1), pages 13-37.

Aquilino, W.S. (1996), 'The Life Course of Children Born to Unmarried Mothers: Childhood Living Arrangements and Young Adult Outcomes'. *Journal of Marriage and the Family*, 58, pages 293-310.

Atkinson, Anthony (1989), *Poverty and Inequality*. London: Harvester Wheatsheaf.

Atkinson, Anthony and John Micklewright (1992), *Economic Transformation in Eastern Europe and the Distribution of Income*. Cambridge, UK: Cambridge University Press.

Australian Bureau of Statistics (1998), *1998 Year Book Australia*. Canberra: Australian Bureau of Statistics.

Avdeev, Alexandre and Alain Monnier (1996), 'Mouvement de la population de la Russie 1959-1994: Tableaux demographiques'. Paris: Institut National d'Etudes Demographiques.

Bane, Mary Jo (1986), 'Household Composition and Poverty' in Sheldon Danziger and Daniel Weinberg (eds), *Fighting Poverty: What Works and What Doesn't*. Cambridge, MA: Harvard University Press, pages 209-231.

Barr, Nicholas (1994), *Labor Markets and Social Policy in Central and Eastern Europe: the Transition and Beyond*. New York: Oxford University Press.

Bartlema, J. and A. Vossen (1988), 'Reflections on Household Modelling' in Nico Keilman, Anton Kuijsten and Ad Vossen (eds), *Modelling Household Formation and Dissolution*. Oxford: Clarendon Press, pages 243, 249-250.

Beaton, A.E., I.V.S. Mullis, M.O. Martin, E.J. Gonzalez, D.L. Kelly and T.A. Smith (1996a), *Mathematics Achievement in the Middle School Years: IEA's Third International Mathematics and Science Study*. Chestnut Hill, MA: Centre for the Study of Testing, Evaluation and Educational Policy, Boston College.

Beaton, A.E, M.O. Martin, I.V.S. Mullis, E.J. Gonzalez, T.A. Smith and D.L. Kelly (1996b), *Science Achievement in the Middle School Years: IEA's Third International Mathematics and Science Study*. Chestnut Hill, MA: Centre for the Study of Testing, Evaluation and Educational Policy, Boston College.

Becker, Gary S. (1981), *A Treatise on the Family*. Cambridge, MA: Harvard University Press.

Becker, Gary S. and N. Tomes (1986), 'Human Capital and the Rise and Fall of Families'. *Journal of Labour Economics*, 4 (3), pages S1-39.

Behrman, J.R. (1992), *The Economic Rationale for Investing in Nutrition in Developing Countries*. Washington, D.C.: U.S. Agency for International Development.

Bianchi, Suzanne and Daphne Spain (1996), 'Women, Work and Family in America'. *Population Bulletin*, 51 (3), Washington, D.C.: Population Reference Bureau.

Björklund, Anders and Richard Freeman (1995), 'Generating Equality and Eliminating Poverty the Swedish Way'. Centre for Economic Performance, Discussion Paper No. 228.

Bonoli, Giuliano (1997), 'Classifying Welfare States: A Two-Dimension Approach'. *Journal of Social Policy*, 26 (3), pages 351-372.

Borisov, B. and A. Sinel'nikov (1996), *Brachnost' i rozhdayemost' v Rossii: demograficheskiy analiz [Marriage and Fertility in Russia: A Demographic Analysis]*. Moscow: Family Research Institute, Ministry of Social Protection.

Bradbury, Bruce and Markus Jännti (1999), 'Child Poverty Across Industrialized Nations'. *Innocenti Occasional Papers*, EPS 71. Florence: UNICEF Innocenti Research Centre.

Bradshaw, Jonathan, et al. (1996), *The Employment of Lone Parents: A Comparison of Policy in 20 Countries*. London: Family Policy Studies Centre.

Braithwaite, Jeanine D. (1997), 'The Old and New Poor in Russia' in Jeni Klugman (ed.), *Poverty in Russia: Public Policy and Private Responses*. Washington, D.C.: Economic Development Institute, The World Bank, pages 34-35.

Bumpass, Larry L. and R. Kelly Raley (1995), 'Redefining Single-Parent Families: Cohabitation and Changing Family Reality'. *Demography*, 32, pages 97-109.

Bumpass, Larry L., James A. Sweet and Andrew J. Cherlin, (1991), 'The Role of Cohabitation in Declining Rates of Marriage'. *Journal of Marriage and the Family*, 53, pages 913-927.

Bumpass, Larry and Sara McLanahan (1989), 'Unmarried Motherhood: Recent Trends, Composition, and Black-White Differences'. *Demography*, 26 (2), pages 279-286.

Bumpass, Larry and James A. Sweet (1989), 'Children's Experience in Single-Parent Families: Implications of Cohabitation and Marital Transitions'. *Family Planning Perspectives,* 21 (6), pages 256-260.

Burch, Thomas K. (1995), 'Theories of Household Formation: Progress and Challenges' in E. van Imhoff et al. (eds), *Household Demography and Modelling*. New York: Plenum Press.

Bureau of the Census (1995), *Who Receives Child Support?* Statistical Brief, No. 95-16. Washington, D.C.: U.S. Department of Commerce.

Carlson, Elwood (1992), 'Inverted Easterlin Fertility Cycles and Kornai's 'Soft' Budget Constraint'. *Population and Development Review*, 18 (4).

Casterline, John, Ronald Lee and Karen Foote (eds) (1996), *Fertility in the United States: New Patterns, New Theories*. New York: The Population Council.

Castro-Martin, Theresa and Larry Bumpass (1989), 'Recent Trends and Differentials in Marital Disruption'. *Demography*, 25 (1), pages 37-51.

Chen, Lincoln, F. Wittgenstein and E. McKeon (1996), 'The Upsurge of Mortality in Russia: Causes and Policy Implications'. *Population and Development Review*, 22 (3).

Chinn, Jeff (1977), *Manipulating Soviet Population Resources*. London: Macmillan.

Clarke, Lynda and Melanie Henwood (1997), 'Great Britain: The Lone Parent as the New Norm?' in F.-X. Kaufmann et al., *Family Life and Family Policies in Europe: Structures and Trends in the 1980s*. Oxford: Clarendon Press.

Coleman, David (1996), 'New Patterns and Trends in European Fertility: International and Sub-National Comparisons' in D. Coleman (ed.) *Europe's Population in the 1990s*. Oxford: Oxford University Press.

Coleman, David (1993), 'Contrasting Age Structures of Western Europe and of Eastern Europe and the Former Soviet Union: Demographic Curiosity or Labour Resource?'. *Population and Development Review*, 19 (3).

Coleman, David (1992), 'European Demographic Systems of the Future: Convergence or Diversity?' in *Proceedings of the Conference on Human Capital in Europe at the Dawn of the 21st Century*. Luxembourg: Eurostat.

Commander, Simon, Andrei Tolstopiatenko and Ruslan Yemstov (1997), 'Channels of Redistribution: Inequality and Poverty in the Russian Transition'. *Economics of Transition*, 7 (2).

Commander, Simon and Ruslan Yemtsov (1997), 'Russian Unemployment: Its Magnitude, Characteristics and Regional Dimensions' in J. Klugman (ed.) *Poverty in Russia: Public Policy and Private Responses.* Washington D.C.: Economic Development Institute, The World Bank.

Commission of the European Community (1994), 'Employment in Europe'. *COM,* No. 314. Luxembourg: Directorate General for Employment, Industrial Relations and Social Affairs, Commission of the European Community.

Committee on Ways and Means (1996), U.S. House of Representatives. *Green Book: Background Material and Data on Programs within the Jurisdiction of the Committee on Ways and Means.* Washington, D.C.: Government Printing Office.

Cornia, Andrea and Renato Paniccià (1995), 'The Demographic Impact of Sudden İmpoverishment: Eastern Europe during the 1989-94 Transition'. *Innocenti Occasional Papers,* EPS 49. Florence: UNICEF International Child Development Centre.

Coudouel, Aline, Alastair McAuley and John Micklewright (1997), 'Transfers and Exchanges Between Households in Uzbekistan' in J. Falkingham, J. Klugman, S. Marnie and J. Micklewright (eds), *Household Welfare in Central Asia.* London: Macmillan.

Council of Europe (1998), *Recent Demographic Developments in Europe and North America.* Strasbourg: Council of Europe Press.

Council of Europe (1997), *Recent Demographic Developments in Europe and North America.* Strasbourg: Council of Europe Press.

Council of Europe (1993), *Recent Demographic Developments in Europe and North America.* Strasbourg: Council of Europe Press.

Cox, D., Z. Eser and E. Jimenez (1997), 'Family Safety Nets During Economic Transition' in J. Klugman (ed.) *Poverty in Russia: Public Policy and Private Responses.* Washington, D.C.: Economic Development Institute, The World Bank.

Cusan, Alessandra and Albert Motivans 1998, 'Education in Central and Eastern Europe: Adjustment and Implications for Access and Quality', mimeo. Florence: UNICEF Innocenti Research Centre.

Czap, Peter Jr. (1983), 'A Large Family: the Peasant's Greatest Wealth': Serf Households in Mishino, Russia, 1814-1858' in Richard Wall (ed.), *Family Forms in Historic Europe.* Cambridge U.K.: Cambridge University Press.

DaVanzo, Julie (ed.) (1996), *Russia's Demographic 'Crisis'.* Santa Monica, CA: Rand Corp.

Duncan, Greg J., R. Coe and Martha S. Hill (1984), *The Dynamics of Poverty,* in G. Duncan (ed.), *Years of Poverty, Years of Plenty.* Ann Arbor, Michigan: University of Michigan, Survey Research Centre.

Duncan, Greg J. and Martha S. Hill (1985), 'Conceptions of Longitudinal Households: Fertile or Futile?'. *Journal of Economic and Social Measurement,* 13, pages 361-375.

Duncan, Greg J. and Willard Rodgers (1990), 'Lone-Parent Families and Their Economic Problems: Transitory or Persistent?' in E. Duskin (ed.), *Lone-Parent Families: The Economic Challenge,* Social Policy Studies, No. 8. Paris: OECD.

Duskin, Elizabeth (1990), 'Overview' in E. Duskin (ed.) *Lone-Parent Families: The Economic Challenge,* Social Policy Studies, No. 8. Paris: OECD.

Eberstadt, Nicholas (1994), 'Demographic Disaster: the Soviet Legacy'. *The National Interes*t, (Summer), pages 53-57.

Elizarov, Valery (1996), 'The Socio-Economic Potential of Families'. Report prepared for the MONEE Project, Florence: International Child Development Centre.

Ellwood, David T. (1990), 'Valuing the United States Income Support System for Lone Mothers' in E. Duskin (ed.), *Lone-Parent Families: The Economic Challenge,* Social Policy Studies, No. 8. Paris: OECD.

Entwisle, B., L. Watterson and D. Donohue (1997), 'Family Planning and Abortion in the Russian Federation: Trends 1992-1996'. Report submitted to USAID. Carolina: Population Centre, University of North Carolina.

Entwhistle, D.R. and K.L. Alexander (1995), 'A Parent's Economic Shadow: Family Structure versus Family Resources as Influences on Early School Achievement'. *Journal of Marriage and the Family,* 57, pages 399-409.

Ermisch, John (1991), *Lone Parenthood: An Economic Analysis.* Cambridge, UK: Cambridge University Press.

Ermisch, John (1990), 'Demographic Aspects of the Growing Numbers of Lone-Parent Families' in E. Duskin (ed.), *Lone Parent Families: The Economic Challenge,* Social Policy Studies, No. 8. Paris: OECD.

Ermisch, J.F. and M. Francesconi (1997), 'Family Matters'. Discussion Paper No. 1591. London: Centre for Economic Policy Research.

Ermisch, John and N. Ogawa (eds) (1997), *The Family, the Market and the State in Ageing Societies.* Oxford: Clarendon Press.

Esping-Anderson, Gøsta (1990), *The Three Worlds of Welfare Capitalism.* Princeton: Princeton University Press.

European Bank for Reconstruction and Development (1999), *Transition Report.* London: European Bank for Reconstruction and Development.

European Bank for Reconstruction and Development (1997), *Transition Report 1997: Enterprise Performance and Growth*. London: European Bank for Reconstruction and Development.

European Observatory on National Family Policies (1990), *Families and Policies, Evolutions and Trends in 1988-89*, Interim Report. Luxembourg: Commission of the European Communities.

Eurostat (1998a), *Demographic Statistics 1997*. Luxembourg: Eurostat.

Eurostat (1998b), 'Population and Social Conditions'. *Statistics in Focus*, No. 12. Luxembourg: Office for Publications of the European Communities.

Eurostat (1997a), *Eurostat Yearbook '97: A Statistical Eye on Europe, 1986-96*. Luxembourg: Office for Publications of the European Communities.

Eurostat (1997b), 'EU Divorce at Record High: Nearly a Third of EU Marriages Could Fail'. *Memo 9/97*. Luxembourg: Eurostat Press Office.

Fajth, Gáspár (1996), 'Family Support Policies in Central and Eastern Europe'. Paper presented at the workshop *Economic Transformation, Institutional Change and Social Sector Reform*, Task Force on Economies in Transition, National Research Council, Washington, D.C., September 1996.

Fajth, Gáspár (1994), 'Family Support Policies in Transitional Economies: Challenges and Constraints'. *Innocenti Occasional Papers*, EPS 43. Florence: UNICEF International Child Development Centre.

Farrell, C. (1978), *My Mother Said: The Way Young People Learned about Sex and Birth Control*. London: Routledge, Kegan and Paul.

Festi, Patrick and Lydia Prokofieva (1996), 'Alimenty, posobiya i dokhody semey posle razvoda' ['Alimony, benefits and family income after divorce']. *Naseleniye i Obshchestvo*, [Population and Society], No. 15. Moscow: Centre for Demography and Human Ecology.

Flemming, John and John Micklewright (1999), 'Income Distribution, Economic Systems and Transition'. *Innocenti Occasional Papers*, EPS 70. Florence: UNICEF Innocenti Research Centre.

Foley, Mark (1997), 'Poverty in Russia: An Econometric Analysis' in J. Klugman (ed.) *Poverty in Russia: Public Policy and Private Responses*. Washington, D.C.: Economic Development Institute, The World Bank.

Foley, Mark and Jeni Klugman (1998), 'The Impact of Social Support: Errors of Leakage and Exclusion' in J. Klugman (ed.), *Poverty in Russia: Public Policy and Private Responses*. Washington, D.C.: Economic Development Institute, The World Bank.

Ford, Reuben (1996), *Child Care in the Balance: How Lone Parents Make Decisions about Work*. London: Policy Studies Institute.

Forssén, Katja (1998), 'Child Poverty and Family Policy in OECD Countries'. Luxembourg Income Study Working Paper, No. 178. LIS: Luxembourg

Frolova, Elena B. (1998), 'Problems in Poverty Measurement and Income Inequality in the Russian Federation: Methodological Issues and Conclusions'. Paper presented at the Joint Conference of the International Association of Survey Statisticians and the International Association for Official Statistics, Aguascalientes, Mexico, 1-4 September, 1998.

Garfinkel, Irwin and Sara McLanahan (1986), *Single Mothers and their Children: A New American Dilemma.* Washington D.C.: Urban Institute Press.

Gimpleson, Vladimir and Douglas Lippoldt (1998), 'Private Sector Employment in Russia: Scale, Composition and Performance - Evidence from the Russian Labour Force Survey', mimeo. Moscow: IMEMO.

Goldman, Wendy Z. (1993), *Women, the State and Revolution: Soviet Family Policy and Social Life, 1917-1936.* Cambridge: Cambridge University Press.

Gomulka, Joanna and Nicholas Stern (1989), 'The Employment of Married Women in the United Kingdom, 1970-83'. *Economica,* 57.

Gongola, Patricia and Edward Thompson (1987), 'Single-Parent Families' in M. Sussman and S. Steinmetz (eds.), *Handbook of Marriage and the Family.* New York: Plenum Press.

Gornick, Janet C., Marcia C. Meyers and Katherin E. Ross (1996), 'Supporting the Employment of Mothers: Policy Variation Across Fourteen Welfare States'. Luxembourg Income Study, Working Paper No. 139. LIS: Luxembourg.

Goskomstat Rossii (1998), *Sotsial'noye polozheniye i uroven' zhizni naseleniya Rossii* [*The Social Situation and Standard of Living of the Population of Russia*]. Moscow: Goskomstat Rossii.

Goskomstat Rossii (1997), *Sotsial'noye polozheniye i uroven' zhizni naseleniya Rossii* [*The Social Situation and Standard of Living of the Population of Russia*], page 72 ff. Moscow: Goskomstat Rossii.

Goskomstat Rossii (1996a), *Demograficheskiy ezhigodnik* [*Demographic Yearbook*]. Moscow: Goskomstat Rossii.

Goskomstat Rossii (1996b), *Rossiyskiy statisticheskiy ezhigodnik: 1996* [*Russian Statistical Yearbook: 1996*]. Moscow: Logos.

Goskomstat Rossii (1996c), *Sem'ya v Rossii: 1996* [*The Family in Russia: 1996*]. Moscow: Goskomstat Rossii.

Goskomstat Rossii (1995a), *Typy i sostav domokhozyastv v Rossii* [*Household Types and Structure in Russia*]. Moscow: Goskomstat Rossii.

Goskomstat Rossii (1995b), *Sostoyaniye v brake i rozhdayemost' v Rossii* [*Marital Status and Fertility in Russia*]. Moscow: Goskomstat Rossii.

Goskomstat Rossii (1995c), Statistical Press Release. Moscow: Goskomstat Rossii.

Goskomstat Rossii (1995d): *Tipy i sostav domokhozyaystv v Rossii* [*Types and Composition of Households in Russia*], pages 4-5; 60-61. Moscow: Goskomstat Rossii.

Goskomstat SSSR (1990a), *Demograficheskiy yezhigodnik SSSR* [*Demographic Yearbook USSR*]. Moscow: Finansy i statistika, Information-publication Centre.

Goskomstat SSSR (1990b), *Problemy molodezhi i molodoy sem'yi* [*Problems of Youth and Young Families*]. Moscow: Information-publication Centre.

Goskomstat SSSR (1990c), *Sotsial'noye razvitiye SSSR* [*Social Development in the USSR*]. Moscow: Finansy i statistika.

Goskomstat SSSR (1987), *Naseleniye SSSR* [*Population of the USSR*]. Moscow: Finansy i statistika.

Gottschalk, Peter and Timothy Smeeding (1997), 'Cross-National Comparisons of Earnings and Income Inequality'. *The Journal of Economic Literature*, 35, pages 633-687.

Greenstein, Robert and Isaac Shapiro (1998), 'New Research Findings on the Effects of the Earned Income Tax Credit'. Washington, D.C.: Center on Budget and Policy Priorities.

Gregory, R.G., E. Klug and Y.M. Martin (1998), 'Labour Market Deregulation, Relative Wages and the Social Security System', mimeo, Research School of Social Sciences. Canberra: Australian National University.

Grootaert, Christiaan and Jeanine Braithwaite (1998), 'Poverty Correlates and Indicator-based Targeting in Eastern Europe and the Former Soviet Union', mimeo. Washington, D.C.: World Bank.

Haddad, L. and R. Kanbur (1990), 'How Serious is the Neglect of Intra-Household Inequality?'. *Economic Journal*, 100, pages 866-881.

Hajnal, J. (1983), 'Two Kinds of Pre-Industrial Household Formation System' in Richard Wall (ed.), *Family Forms in Historic Europe.* Cambridge: Cambridge University Press.

Harwin, Judith (1996), *Children of the Russian State: 1917-95.* Aldershot, UK: Avebury.

Haub, Carl (1994), 'Population Change in the Former Soviet Republics'. *Population Bulletin*, 49 (4), Washington, D.C.: Population Reference Bureau.

Haveman, Robert and Barbara Wolfe (1995), 'The Determinants of Children's Attainments: A Review of Methods and Findings'. *Journal of Economic Literature*, 33, pages 1829-1878.

Haveman, Robert, Barbara Wolfe and J. Spaulding (1991), 'Childhood Events and Circumstances Influencing High School Completion'. *Demography*, 28 (1), pages 133-157.

Headey, Bruce, Robert E. Goodin, Ruud Muffels and Henk-Jan Dirven (1997), 'Welfare Over Time: Three Worlds of Welfare Capitalism in Panel Perspective'. *Journal of Public Policy*, 17 (3), pages 329-359.

Heleniak, Tim (1995), 'Economic Transition and Demographic Change in Russia, 1989-1995'. *Post-Soviet Geography*, 36 (7), pages 446-458.

Hemming, R., Adrienne Cheasty and Ashok Lahiri (1995), 'The Revenue Decline in Policy Experiences and Issues in the Baltics, Russia and Other Countries of the Former Soviet Union'. Occasional Paper No. 133. Washington, D.C.: International Monetary Fund.

Hernandez, Donald (1993), *America's Children: Resources from Family, Government and the Economy*. New York: Russell Sage Foundation.

Hill, Martha S. (1995), 'When is a Family a Family? Evidence from Survey Data and Implications for Family Policy'. *Journal of Family and Economic Issues*, 16 (1), pages 35-64.

Hoem, Britta and Jan M. Hoem (1988), 'The Swedish Family: Aspects of Contemporary Development'. *Journal of Family Issues*, 9 (3), pages 397-424.

Imhoff, Evert van, Anton Kuijsten, Pieter Hooimeijer and Leo van Wissen (eds) (1995), *Household Demography and Household Modeling*. New York: Plenum Press.

Institute for Family Research (1997), 'Sotsial'no-demograficheskiye kharakter-istiki zhiznedeyatel'nosti semey' [*Socio-Demographic Characteristics of Family Life*], *Sem'ya v Rossii* [*Family in Russia*], No. 2. Moscow: Institute for Family Research.

ILO (1997), *Yearbook of Labour Statistics*. Geneva: International Labour Organization.

ILO (1992), *Yearbook of Labour Statistics*. Geneva: International Labour Organization.

IMF (1998), *Government Finance Statistics Yearbook*. Washington, D.C.: International Monetary Fund.

Ivanova, Elena (1997), 'Braky i razvody' ['Marriage and Divorce'] in A. Vishnevskiy (ed.), *Naseleniye Rossii: 1996* [*Population of Russia, 1996*], pages 54-74. Moscow: Centre for Human Demography and Ecology.

Jäntti, Markus and Sheldon Danziger (1994), 'Child Poverty in Sweden and the United States: The Effect of Social Transfers and Parental Labor Force

Participation'. *Industrial and Labor Relations Review*, 48, pages 48-64.

Jarvis, Sarah and Stephen Jenkins (1997), 'Marital Splits and Income Change: Evidence for Britain'. *Innocenti Occasional Papers*, EPS 60. Florence: UNICEF International Child Development Centre.

Jencks, C. and S. Mayer (1990), 'The Social Consequences of Growing up in a Poor Neighbourhood' in L. Lynn and M. McGeary (eds), *Inner-City Poverty in the United States*. Washington, D.C.: National Academy Press.

Jenkins, Stephen (1995), 'Accounting for Inequality Trends: Decomposition Analyses for the UK, 1997-86'. *Economica*, 62.

Kamerman, Sheila B. (1995), 'Gender Role and Family Structure Changes in the Advanced Industrialized West: Implications for Social Policy' in K. McFate, R. Lawson and W.J. Wilson (eds), *Poverty, Inequality and the Future of Social Policy: Western States in the New World Order*. New York: Russell Sage Foundation.

Kamerman, Sheila B. and Alfred J. Kahn (1988), 'What Europe Does for Single-Parent Families'. *The Public Interest*, 93, pages 70-86.

Kamerman, Sheila B. and Alfred J. Kahn (1989), 'Single-Parent, Female-Headed Families in Western Europe: Social Change and Response'. *International Social Security Review*, 1.

Karelova, G. N. (1997), *O polozhenii detey v Rossiyskoy Federatsii: 1996 [On the situation of children in the Russian Federation: 1996]*, pages 106-107. Annual Report of Ministry of Labor and Social Development. Moscow: Sinergiya International Publishing House.

Katz, Katarina (1996), 'Gender, Wages and Discrimination in the USSR: A Study of a Russian Industrial Town.' Gothenburg: University of Gothenburg.

Katz, Katarina (1994), 'Gender Differentiation and Discrimination: A Study of Soviet Wages', Economic Studies, 54. Gothenburg: University of Gothenburg.

Keilman, Nico (1995), 'Household Concepts and Household Definitions in Western Europe: Different Levels but Similar Trends in Household Developments' in Evert van Imhoff, Anton Kuijsten, Pieter Hooimeijer, and Leo van Wissen (eds), *Household Demography and Household Modelling*. New York: Plenum Press.

Keilman, Nico and Nathan Keyfitz (1988), 'Recurrent Issues in Dynamic Household Modelling' in Nico Keilman, Anton Kuijsten and Ad Vossen (eds), *Modelling Household Formation and Dissolution*. Oxford: Clarendon Press.

Khmelevskaya, Anna (1997), *Increasing the Efficiency of the Social Benefit*

System in Russia, MA Dissertation. Moscow: New Economic School.

Kiernan, Kathleen E. (1996), 'Partnership Behaviour in Europe: Recent Trends and Issues' in D. Coleman (ed.), *Europe's Population in the 1990s.* Oxford: Oxford University Press.

Kiernan, Kathleen E., Hilary Land and Jane Lewis (1998), *Lone Motherhood in Twentieth-Century Britain: From Footnote to Front Page.* Oxford: Clarendon Press.

Kingkade, Ward (1994), *The Recent Increase in Russian Mortality,* mimeo. Washington, D.C.: Centre for International Research, US Census Bureau.

Klugman, Jeni (ed.) (1997), *Poverty in Russia: Public Policy and Private Responses.* Washington, D.C.: Economic Development Institute, The World Bank.

Klugman, Jeni and Jeanine Braithwaite (1998), 'Poverty in Russia: An Overview'. *World Bank Research Observer,* 13 (1), pages 37-58.

Klugman, J., S. Marnie, J. Micklewright and P. O'Keefe (1997), 'The Impact of Kindergarten Divestiture on Household Welfare in Central Asia' in J. Falkingham, J. Klugman, S. Marnie and J. Micklewright (eds), *Household Welfare in Central Asia.* London: Macmillan.

Kolev, Alexandre (1998), 'Labour Supply in the Informal Economy during Transition in Russia'. Centre for Economic and Policy Research, Discussion Paper Series, No. 2024. London: Centre for Economic and Policy Research.

Kolev, Alexandre (1996), 'Poverty in Russia: What Can We Learn from Round VI of the RLMS?', mimeo. Florence: European University Institute.

Korpi, Walter and Joakim Palme (1998), 'The Paradox of Redistribution and Strategies of Equality: Welfare State Institutions, Inequality and Poverty in Western Countries'. Luxembourg Income Study, Working Paper No. 174. Luxembourg: LIS

Krein, S.F. and A.H. Beller (1988), 'Educational Attainment of Children From Single-Parent Families: Differences by Exposure, Gender and Race'. *Demography,* 25 (2), pages 221-234.

Kuijsten, Anton (1995), 'Recent Trends in Household and Family Structures in Europe: An Overview' in E. van Imhoff et al. (eds), *Household Demography and Household Modelling.* New York: Plenum Press.

Kuprianova, Elena (1998), 'Gender Policies in Transition'. Report prepared for the MONEE Project. Florence: UNICEF International Child Development Centre.

Land, Hilary and Jane Lewis (1997), 'The Emergence of Lone Motherhood as a Problem in Late 20th Century Britain', Discussion paper WSP/134. London: London School of Economics/STICERD.

Lanjouw, Peter and Martin Ravallion (1996), 'Poverty and Household Size'. *Economic Journal*, 105.

Lefaucher, Nadine (1995), 'French Policies Toward Lone Parents: Social Categories and Social Policies' in K. Mc Fate, R. Lawson and W.J. Wilson (eds), *Poverty, Inequality and the Future of Social Policy: Western States in the New World Order.* New York: Russell Sage Foundation.

Lerman, Robert (1996), 'The Impact of Changing U.S. Family Structure on Child Poverty and Income Inequality'. *Economica*, 63, pages 119-139.

Lesthaege, Ron (1998), 'On Theory Development: Applications to the Study of Family Formation'. *Population and Development Review*, 24 (1).

Lewis, Jane (ed.) (1997), *Lone Mothers in European Welfare Regimes.* London and Philadelphia: Jessica Kingsley Publishers.

Lichter, Daniel T., Felicia B. Le Clere and Diane K. Mc Laughlin (1991), 'Local Marriage Market Conditions and the Marital Behaviour of Black and White Women'. *American Journal of Sociology*, 96, pages 843-867.

Liegle, Ludwig (1975), *The Family's Role in Soviet Education.* New York: Springer Publishing.

Longfellow, C. (1979), 'Divorce in Context: Its Impact on Children' in G. Levinger and O. Moles (eds), *Divorce and Separation: Context, Causes and Consequences.* New York: Basic Books.

Lutz, Wolfgang, Sergei Scherbov and Andrei Volkov (eds) (1994), *Demographic Trends and Patterns in the Soviet Union Before 1991.* London: Routledge.

Marnie, Sheila and Albert Motivans (1992), 'Women in the Labour Market in the Former Soviet Union: Project Report', mimeo. Washington D.C.: World Bank.

Marx and Engels (1962), *Karl Marx and Frederick Engels, Selected Works*, Vol. II. Moscow: Foreign Languages Publishing House, excerpted in *Population and Development Review*, 14 (4), page 725.

Mason K. and A.-M. Jensen (eds) (1995), *Gender and Family Change in Industrialised Countries.* Oxford: Clarendon Press.

Mauldon, J. (1990), 'The Effect of Marital Disruption on Children's Health'. *Demography*, 27 (3), pages 431-446.

McAuley, Alastair (1996), 'Social Policy and the Labour Market in Russia during Transition'. Paper prepared for *Economic Transformation: Institutional Change and Social Sector Reform.* Washington, D.C.: National Academy of Sciences.

McAuley, Alastair (1991), 'The Welfare State in the USSR' in T. Wilson and D. Wilson (eds.), *The State and Social Welfare: the Objectives of Policy.* London: Longman.

McAuley, Alastair (1987), 'Social Policy' in M. McCauley (ed.) *Khrushchev and Khrushchevism*. London: Macmillan.

McAuley, Alastair (1981), *Women's Work and Wages in the Soviet Union*. London: George Allen and Unwin.

McAuley, Alastair (1979), *Economic Welfare in the Soviet Union*. London: George Allen and Unwin.

McLanahan, Sara and Karen Booth (1989), 'Mother-Only Families: Problems, Prospects and Politics'. *Journal of Marriage and the Family*, 51, pages 557-580.

McLanahan, Sara and Lynne Casper (1995), 'Growing Diversity and Inequality in the American Family' in R. Farley (ed.), *State of the Union: America in the 1990s*. New York: Russell Sage Foundation.

McLanahan, Sara, Lynne Casper and Anne Sorenson (1995), 'Women's Roles and Women's Poverty' in K. Mason and A.-M. Jensen, (eds), *Gender and Family Change in Industrialised Countries*. Oxford: Clarendon Press.

McLanahan, Sara and Gary Sandefur (1994), *Growing Up With a Single Parent: What Hurts, What Helps*. Cambridge, MA: Harvard University Press.

Ministry of Social Protection (1996), *O polozheniye detey v Rossiyskoy Federatsii: 1995 [The Situation of Children in the Russian Federation: 1995]*, State Report. Moscow: Ministry of Social Protection.

Mitterauer, M. and Alexander Kagan (1982), 'Russian and Central European Family Structures: A Comparative Review'. *Journal of Family History* (Spring), pages 103-131.

Moffitt, Robert A. (1997), 'The Effect of Welfare on Marriage and Fertility: What Do We Know and What Do We Need to Know?', Discussion paper No. 1153-97. University of Wisconsin, Institute for Research on Poverty.

Moore, Kristin (1995), 'Nonmarital Childbearing in the United States' in *Report to Congress on Out-of-Wedlock Childbearing*, Department of Health and Human Services. Washington, D.C.: Government Printing Office.

Moore, Kristin A., Brent C. Miller, Barbara W. Sugland, Donna Ruane Morrison, Dana A. Glei and Connie Blumenthal (1998), *Beginning Too Soon: Adolescent Sexual Behavior, Pregnancy and Parenthood*. Washington, D.C.: Child Trends, Inc.

Morgan, D. H. J. (1985), *The Family, Politics and Social Theory*. London: Routledge, Kegan and Paul.

Mozhina, Marina and Elena Prokofieva (1997), 'Living Standards of Families in Russia', Report prepared for the MONEE Project. Florence: UNICEF International Child Development Centre.

Mroz, T., D. Mancini and B. Popkin (1999), 'Monitoring Economic Conditions in the Russian Federation: The Russia Longitudinal Monitoring Survey 1992-1998.' Report submitted to the U.S. Agency for International Development, Carolina Population Center, University of North Carolina. Found at http: //www.cpc. unc.edu/projects/rlms

Mroz, Thomas and Barry Popkin (1996), 'Monitoring Economic Conditions in the Russian Federation'. Chapel Hill, NC: Carolina Population Center.

Muller-Escoda, Béatrice and Ulla Vogt (1997), 'France: The Institutionalization of Plurality' in F.-X. Kaufmann, A. Kuijsten, H.-J. Schulze and K.P. Strohmeier (eds), *Family Life and Family Policies in Europe, Volume I, Structures and Trends in the 1980s*. Oxford: Clarendon Press.

National Center for Education Statistics (1993), *Youth Indicators 1993: Trends in the Well-Being of American Youth*, NCES 93-242. Washington D.C.: U.S. Department of Education.

Newell, Andrew and Barry Reilly (1999), 'Returns to Educational Qualifications in the Transitional Economies'. *Education Economics*, 7 (1), pages 67-84.

Newell, Andrew and Barry Reilly (1996), 'Returns to Education in Transition', Report prepared for the MONEE Project. Florence: UNICEF International Child Development Centre.

Ni Broclchain, M., R. Chappel and I. Diamond (1994), 'Scolarité et autres caractéristiques socio-économiques des enfants de mariages rompus', *Population*, 49, pages 1585-1612.

Nichols-Casebolt, Ann and Judy Krysik (1995), 'The Economic Well-Being of Never- and Ever-Married Single Mothers: A Cross-National Comparison', Luxembourg Income Study, Working Paper No. 131. Luxembourg: LIS.

Ofer, Gur and Aaron Vinokur (1992), *The Soviet Household under the Old Regime: Economic Conditions in the 1970s*. Cambridge, U.K.: Cambridge University Press.

Organization for Economic Cooperation and Development (1998), *The Caring World: An Analysis*. Background Documents, Meeting of the Employment, Labor and Social Affairs Committee at the Ministerial Level on Social Policy, June 23-24, 1998.

Organization for Economic Cooperation and Development (1997), *CCET Labour Market Indicators Database*. Paris: OECD. Available on diskette.

Organization for Economic Cooperation and Development (1996), Labour Force Statistics 1974-1994. Paris: OECD. Found at http://www.oecd.org/.

Ott, Notburga (1995), 'The Use of Panel Data in the Analysis of Household Structures' in Evert van Imhoff, Anton Kuijsten, Pieter Hooimeijer and Leo van Wissen (eds), *Household Demography and Household Modeling*. New York: Plenum Press.

Oxenstierna, Sylvana (1990), *From Labour Shortages to Unemployment? The Soviet Labour Market in the 1980s*. Stockholm: Almquist and Wicksell.

Paci, Pierella (1999), 'A Bundle of Joy or an Expensive Luxury: A Comparative Analysis of the Economic Environment for Family Formation in Western Europe', Social Protection Discussion Paper, No. 9903. Washington, D.C.: World Bank.

Pascal, Anne (1998), 'L'offre de travail des femmes en Russie pendant la période de transition', mimeo. Paris: Université de Paris.

Phillips, Roderick (1988), *Putting Asunder: A History of Divorce in Western Society*. Cambridge: Cambridge University Press.

Plotnick, R. (1992), 'The Effects of Attitudes on Teenage Premarital Pregnancy and its Resolution'. *American Sociological Review*, 57 (6), pages 800-811.

Popenoe, David (1988), *Disturbing the Nest: Family Change and Decline in Modern Societies*. New York: A. de Gruyter.

Popkin, Barry, Alexander K. Baturin, Marina Mozhina, and Tom Mroz (1996), 'The Russian Federation Subsistence Income Level: The Development of Regional Food Baskets and Other Methodological Improvements'. Carolina: University of North Carolina. Found at http: //www.cpc. unc.edu/projects/rlms

Porter, Kathleen, Wendell Primus, Lynette Rawlings and Esther Rosenbaum (1998), *Strengths of the Safety Net: How the EITC, Social Security, and Other Government Programs Affect Poverty*. Washington, D.C.: Center on Budget and Policy Priorities.

Powell, M.A. and T.L. Parcel (1997), 'Effects of Family Structure on the Earnings Attainment Process: Differences by Gender'. *Journal of Marriage and the Family*, 59, pages 419-433.

Rainwater, Lee and Timothy M. Smeeding (1995), 'Doing Poorly: The Real Income of American Children in a Comparative Perspective', Luxembourg Income Study Working Paper 127. Luxembourg: LIS.

Ravallion, Martin (1996), 'Issues in Measuring and Modelling Poverty'. *The Economic Journal*, 106.

Ravallion, Martin (1994), 'Poverty Comparisons' in *Fundamentals of Pure and Applied Economics*, 56. Chur, Switzerland: Harwood Academic Press.

Ravallion, Martin (1992), *Poverty Comparisons: Living Standards Measurement Survey Study*. Washington D.C.: World Bank.

Rendall, Michael S. (1992), 'Transition, Probability, Change and the Growth of

Female Family Headship in the United States, 1968-88'. Brown University Population Studies and Training Center, Working Paper Series 92-02.

Richards, Toni, Michael J. White, and Amy Ong Tsui (1987), 'Changing Living Arrangements: A Hazard Model of Transitions among Household Types'. *Demography,* 24, page 80.

Rossiyskaya Federatsiya (1997), *Proyekt Federal'nogo Zakona: O vnesenii izmeneniy v federal'nyy zakon 'O gosudarstvennykh posobiyakh grazhdanam imeyushchim detey'* [*Proposed Federal Law: On the introduction of changes in the Federal law on state benefits to citizens with children*]. Moscow: Rossiyskaya Federatsiya.

Rossiyskaya Federatsiya (1996), *Semeyniy Kodeks Rossiyskoy Federatsii* [*Family Code of the Russian Federation*]. Moscow: Yuridicheskaya Literatura.

Russian European Centre for Economic Policy (RECEP) (1998), *Russian Economic Trends,* 7 (4).

Rutkowski, Jan (1996), 'Changes in the Wage Structure During Economic Transition in Central and Eastern Europe'. World Bank Technical Paper No.340. Washington, D.C.: The World Bank.

Sainsbury, Diane (1996), *Gender, Equality and Welfare States.* Cambridge U.K.: Cambridge University Press.

Sandefur, Gary (1996), 'Family Structure, Stability and the Well-Being of Children' in *Indicators of Child Well-Being: Conference Papers*, Volume III. Madison, WI: Institute for Research on Poverty.

Sandefur, Gary D., Sara McLanahan, and Roger Wijtkiewicz (1992), 'The Effects of Parental Marital Status during Adolescence on High School Graduation'. *Social Forces,* 71 (1), pages 103-122.

Schofield, M. (1968), *The Sexual Behaviour of Young People.* Harmondsworth, England: Penguin.

Seltzer, J.A. (1994), 'Consequences of Marital Dissolution for Children'. *Annual Review of Sociology*, 20, pages 235-266.

Sen, Amartya (1992), *Inequality Re-Examined.* Oxford: Clarendon Press.

Sen, Amartya (1985), 'The Standard of Living'. *The Tanner Lectures*, Clare Hall, Cambridge, UK: Cambridge University Press.

Shapiro, Judith (1995), 'The Russian Mortality Crisis and Its Causes' in A. Aslund (ed.), *Russian Economic Reform at Risk*, London: Pinter.

Shkolnikov, Vladimir and France Mesle (1996), 'The Russian Epidemiological Crisis as Mirrored by Mortality Trends', mimeo. Berkeley, CA: Rand.

Sinel'nikov, Aleksandr (1997), 'Perspektivy izmeneniya norm brachnosti i razvodimosti v Rossiyskoy Federatsii' ['Perspectives on Changes in

Marriage and Divorce Norms in the Russian Federation'], *Sem'ya v Rossii* [*Family in Russia*], No. 2. Moscow: Institute for Family Research.

Sinel'nikov, Aleksandr (1996), 'Novyye tendentsii strukturnykh izmeneniy sem'yi' ['New Trends in Family Structure']. *Sem'ya v Rossii* [Family in Russia], No. 2. Moscow: Institute for Family Research.

Skocpol, Theda (1992), *Protecting Mothers and Soldiers: The Political Origins of Social Policy in the United States*. Cambridge: Harvard University Press.

Skocpol, Theda (1990), 'Sustainable Social Policy: Fighting Poverty without Poverty Programs'. *The American Prospect*, 2, pages 58-70.

Sorrentino, Constance (1990), 'The Changing Family in International Perspective'. *Monthly Labor Review*, 113 (3).

Standing, Guy (1997), 'Social Protection in Central and Eastern Europe: A Tale of Slipping Anchors and Torn Safety Nets' in G. Esping-Anderson (ed.), *Welfare States in Transition: National Adaptations in Global Economies*. London: Sage Publications.

Statistics Canada (1996), Nation Tables from 1996 Census data. Found at http://www.statcan.ca.

Statistics New Zealand (1998), *New Zealand Official Yearbook 1998*. Wellington: GP Publications.

Statistiska Centralbyrån (Statistics Sweden) (1998). Found at http://www.scb.se.

Stewart, Kitty (1997), 'Are Intergovernmental Transfers in Russia Equalizing?'. *Innocenti Occasional Papers*, EPS 59. Florence: UNICEF International Child Development Centre.

Stoker, T.M (1985), 'Aggregation, Structural Change, and Cross-Section Estimation'. *Journal of the American Statistical Association*, 80.

Streeten, P. and Burki, S. (1978), 'Basic Needs: Some Issues'. *World Development*, 6.

Sussman, M. and S. Steinmetz (eds) (1987), *Handbook of Marriage and the Family*. New York: Plenum Press.

Swafford, Michael S. and Mikhail Kosolapov (1999), 'Sample of the Russian Federation: Rounds 5-8 of the Russian Longitudinal Monitoring Survey'. Carolina Population Center of the University of North Carolina, Chapel Hill, NC. Found at http://www.cpc. unc.edu/projects/rlms.

Swedish Institute (1994), *Fact Sheets on Sweden*. Stockholm: Svenska Institutet.

Tchernina, Natalia (1996), 'Economic Transition and Social Exclusion in Russia'. International Institute for Labour Studies, Research Series Number 108. Geneva: United Nations Development Programme.

Thornton, A. (1989), 'Changing Attitudes Toward Family Issues in the United States'. *Journal of Marriage and the Family*, 51, pages 873-893.

Thornton, Arland (1985), 'Changing Attitudes toward Separation and Divorce: Causes and Consequences'. *American Journal of Sociology*, 90 (4), pages 856-872.

Tilly, Chris and Randy Albeda (1994), 'Family Structure and the Determinants of Earnings Among Different Family Types'. *Industrial Relations*, 33 (2).

United Nations 1974, 1989, 1996, 1997. *Demographic Yearbook*. New York: United Nations Publishing Division.

UNICEF (1999), 'Women in Transition'. *Regional Monitoring Report*, No. 6. Florence: UNICEF International Child Development Centre.

UNICEF (1998a), 'Education for All?'. *Regional Monitoring Report*, No. 5. Florence: UNICEF International Child Development Centre.

UNICEF (1998b), *The State of the World's Children 1998: Focus on Nutrition*. New York: Oxford University Press.

UNICEF (1997), 'Children at Risk in Central and Eastern Europe: Perils and Promises'. *Regional Monitoring Report*, No. 4. Florence: UNICEF International Child Development Centre.

UNICEF (1994), 'Crisis in Mortality, Health and Nutrition'. *Regional Monitoring Report*, No. 2. Florence: UNICEF International Child Development Centre.

UNICEF (1993), 'Public Policy and Social Conditions'. *Regional Monitoring Report*, No. 1. Florence: UNICEF International Child Development Centre.

U.S. Department of Health and Human Services (DHHS) (1998), *Social Security Programs throughout the World—1995*, SSA Publication No. 61-006. Washington D.C.: Social Security Administration.

U.S. Department of Health and Human Services (DHHS) (1995a), *Social Security Programs throughout the World—1991*, SSA Publication No. 13-11805. Washington D.C.: Social Security Administration.

U.S. Department of Health and Human Services (1995b), *Report to Congress on Out-of-Wedlock Childbearing*. Washington, D.C.: U.S. Government Printing Office.

U.S. National Center for Health Statistics (1996), *Vital Statistics of the United States 1992, Volume I – Natality*. Hyattsville, MD: National Center for Health Statistics.

Van de Kaa, Dirk (1987), 'Europe's Second Demographic Transition', *Population Bulletin*, 4 (1). Washington D.C.: Population Reference Bureau.

Van de Walle, Dominique (1998), 'Targeting Revisited'. *World Bank Research Observer*, 13 (1). Washington D.C.: World Bank.

Vari, P. (1997), *Are We Similar in Maths and Science? A Study of Grade 8 in*

Nine Central and Eastern European Countries. Amsterdam: International Association for the Evaluation of Educational Achievement.

Vishnevskiy, Anatoliy (ed.) (1997), *Naseleniya Rossii: 1996 [The Population of Russia: 1996]*. Moscow: Population and Society.

Vishnevsky, Anatoly (1996), 'Family, Fertility, and Demographic Dynamics in Russia: Analysis and Forecast', Conference Paper. Santa Monica, CA: Rand.

VTsIOM (1995), *Ekonomicheskiye i sotsial'nyye peremeny: monitoring obshchestvennogo mneniya [Economic and Social Changes: Public Opinion Monitoring]*, Information Bulletin. Moscow: VTs IOM.

Wallerstein, J.S. and S. Blakeslee (1989), *Second Changes: Men, Women and Children a Decade after Divorce*. New York: Ticknor and Fields.

Watts, Harold W. (1985), 'The Scientific Potential of SIPP for Analysis of Living Arrangements for Families and Households'. *Journal of Economic and Social Measurement*, 13.

Wennemo, Irene (1994), *Sharing the Costs of Children: Studies on the Development of Family Support in the OECD Countries*. Stockholm: Swedish Institute for Social Research, Dissertation Series.

Willekens, Frans (1988), 'A Life Course Perspective on Household Dynamics' in Nico Keilman, Anton Kuijsten and Ad Vossen (eds), *Modelling Household Formation and Dissolution*. Oxford: Clarendon Press.

Wimperis, Virginia (1960), *The Unmarried Mother and Her Child*. London: George Allen and Unwin.

Wong, Yin-Ling Irene, Irwin Garfinkel and Sara McLanahan (1993), 'Single-Mother Families in Eight Countries: Economic Status and Social Policy'. *Social Service Review*, 67 (2).

World Bank (1994), *Russia: Poverty, Policy and Responses*. Washington D.C.: World Bank.

World Bank (1999), *Russia's Social Protection Malaise: How to Begin a Turnaround*, mimeo. Washington D.C.: World Bank.

WHO (1998), *Health-for-All Database*, European Region. Copenhagen, Denmark: World Health Organization, Regional Office for Europe.

Yakovleva, Galena V. (1979), *Okhrana prav nezamuzhnoy materi [Protecting the Rights of Unmarried Mothers]*. Minsk: Izdatelstvo Belorusskogo Gosudarstvennogo Universiteta.

Zakharov, Sergei and Elena Ivanova (1996), 'Fertility Decline and Recent Changes in Russia: on the Threshold of the Second Demographic Transition'. Santa Monica, CA: Rand.

Zohoori, N., L. Kline, B. Popkin, and L. Kohlmeier (1997), 'Monitoring Health
    Conditions in the Russian Federation: The Russian Longitudinal
    Monitoring Survey, 1992-96'. Chapel Hill, NC: Carolina Population
    Centre, University of North Carolina.
Zubova, L. and N. Kovalyova (1997), 'Public Opinion about Social Issues' in J.
    Klugman (ed.), *Poverty in Russia: Public Policy and Private Responses.*
    Washington, D.C.: Economic Development Institute, The World Bank.

Index

abortion 32, 40–1, 92, 127, 128, 218–9
adoption 126, 128
alimony 126-7, 136, 178-9
anthropometric measurement 200, 207-9

benefit exclusions 173–7, 188
birth rates 28-30, 40

census (1937) 124
census data 161–5
censuses, families within 60
child
    abandonment 80
    allowances 128, 138–9, 141–4, 173, 175
    support enforcement 117–18, 126, 129, 136–7, 179
    welfare, deterioration in transition period 192–5, 220
    welfare indicators 192
childcare services 15, 56, 109, 144, 168, 172
children's living arrangements 63 ff.
cohabitation 29–30, 42, 62, 70, 93
Committee on Ways and Means 113–14
crime rate 218
criminal activities, children and 193, 218

decentralisation of social expenditures 13

demographic trends 27–31, 55
diptheria 208
divorce 41–2, 44, 75, 91, 94, 126, 135–6, 196
divorce rates 30, 43–4, 55, 80, 92, 93

economic independence, women 11, 32, 98
education, non-attendance 213
EITC (Earned Income Tax Credit) 114, 117
employment
    and gender 166
    formal sector 180
    informal sector 164
enrolment
    compulsory education 213
    pre-school 193, 205, 210
    tertiary education 215

families
    complex 55-7
    extended 33, 37, 55
    incomplete 60, 147, 153, 177
    nuclear 63
Family Code (1996) 44, 135
family policy 123, 125, 132
family structure 33
    and child welfare 195 ff., 206 ff.
female unemployment 10, 16-18, 98
    state policies and 32–3, 145–6
fertility 28–30, 40, 45, 56, 79, 95
fiscal constraint 133

fiscal crisis, transition period 133–4, 140, 150
Food Stamp Programme 113
foster families 38

gender wage gap 7, 11, 129, 169, 180
gross domestic product (GDP) 13

health and educational status of children
    compulsory school age, 211–14
    post-compulsory school age, 215–19
    pre-school, 206–11
household
    composition 55
    definition 4, 34
    types 200–3
housing
    benefit 109, 114
    shortage 12, 31, 56
illegitimacy 70, 126
immunisation 205, 207
income
    and family structure 166–72
    distribution 13, 166, 169
    household 195
    inequality 94, 166, 171-2
    informal 136
    in-kind 143, 194
infectious diseases 208
infertility 32
inflation 79, 132, 158
institutionalized children 80

Khrushchev, family policies and 124, 128
kindergartens 10, 210

labour force participation, female 98
Land Code 126
local authorities, payment of benefits 138-42

marriage 11, 124, 135
    mean age of first, 30
    rates 41, 91
Marriage Code (1918) 11–12, 124, 125–6, 132
Marriage Code (1968) 129
maternity
    benefits 130, 139
    leave 129, 145
measures of child welfare outcomes 203–206
Minimum Subsistence Income (MSI) 157
monetary indicators 199
mortality rate 55, 192
    parents 78-9
    teenage 193
    young children 207

non-marital fertility 45–7, 95

orphans, social 38
parental education 70 ff., 163, 196, 216
parental mortality 39, 47–9, 78–9
part-time employment 16, 168
paternity 47, 117, 126, 127, 135
peasant *dvor* (household) 57
pensions 49, 56, 128, 134, 144, 173
planned socialist economy framework 122, 125, 132
poverty
    among single-parent families 153 ff.

and family type 158–66
causes 7
gender differences 163, 179
incidence 2, 15
measures of 104, 157, 182–3
reduction 124
regional thresholds 159
pregnancy 31, 218-19
adolescent 32, 40, 42, 198
pre-nuptial 31
private transfers of income 177–9, 189
privatization 17
pro-natalist policies 110, 124, 127

real wage levels 13
reconstructed households 194, 198, 201
remarriage 30, 38, 41, 72
risk factors
to behaviour 206, 218
to well-being 203-4
role models 196
rural households 33, 36, 67-9
Russian Longitudinal Monitoring Survey (RLMS) 5, 36, 58–9, 152, 199–200
Russian micro-census (1994) 5–6, 33, 60

Second World War 28, 108, 110, 127
self-employment among women 18

separation 43, 91
single-parent family, definition 5, 34, 153
single-parenthood in Western countries 6–9, 11, 89 ff.
social welfare programmes (Western) 100–4
social welfare state typologies 105–15
France 110–12
Sweden 108–10
United States 112–15
state family policy 197
Soviet 123–33
transition period 133–47
step-parents 194, 195, 201
stress 12, 196, 219
student benefit 176
suicide 193
syphilis 193, 218

transfers
exclusion from 176, 180
means-tested 102, 112, 118
private 133, 152, 173-5, 177-9
public 133, 137-8, 154, 173-5

tuberculosis 208-9

unemployment benefits 180, 193
urban households 36, 67-9

vocational schools 215